AL —

GOOD LUCK IN YOUR 6σ
EFFORTS.

(signature)

THE
SIX SIGMA
REVOLUTION

THE

SIX SIGMA REVOLUTION

How General Electric and Others Turned Process Into Profits

GEORGE ECKES

JOHN WILEY & SONS, INC.

New York ➤ Chichester ➤ Weinheim ➤ Brisbane ➤ Singapore ➤ Toronto

ISBN 0-471-38822-X

Printed in the United States of America.
10 9 8 7 6 5 4 3 2 1

To Lucia Della Malva and
her Grandsons, Joe and Temo

Contents

Foreword

As the Business Leader for General Electric's Access, one of GE businesses, I am keenly aware of the impact Six Sigma has had since Jack Welch announced his commitment to it in 1995.

In that year I heard Jack proclaim that "Six Sigma is the most important initiative GE has ever undertaken . . . it is part of the genetic code of our future leadership." When he made formal the edict that 40 percent of a business leader's bonus was going to be determined by his or her Six Sigma performance, it was quite apparent that Jack was not just committed to Six Sigma, he was making it a way of life at GE.

While working at GE Access, I came across George Eckes, an external consultant that GE Capital had hired to assist in their course design and delivery. George's knowledge and experience in Six Sigma was obvious, but the key for me in hiring him was how practical and easy he made what could be such a difficult subject. While some make it difficult and awkward, George not only made Six Sigma practical, he made it fun. He also was particularly good at getting my attention as a business leader and challenging me personally to get involved in the initiative.

Reading this book, *The Six Sigma Revolution,* is like attending one of George's seminars. In easy-to-read chapters, he has successfully turned this cutting edge management approach into easy-to-understand language.

He begins with a history of the quality movement in the twentieth century and shows how Six Sigma contrasts and compares with previous efforts. He goes on to explain the key ingredients of Six Sigma. In Chapter 2 he covers the strategic component of Six Sigma: Business Process Management. This chapter is one that other books on Six Sigma do not include with the detail that

George does. Chapter 2 covers how an executive can create the infrastructure for Six Sigma to be successful in an organization.

Chapters 4 through 9 describe the tactics that project teams use to apply the tools and techniques that drive improved performance in a Six Sigma organization. From how to charter a team to how a team ends its work and turns over an improved process to the workforce, each element of the methodology is explained clearly and with examples.

The latter part of Chapter 9 returns to the strategic element of Six Sigma, giving executives multiple suggestions on how to sustain and manage an on-going Six Sigma initiative.

In his last chapter, "How Six Sigma Initiatives Fail and How to Avoid Mistakes," George reviews 10 ways in which an organization can fail to achieve the results that GE has obtained with Six Sigma.

Each chapter is filled with the actual case studies and stories that George has used in his seminars. They make for both thoughtful and quick reading.

We at GE Access have utilized the concepts found in this book to improve our performance. You will find this book a significant tool in your understanding of Six Sigma. Enjoy.

Perry Monych
President and CEO
GE Access

Preface

The Six Sigma Revolution chronicles the pragmatic journey through a new management approach that is helping drive improved productivity and profits.

Six Sigma is a quantitative approach that fuels improved effectiveness and efficiency in an organization. This approach was first created in the 1980s by Motorola. Then, in the 1990s, companies like AlliedSignal and General Electric contributed to making Six Sigma the most popular quality improvement methodology in history.

This book is different than any other on the market. Rather than tout how important Six Sigma is, *The Six Sigma Revolution* addresses those executives and implementers interested in creating and sustaining a Six Sigma initiative in their organization.

This book begins with a discussion of the quality movement in the twentieth century, describing the limitations with previous efforts, and how Six Sigma came to be the management approach of choice for those interested in making their organizations world class.

What makes Six Sigma different, in part, is its focus on the involvement of management at all levels of an organization. This book addresses the elements management must institute to create an infrastructure for Six Sigma to work.

The second major component of Six Sigma addresses the tactics that drive improved effectiveness and efficiency in an organization. This method uses a simple but detailed approach to improve the performance of existing processes.

The journey through the tactical aspects of Six Sigma begins with how to charter teams so they are working on processes that directly impact the strategic business objectives of the organization.

Later chapters address how to calculate sigma at the process level, how to create specific, measurable problem statements that the project team will then attempt to improve, as well as how to utilize the analysis and improvement tools that will assist teams in their efforts to improve sigma performance. The final tactical chapter describes how a team transfers an improved process so that improvement will be sustained over time.

Another aspect of this book that you will not see elsewhere is the recognition of managing cultural change in the Six Sigma initiative. Six Sigma initiatives involve a cultural transformation toward managing with facts and data. For some organizations, this transformation will be a dramatic change from current management methods. It is probable that there will be resistance. This book addresses four major types of resistance, indicating how to diagnose the type of resistance and then providing strategies to overcome resistance.

The later chapters provide both executives and implementers with methods on how to sustain Six Sigma initiatives. The reader will learn how to create and manage Business Quality Councils where management has continuing responsibilities for the success of Six Sigma within their organization. We discuss how to change the systems and structures of an organization so that Six Sigma is successful.

Finally, the last chapter addresses 10 ways in which Six Sigma initiatives fail. Each failure is discussed to illustrate how to overcome failure to create a Six Sigma success story.

GEORGE ECKES

Acknowledgments

This book would not have been possible without the assistance of many people. During a seminar given at General Electric, Brian Swayne, a GE Master Black Belt recommended I contract with his wife, Lisa Swayne of the Swayne Agency. As my book agent, Lisa provided suggestions that made this a broad book and not just another text on Six Sigma. Jeanne Glasser, my editor at John Wiley, supported me throughout the publishing process. Thanks to the staff at Publications Development Company for their effective and efficient editing.

Thanks to the host of business leaders who influenced my beliefs in the strategic elements of process management, most notably Ross Leher of Waxman, whose progressive process thinking was ahead of its time, to Perry Monych of GE Access who combines process and strategic thinking in a way I have never seen, and to Bill Dougherty for the opportunity to use the Westin Hotel as a process improvement laboratory.

Thanks to D. Chris Anderson, my favorite Notre Dame professor whose teaching style made me the successful consultant I am today, and to another Notre Dame professor, Richard Sebastian, who taught me the rigor and discipline of research. Those lessons served me well in my continued interest in statistics that led to my involvement in Six Sigma process improvement before it became popular.

Thanks to the Destra Consulting Group, specifically Meg Hartzler, Laurie Dodd, and their founder Pam Dennis, who asked me to begin working with General Electric in 1991.

On a personal note, to the memory of Bill Lindenfelder whose intelligence, humor, and belief in me made working with

General Electric one of my favorite memories. I miss you, Bill. Thanks also to Rick Holley who proved friendship doesn't end at midnight, to Charlotte Reece Eskildsen and Don Hartshorn who provided me the greatest gift of all, their daughter Debbie, and finally, to my brother Mike, may I see you again someday.

G.E.

Chapter 1

Introduction to Six Sigma

Organizations are constantly on the alert to gain a competitive edge, using the many tools that have long been touted as a way to beat the competition. Yet, despite the focus on innovative ways of making products and providing services, there remains one constant: Organizations that produce better quality products and services than their rivals beat the competition time and again. Six Sigma Improvement is a tried-and-tested method that has been effective in helping businesses dominate their competition.

Achieving high quality has been a concern since the beginning of the twentieth century, when there was a massive shift away from an agrarian culture toward an industrial culture. As the United States evolved from a culture of craftsmanship toward one of mass production, assurance of product quality shifted from individuals personally inspecting their products to the development of a group of specialists who inspected parts and products after they were made.

This approach to quality control and its fit with customer needs worked well for many years for a variety of reasons. First, as the century progressed, the U.S. consumer's appetite for goods and services became nearly insatiable. Beginning with Henry Ford and the mass production of the automobile to William Levit's post–World War II creation of reasonably priced homes for returning veterans, Americans everywhere desired the material goods that would contribute to making their lives better.

The emphasis on quantity of goods and services superceded the emphasis on quality. Americans at that time were more accepting, willing to put up with a creaky window or a car door that occasionally had trouble closing. Additionally, in 1950, only a small percentage of women worked outside the home. Today, when 50 percent[1] of women work outside the home, it is more difficult to find the time to get the car repaired or wait for the repairman at home.

As Americans entered the 1970s, the definition of quality began to change. Traditionally, quality had referred to features, such as the difference between a Chevrolet Impala and a Cadillac Seville. But, several key events changed the perception of Americans toward quality.

As more and more women entered the workforce, there was less time to focus on maintenance of the home and the various products that were found in it. More immediate in its effect was the gas shortage of the mid-1970s. As the gas-guzzlers produced by Detroit proved too expensive, Americans migrated to foreign imports, particularly Japanese automobiles that were fuel-efficient. While enjoying these Japanese products, Americans found an added benefit. Japanese cars performed better in terms of durability and reliability. Gone were the major service problems that had historically plagued Detroit's offerings.

Japan had a different approach to and attitude toward quality. Since the days of mass production, Americans' approach to and attitude toward quality was based on mass inspection to find and sort out nonconforming parts or products. Starting with the famed assembly line of Ford, most production in American factories was based on mass producing something and inspecting key characteristics at the "end of the production line." This approach to quality improvement was found to be highly ineffective. Experts have determined that 100 percent inspection not only adds to the cost of the product, but is 80 percent effective at best. Take the quiz below to give yourself a feel for this ineffectiveness. In the text below, identify (inspect) the number of f's that appear:

Count the number of times the letter f appears in the following:

Finished files are the result of years of scientific study combined with the experience of years.

How long did it take to identify the 9 f's? Oh, you didn't get all 9? You may have missed f's that sound like v's. Or you may have misinterpreted the instuctions and just read below the first paragraph. If you did catch all the f's, how long did it take you? Either way, inspecting something is no guarantee that you will find defective parts or product. Second, think of the costs associated with inspection. The act of inspection does not add to the quality of the part or product. It simply verifies that it meets some specification or function. It's like going to the coroner when you are sick. The coroner will only tell you if you are dead or alive. Inspection alone does not add value and can be prohibitively expensive, whether we are talking about labor costs or the machines that are used to inspect. Furthermore, if you rely on inspection alone, there is no guarantee that you will improve performance.

On the other hand, the Japanese automobile was produced using an entirely different approach. Instead of mass producing a part or product and inspecting it after the fact, the Japanese automakers were committed to never-ending improvement of the product and the process that created it. (What is a process? A process is defined as those series of steps and activities that take inputs, add value, and produce an output.)

The way the Japanese were producing cars at that time was revolutionary. Their approach made management and autoworkers focus on continually making something better.

Measurement methods began to focus on the amount of variation that existed in a process and its subsequent part or product. Instead of measuring something to see if it was good or bad, the measurement of the part was an indicator of how well the process was performing.

This dramatic approach to production remained largely a Japanese phenomenon until 1980. In that year, NBC produced a documentary entitled *If Japan Can, Why Can't We?* Journalist Lloyd Dobbins profiled how an American statistician had a major impact on Japanese organizations. The man was W. Edwards Deming, a statistician who in the 1930s and 1940s had worked in the Census Bureau. As part of the armistice with the Japanese in 1945, the United States agreed to provide Japan with assistance in demilitarizing their country while simultaneously rebuilding their economic base. Deming was one of many who visited Japan and conducted seminars, at first primarily on statistics, to assist the Japanese in their effort to re-industrialize.

Deming made repeated trips to Japan and gradually shaped his message to include various management principles that company after company embraced.

While *If Japan Can, Why Can't We?* highlighted many of Deming's later theories of management, his original work strongly influenced Japanese companies in the strategies of analyzing the variations of the processes that resulted in production. Today, the highest technological award given in Japan is the Deming Prize.

As a result of Deming's contributions to the Japanese economy, nearly overnight, Deming's philosophy was adopted in the United States.

The 1980s were marked by rapid attempts to change the approach to quality in the United States, ranging from well intentioned but nonsustainable approaches to technically correct while limiting styles (e.g., the auto industry's initial Statistical Process Control efforts).

Desperate to mimic the results of Japan domestically, America latched onto virtually every approach that had quality in its title. Statistical Process Control (SPC) was followed by Total Quality Management (TQM) which was followed by Just-in-Time Manufacturing (JIT) which was followed by other more international approaches like Kaizen or Hoisin Planning. Each of these were sound, principled approaches toward improving the way a part or product was produced. Proponents of these approaches made them seem easy and that was good since those receiving the message wanted a quick fix. Just a few training classes from the appropriate consultant and the organization would be magically transformed.

Recognizing that quality had to be a companywide initiative, a national quality effort was conceived and implemented in the late 1980s and named after the commerce secretary reporting to President Ronald Reagan, Malcolm Baldrige. This comprehensive set of guidelines when implemented would involve everyone in the organization. Prior to this, quality efforts tended to be directed by quality professionals in an organization, who often would be perceived as internal evangelists, frequently ignored by management.

The Baldrige criteria was based on winning an award after an organization made a formal, detailed, and highly documented application. If warranted, the application would trigger a site visit by a group of Baldrige examiners, who would sift through the organization, verifying on site what the organization had written in their application.

In the late 1980s, the first awards were given to three organizations. The high profile awards were personally given by the

President himself, because Malcolm Baldrige had died in an accident. Among the first winners, in the late 1980s, was Xerox, a company that began the decade of the 1980s with their competition selling a product for what it cost Xerox to manufacture theirs. While Xerox was a genuine success story, the bloom on the Malcolm Baldrige Award quickly dispersed for three major reasons. Often, more work was focused on the documentation required for winning the award than the underlying activity that the documentation was to represent. Second, the concept of an award, while strongly compatible with the American love of a winner, left many an organization with the belief that quality was a destination to arrive at, and then once there, they could go back to how they traditionally ran their business. Finally, within the first several years, several winners turned out to be questionable at best, including at least one company (Wallace Company, Inc.)[2] who filed for bankruptcy protection from the same government who the year before had awarded them the Baldrige Award recognizing them as a great company.

At the same time, an engineer working at Motorola began focusing on Deming's concept of process variation. This engineer and trained statistician, Mikel Harry, began influencing his organization to study variation as a way to improve performance. These variations when measured statistically are the standard deviation around the mean, represented by the Greek symbol, sigma. The sigma approach became the focal point of Motorola's quality effort, particularly when Harry's initial efforts caught the attention of Bob Galvin, Motorola's chief executive officer. With Galvin's support, the sigma initiative became a way of doing business at Motorola. While the focus was on analysis of variation in everything Motorola did, far more important was the emphasis on continuous improvement. Motorola adopted a Six Sigma goal in everything they did, roughly equivalent to a process producing only 3.4 defects (defined as something not meeting the customer's requirement) per million opportunities; near perfection.

Virtually everywhere he went, Galvin talked of the successes of continuous improvement in everything Motorola did. One of the people who heard Galvin's message was Lawrence Bossidy. In 1991, after a successful career at General Electric, Bossidy took the reins of AlliedSignal, at the time a troubled conglomerate that needed a turnaround expert. Bossidy soon realized that this sigma approach could make AlliedSignal into the organization he envisioned.

Soon, AlliedSignal was using the Six Sigma approach to radically change the way it did business. During the 1990s, when Bossidy drove Six Sigma into his organization, sales repeatedly rose in double digits while productivity and earnings rose dramatically.[3] The Six Sigma approach was adopted by Texas Instruments with equal success. Then, in the summer of 1995, General Electric's (GE) CEO, Jack Welch, asked Lawrence Bossidy about his success. Welch's tenure at GE has been marked by a series of innovative approaches toward improvement since taking the reins of the conglomerate in 1980. Listening to Bossidy that summer, he became a quick convert to seeing how becoming a Six Sigma organization could leave a lasting legacy when he retires in April 2001.

General Electric's dedication to Six Sigma has already resulted in significant improvements. Jack Welch credits the Six Sigma initiative with raising the company's operating profit margins. Success stories abound within GE. GE Medical Systems recently introduced a $1.25 million diagnostic scanner, a product designed from start to finish using Six Sigma design principles. The chest scan that took 3 minutes (180 sec.) now takes only 17 seconds. At GE Plastics, a Six Sigma team improved a process to increase production of plastic by 1.1 billion pounds. Not only did this add to general increased revenue, but the increased production influenced acquisition of the contract for the coverings of the new Apple product, iMac.

GE has attributed a host of other benefits to Six Sigma. Inventory turns were at 5.8 and now are at 9.2, and getting better. At the core of Six Sigma is improvement in effectiveness and efficiency. The ratio of plant and equipment expenditures to depreciation is one measure of efficiency. At GE this number dropped to 1.2 and is anticipated to be below 1 as Six Sigma projects uncover and remove the "hidden factory" of processes that have to rework parts and services.[4] Six Sigma is assisting General Electric improve their standing as the most successful corporation in history.

How does an organization achieve Six Sigma methodology? Many of its proponents have made this approach seem more difficult than it needs to be. A common theme that Jack Welch has echoed in his many talks to GE employees is practicing the "rigor and discipline" of Six Sigma. Some have misinterpreted this to mean greater use and many times misuse of the various statistics involved in Six Sigma. This book will teach you how to use rigor and discipline to ensure that the steps and methods of improvement are always used. In my experience as a Six Sigma consultant, I have seen project teams make assumptions without really looking at the data they have collected. I will teach you how to apply the rigor and discipline that makes Six Sigma the most powerful management tool to improve your products, services, and profits.

The book, like the consultant's lectures that it is based on, uses adult learning theory to ensure that four elements regarding each topic are covered. Those four elements are:

1. *Conceptual.* In each chapter, the concept is defined and explained using simple but accurate terminology.

2. *Practical.* To appreciate a concept, you must understand its practical use.

3. *Technical.* This book can be used by a variety of personnel in an organization attempting to implement Six Sigma. Thus, this book emphasizes the technical elements necessary to successfully implement Six Sigma.

4. *Example.* Every concept is highlighted by a real life example. Through these examples, which come from manufacturing, service, and even family applications, you will gain the confidence to see Six Sigma as a useful hands-on tool to use to achieve quality improvement.

This book was written by someone working with clients ranging from large manufacturing firms like Honeywell and Bay Networks to pharmaceutical companies like Pfizer and SmithKline Beecham.

After several years in practice as a licensed psychologist, I became involved in quality consulting in the business world. After the airing of *If Japan Can, Why Can't We?* one of the approved consulting firms to the automotive industry was desperate for consultants to sate the growing thirst for quality training and implementation. They had two simple requirements: manufacturing experience and teaching experience.

I was fortunate to have worked at Saginaw Steering Gear (SSG) in the mid-1970s as a summer intern. SSG made all of the tilt wheel steering columns for all GM cars. Those were the days of mass inspection of everything. On my first day of work, my boss greeted me after a brief orientation from Human Resources and told me to inspect bar stock (cylindrical pieces of steel) for burrs. As I waited for my boss to explain what a burr was, he turned and began to talk to the next intern.

"Excuse me, sir, what is a burr?"

With a look that indicated I had just insulted his mother, my new boss returned to my work area, picked up a piece of bar stock and said, "This is a piece of bar stock. If you rub your finger on it and it bleeds . . . that's a burr."

As he walked off, I made a note to myself not to ask him any more questions. This experience chastened me. Like all college kids, I was anxious to make a good impression. I wanted to work hard. But I was amazed that they would put their most inexperienced person in a position to determine whether something met some customer requirement. For years afterward, I read the paper diligently thinking I would see some massive recall of Buicks based on some burr problem resulting from poor inspection practices in Saginaw, Michigan.

The other requirement that the consulting company was looking for was training experience. The consulting company, Gilbert Commonwealth, recognized that massive training would be requested, thus, training experience would be a prerequisite of being hired as a consultant.

While I met the letter of the law on this requirement, I didn't meet the spirit of this requirement. While still a psychologist, I would teach psychology in the evenings at a local community college, a required class for nursing students. While I thought this would be my ruin in the interview, I had been taught by my mother that integrity is doing the right thing when no one is watching. When asked if I had teaching experience, I freely admitted that I had been a psychology professor at Delta College near Bay City, Michigan. My soon-to-be boss replied, "Ah hell, in the business world you will still be dealing with crazy people, they just wear better clothing."

In the early months of working for Gilbert Commonwealth, I had the opportunity to meet Deming himself while waiting for a client at Ford Motor Headquarters in Dearborn, Michigan. In his early 80s, Deming exuded a sense of stature and purpose. Recognizing this was the opportunity to receive first-hand knowledge from the "godfather" of quality himself, I quickly went over to him, introduced myself, and proceeded to ramble a series of questions that I had been hearing frequently from my new client base. I finished with "So, Dr. Deming, what is your answer?"

As I looked up at this 80-year-old guru expecting to hear the same pearls of wisdom that had transformed the Japanese economy, I was astounded with his response. "Those are the most stupid questions I have ever heard! Go read some of my books."

Speechless with his response, he was 10 yards away before I regained my composure. While our paths would cross again several times before his death in 1993, I vowed never to be left looking flat-footed again. I committed myself to learning every tool, technique, and methodology of improvement, while retaining the valuable lessons I had learned as a psychologist. You, too, will learn not only the technical aspects of Six Sigma methodology, but also learn the psychology of how to implement this important philosophy of business in a way that it becomes a part of the organization's culture.

This book is divided into two major components. The first segment of the book addresses the strategic component of Six Sigma, *Business Process Management*. For Six Sigma methodology to work, management at all levels of an organization must be actively involved. *Business Process Management* is the vehicle by which management's involvement is initiated and sustained. The key elements of Business Process Management are:

1. Creation and agreement of strategic business objectives.
2. Creation of core, key sub- and enabling processes.
3. Identification of process owners.
4. Creation and validation of the key measures of effectiveness and efficiency for each process (also known as measurement "dashboards").
5. Collection of data on agreed dashboards.
6. Creation of project selection criteria.
7. Using the project selection criteria for project selection.
8. Continual management of the processes to achieve strategic objectives of the organization.

The second major component of Six Sigma addresses *Process Improvement Methodology*. There are two methodologies: One method takes already existing processes and uses a simple but detailed method to improve them. Another method is used to create new processes. Since most organizations' first emphasis is on improvement, we will focus on process improvement.

The method GE and several other organizations use to improve processes is summarized by the initials DMAIC or:

➤ *Define.* Defining the team to work on improvement, defining the customers of the process, their needs and requirements, and creating a map of the process to be improved.

➤ *Measure.* Identifying key measures of effectiveness and efficiency and translating them into the concept of sigma.

➤ *Analyze.* Through analysis, the team can determine the causes of the problem that needs improvement.

➤ *Improve.* The sum of activities that relate to generating, selecting, and implementing solutions.

➤ *Control.* Ensuring that improvement sustains over time.

Referenced throughout this book will be the importance of *managing change.* So many change quality efforts fail because too much effort is put into the technical change while not enough effort is put into ensuring acceptance of the quality effort. Resistance is to be expected. Thus, the need for the quality effort must be established and a vision of what a Six Sigma organization looks like must occur. A key element of the change initiative is mobilizing commitment to the Six Sigma organization. This means identifying the sources of resistance to Six Sigma and planning a strategy to overcome that resistance.

KEY LEARNINGS

➤ Improving the quality of products and services will help you gain a competitive advantage.

➤ The history of U.S. quality improvement in the twentieth century is based on inspection—a highly inefficient method that is competitive only when everyone else is practicing the same method.

➤ The decade of the 1980s was marked by frantic efforts to become more efficient in improving quality.

➤ While many approaches to improvement can work, fact-based, data-driven improvement is best.

➤ In the past 20 years, companies like Motorola, AlliedSignal, and now General Electric have used the Six Sigma approach to improvement.

■ NOTES

1. Women in the Work Force, www.uvm.edu/%7ejecarter/robinson .html.
2. ASQ, Malcolm Baldrige Award recipients, 1988 to present, www.asq.org/abtquality/awards/baldrige/mbrecipients.html.
3. AlliedSignal, press releases and financial summaries, aol net find.
4. 1998 General Electric Annual Report.

Chapter 2

The Strategy of Six Sigma

Eight Steps to Strategic Improvement

In my days as a practicing psychologist, I spent time as an *inpatient therapist,* working with severely ill patients, some of whom had to be medicated with drugs to just get them through the day without harming themselves or others. I also worked with out-patients, helping individuals, couples, or families having problems coping with everyday life.

Today, when I first begin working with a new client, I often think of my work as a kind of marital therapy. This is especially true when I think of the odds of a marriage working out through therapy. Typically, either the wife or the husband would make the first appointment and provide details of the marriage while I would document those details in what is referred to as the marital history. I would always end the first session with the pivotal question, "Is your spouse willing to work on the marriage by attend-ing therapy?" If the answer was yes, there was a good chance the marriage could be saved. If the answer was no, the odds of the person meeting with a divorce attorney in a few months grew dramatically.

I ask a similar question when I am called upon to consult with an organization, "Is management willing not only to hire me but more importantly, to *involve* themselves in a quality improvement initiative?"

Organizations that are successful in their quality efforts have vibrant, vocal, knowledgeable, and most importantly, involved management. It doesn't matter what their individual management styles are, whether it be the more dynamic style of a Jack Welch at

GE, the disciplined approach of a Lawrence Bossidy at AlliedSignal, the omnipresent style of a Bob Galvin at Motorola, or the charm of Bill Dougherty at the Westin Hotels. In each case, these individuals recognized that for their quality effort to succeed, their involvement was paramount.

This chapter addresses what management must do to ensure that the implementation of a quality improvement program is successful in the organization. Like the odds for success in marriage therapy being dependent on both parties participating, the odds for an improvement program taking root in an organization is based on management's involvement. The sad fact is most members of management don't want to participate. Like the reluctant spouse, they see no benefit to involvement. I have participated in a number of situations where management was reluctant to involve themselves at the level needed to make the quality program work effectively.

In reality, I rarely blame management for its lack of involvement. Human nature tells us we keep doing the things that work for us. By whatever definition you would use, those who have ascended the management ladder have typically succeeded without a quality initiative. Unfortunately, some have succeeded using barbaric methods to achieve, particularly those that have been placed in turnaround situations. Look at what Al Dunlap as a Chief Executive Officer, "accomplished" in the various businesses he led. But as he learned in 1998 at Sunbeam, his "chain-saw" approach to management backfired and he was given his walking papers.

So, if management has been successful with this approach, why should they use a quality approach to obtain results?

How do you convince management to invest themselves in a quality initative? A few years ago I worked for a computer company that had filed for Chapter 11 bankruptcy protection. Within a few months of the filing, several thousand employees had been given their walking papers. Eventually, this company got back on their feet, but isolated layoffs, euphemistically referred to as RIFs (Reductions in Force), were still prevalent. During one speech given by their CEO, references were made that the "tree cutting" of the organization had stopped, but isolated "pruning" was still going on.

This story highlights how many turnaround artists use cost cutting to get a company back on its feet. Although cost cutting has a direct and immediate impact on the people in the organization, it only indirectly affects the two most important elements that a quality initiative attempts to address: the *effectiveness* and *efficiency* of the organization. Effectiveness is the degree to which an organization meets and preferably exceeds a customer's needs and requirements. Efficiency refers to the resources consumed in attempting to become effective. By becoming more effective and efficient, an organization can achieve its business objectives without the wholesale destruction of the company's most important asset, its "human" resources.

I usually begin each of my seminars with a subjective test of how efficient and effective an organization is. An average organization experiences over 50 percent efficiency and only 70 percent effectiveness.

Rarely does the quality professional talk about quality improvement as an enabler toward achieving general business results. Yet, if that connection is not made, management ends up seeing quality as an add-on, an extra something to do. Worse yet, if initial efforts don't provide successes that are visible, management ends up viewing their investment in training and project work as a worthless expenditure.

The key for securing management's involvement can be found in the pages that follow. I'll use a proven case study where quality became an unconscious part of management's professional lives.

■ THE EIGHT ESSENTIAL STEPS

In 1994, I gave a speech on Business Process Management (BPM) at a conference in Keystone, Colorado. As I left the speaking platform, I was approached by a well-dressed man named Bill Dougherty. He indicated he had just taken over the position of general manager at the Westin Tabor Center, at the time one of more than 80 Westin Hotels worldwide. Dougherty had worked in the Westin organization nearly all his adult life with stints in Atlanta, Houston, and San Francisco. He had ascended to the top position in Denver because this particular facility had been experiencing difficulties in meeting their business objectives.

As we talked, we agreed to a short consulting contract where I would explain the concepts of BPM to the people who directly reported to him. I had no idea they would end up being one of the more dramatic examples of how this strategic element of quality could transform an organization.

When we met at the Westin, I gave virtually the same presentation that Bill heard in Keystone highlighting the eight key elements of a good BPM system. These same elements apply to a Six Sigma initiative and bear discussion.

➤ Step 1 Creation and Agreement of Strategic Business Objectives

During my presentation to Bill's staff, I stressed that failure for management to become more readily involved in a quality initiative appears to be directly related to management seeing quality as an additional activity, unrelated to the actual "work" of the organization. For a quality effort to be successful, it must have the support and active involvement of senior management. To obtain support and active involvement of management, the quality initiative must be linked to the ongoing strategic business objectives of the organization.

For too long, quality professionals have failed to connect their work with the business demands of senior management. Until and unless senior management can see that quality is the enabler to achieve strategic objectives, management will not only continue to practice an ineffective and inefficient method of goal obtainment, quality professionals will continue to be seen as an expensive burden rather than an asset to the organization.

Creation and agreement of strategic business objectives is a pivotal first step toward ensuring that a quality initiative becomes successful in the organization. This first step was not an issue for the Westin. While the Westin Tabor Center was individually owned and operated, their relationship was predicated on agreement with corporate-dictated business objectives including:

> ➤ *GOPAR.* This primary goal is revenue based. GOPAR stands for Gross Operating Profit per Available Room. This is to be distinguished from occupancy rate. The Westin Hotels cater to an upscale businessman or woman. As such, their goal is not to fill rooms but to fill rooms at the highest rate possible.

> ➤ *Maintenance of Their AAA Four-Star Rating.* The American Automobile Association anonymously visits and rates hotels against a set of criteria to determine if they continue to comply with the requirements needed to be a four-star hotel. The raters indicate if the hotel is in full compliance with the

requirements, in need of corrective action to sustain compliance, should be put on probation, or be denied the four-star rating.

➤ *Employee Satisfaction.* In addition to an employee satisfaction survey, the Westin monitored turnover closely. Customer satisfaction tends to be higher when employee satisfaction is high in all businesses but this is particularly true in the hotel industry.

The Westin Tabor Center needed major improvement in all categories.

➤ Step 2 Creation of Core, Key Sub-, and Enabling Processes

Traditionally, a business is organized by function for efficiency and effectiveness. This is a mistaken belief. Most organizations with a functional perspective may believe they are effective and efficient, but they are not.

An organization that thinks and acts functionally has a vertical mind-set around their work. This approach often results in thinking and acting toward maximization of the sub-goals and objectives of the function which may be at odds with the larger goals of the organization. For example, it may be the goal of an organization's travel department to cut costs. Thus, they may create an edict to fly the cheapest airfare, not realizing that this means employees may no longer be able to fly direct. This affects productivity because more time is spent in travel. Or reflect on the sales and marketing function that meets their quota in May of a given year, leaving the manufacturing group with capacity problems and additional labor costs. The vertical and horizontal nature of business are highlighted in Exhibits 2.1 and 2.2 on page 18.

The maximization of a function at the expense of the goals of the larger organization (a concept called suboptimization) is only one problem. The larger problem of thinking functionally is how it affects the customers of your organization. The major goal of increasing productivity is based on an overriding focus on *customer, process,* and *employee.* Thinking geometrically, how does the customer move through your organization? It certainly is not vertically. Instead, the customer travels through a series of processes in your organization that are reflected by a horizontal viewpoint. As

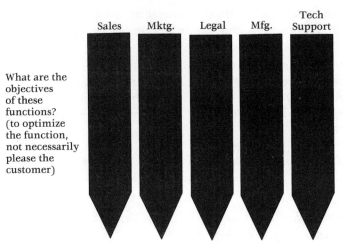

Exhibit 2.1 Functional versus process management.

defined in Chapter 1, process is the series of steps and activities that take inputs, add value, and transform them into outputs.

For example, think of how someone buying electronic equipment travels through an organization. First, they may see an advertisement in a newspaper, which was a result of the marketing department. Then, they visit the sales location, where they are approached by a salesperson. After completion of a sale, they may encounter problems that may require technical assistance. The

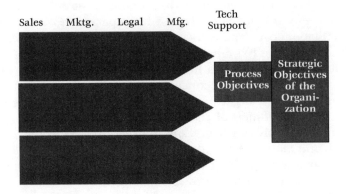

Exhibit 2.2 How do customers go through your organization?

path that the customer travels through this organization is horizontal, not vertical.

Or think of the front desk function at a hotel. If I run the front desk function, there may be a host of tasks that I would like to see accomplished where the customer may be seen as a secondary element or even a hindrance to getting my work done. If instead I think of the check-in process, the customer is seen foremost in the activity of this process rather than secondary.

Thus, an organization must identify the core and key subprocesses that constitute their organization. A core process is a set of cross-functional activities or steps that have a profound impact on achieving strategic business objectives, either directly or indirectly. Key subprocesses constitute the sum of a core process.

Once Bill Dougherty and his direct reports had approved Step 1 of Business Process Management it was time to Identify the Core and Key subprocesses of the hotel. Exhibit 2.3 shows the core processes and its composite subprocesses for Westin. Typically, there are five to seven core processes in a typical organization and five to seven key subprocesses that constitute the core process.

It took some time for us to create and agree on the three core processes at Westin. (Today there are five.) In large part this was a result of the functional mind-set of the executive staff. This is

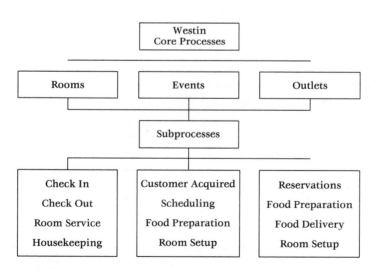

Exhibit 2.3 Example of core and subprocesses: Westin Hotel.

almost a universal phenomenon in my work with executives creating the core processes. What I was asking them to do was equivalent to speaking a foreign language. People tend to repeat behaviors that are successful. Whatever the problems that had existed at the Westin, each person I was working with had risen to his or her management position based on succeeding through managing functions. Thus, it took time for the group to think in terms of the processes that went through their function.

Once agreement on the core processes had been achieved, coming to agreement on the key subprocesses was much easier. I asked the team which of the three core processes most directly impacted the most important of their strategic business objectives—GOPAR. They responded that the *Rooms* core process had the most impact on their revenue measure (GOPAR). I then asked the executive team to pretend they were a customer of the *Rooms* process and identify all the touch points a customer would have. Further, I asked them what process the customer would see first, then second, and so on. Thinking like a customer made it considerably easier to finish this second element of Business Process Management.

Note how the key subprocesses were created by seeing how the customer traveled through the hotel *not* by thinking functionally. The first point of contact was the reservations process and then we move on to the check-in process (as opposed to the front desk function) to room service (as opposed to the food and beverage function) through to check-out.

The last thing to do before going on to the next step in Business Process Management is to identify those processes that do not necessarily belong to any one core process: These types of processes are called *enabling* processes; they only indirectly impact customer satisfaction, but are essential for the business to conduct its work. Typical examples in an organization are the employee acquisition process, the payroll process, the legal resolution process, and so on. At GE Capital, the financial arm of the famed conglomerate, risk management is a typical enabling process.

➤ Step 3 Identification of Process Owner

A process owner should be assigned to each core, key sub- and enabling process. The process owner is not necessarily the functional head of the related department (though functional heads will be process owners). Typically, the process owner will possess the following major core competencies:

➤ Knowledge of the subprocess sufficient to be seen as a subject matter expert.

➤ Leadership skills that include the power of persuasion (since without traditional line authority, the process owner will be required to have an impact based on the power of persuasion).

➤ Understanding and appreciation of Business Process Management.

➤ Experience the pain or gain if the process is not functioning properly or is doing well.

➤ Respect of those individuals in preceding and subsequent processes.

Enabling processes will be managed just as key subprocesses are managed. Some organizations struggle with the concept of considering a set of enabling subprocesses worthy of a core process. If the organization feels that a set of important enabling processes are critical to the operation of that organization (and most do), then creation of a core process (typically called Business Performance Management) is worth considering. While Westin did not do this originally, today one of the Westin's core processes is employee development.

➤ Step 4 Creation and Validation of Measurement "Dashboards"

What started as a short-term consulting contract with Westin was now growing. Our work together began in the late fall of 1994. After several days of consulting, we held a meeting with all the process owners. Thirty-three core, key sub-, and enabling processes were identified. After the executive team identified the process owners, a meeting with 15 individuals was scheduled.

In this session, I explained the concept of the measurement "dashboard." While driving a car, it makes good sense to pay close attention to what you're doing, looking at the road ahead and checking who is on either side of you and who is visible in the rearview mirror. A good driver will glance at the dashboard of the car as they proceed. This dashboard holds the essential information needed to drive the car, the speedometer, the oil pressure gauge, the gas gauge, and few others. Without the dashboard, the driving process could become significantly more dangerous.

Think of driving from point A to point B without the benefit of a speedometer. Similarly, the process owner should create a measurement dashboard for the process he or she owns. What goes into this dashboard can be obtained from customers through tools such as focus groups, interviews, customer complaints, or market research.

After explaining the concept of the dashboard, I asked each process owner to return to the same room in one month with the one to three key dashboard measures of the process he or she owned. At this point the first real resistance to the quality initiative arose.

Up to this point, the Westin managers had been amiable clients, with little disagreement voiced over what I had been asking them to do. The response to this request was almost unanimous. "Look, George, you don't work in the hotel industry. We already know what these measures are. Let's get on with it."

My experience told me that there are many approaches that will work when implementing quality. Allowing the Westin team to indicate their dashboard measures without verifying them independently through customer input was not one of them. I told the process owners that I would make them a friendly wager. If the majority of them brought back dashboards that showed spending the time to validate these measures was a waste of time, I would provide six months of free consulting.

During the following month I didn't lose much sleep thinking I had made a blunder. Experience had taught me that what the service provider thinks is important sometimes is not what the customer thinks is important. For example, with all my traveling I have eaten in many restaurants where the waiter or waitress almost always makes the same mistake: I will get just that right combination of cream and sugar in my coffee. Then, as I proceed to engage in conversation, the server comes by and fills up my coffee cup. The server is trying to be customer-oriented, but he or she does not know my requirements.

This concept applies to virtually every situation. Take the test yourself. Most of you have stayed in a hotel. Many of you have ordered a room service meal. What are the three most important requirements you have of a room service meal? Go ahead. Take a moment and write them down.

The room service process owner claimed that the most important requirement for someone ordering a room service meal was speed of delivery. How did this most important requirement match yours? In all likelihood, yours was the same. It was also the most important requirement when the room service process owner went out to verify his perception with the Westin customers.

The second most important requirement stated by the process owner was food quality. That is, the soup is hot, the iced tea is cold, and the steak is medium rare, if that is what was ordered. Check your list. It was the second most important requirement of the Westin customer. So far, two for two.

The third most frequently mentioned requirement of the customer surprised the process owner. It was menu variety, something that was far down the original list. This pattern existed through virtually every dashboard report from each process owner. The process owner would confidently report that his or her opinion was right for two of the requirements, but almost all the process owners missed out on one of the requirements.

The month to validate these requirements went a long way toward getting greater buy-in from the process owners. They soon realized that they invariably were working hard to improve 33 percent of the requirements that don't matter as much to the customer as something else they were ignoring or downplaying.

Many organizations end up having significant difficulty in collecting measurements because they fall into one of two typical traps. Trap one is not collecting the right data. Trap two is collecting too much data. Data should be used to create information that allows for intelligent decision making. In this case, the measures should help a process owner identify those areas that reveal how well the process is meeting and exceeding customers' needs and requirements (effectiveness).

In addition to finding out what the measures of effectiveness for a process are, it is also important to identify the measures of efficiency. Efficiency usually is measured through cycle time, cost, or value. While the first two are self-explanatory, measuring value is based on a process step being able to comply with the following three criteria:

1. The customer is willing to pay for the process step.

2. The process step physically transforms or changes the product or service.

3. The activity is done right the first time.

As has already been indicated, typical problems are not enough measurement or too much measurement. In the latter case, it is important that process effectiveness and efficiency measures be limited only to those measures that an organization will use. Thus, the Rule of 1 to 3, which states that for any process, only 1 to 3 measures should be targeted. Using the following criteria for measurement will greatly assist in limiting a process to a more manageable number, even if that number exceeds the recommended 1 to 3:

➤ Measure only what is important to the customer.

➤ Only measure those outputs of a process that you can improve.

➤ Measures of effectiveness in which you have no history of customer dissatisfaction should be avoided.

The criteria for measures of efficiency have already been discussed. Only one of the three (value, cycle time, or cost) should be measured.

Note that in the room service example, one measure, speed of delivery is both an effectiveness and efficiency measure. This "double-dipping" concept is prevalent among many processes and helps reduce the overall measures necessary to improve performance.

➤ Step 5 Data Collection on Agreed Dashboards

With a greater appreciation for the power of measurement, the Westin's process owner's were more acceptable to my next request. I asked each process owner to return one month hence with actual data of the agreed to measures on each dashboard.

Thus, the process owner of room service collected data on speed of delivery, food quality, and menu variety.

While I am a strong proponent of measurement and data collection, I also believe that data collection takes time and costs money. If done right it is a wise investment. If done wrong it has been not only wasteful but has taken away from other work that could be done for the customer.

It is also important that what is measured is compared against something else. In the case of effectiveness measures, the measures should be compared against the customers' specification of acceptance. For example, in the room service project, customers were asked when a room service meal was considered late. The vast majority of respondents indicated that while the quicker the delivery of the meal the happier they were, a room service order was considered late if, for lunch or dinner, it arrived past 30 minutes.

For food quality and menu variety a "Likert" Scale (so named for the University of Michigan academician who mathematically proved that people respond more evenly to 1 to 5 or 1 to 7 scales than 1 to 10 scales) was created. A rating of 1 would indicate that the meal did not meet the room service orderer's requirement for taste or temperature of the food. A rating of 3 would indicate that the meal did meet the requirement and a rating of 5 out of 5 would indicate that the meal exceeded their requirements.

During the ensuing month, each process owner collected data on the respective process or processes. Meanwhile, Bill Dougherty, his organizational development director, Elizabeth Ruppe, and his human resource director, Elizabeth Norberg, were deciding on a set of project selection criteria.

➤ Step 6 Creation of Project Selection Criteria and Choosing First Projects

Resources in the most profitable of organizations cannot sustain free-wheeling spending on a quality initiative. Even if it could, management would quickly see that nonfocused activity in the beginning of a quality initiative will result in higher levels of resistance among management and will contribute to the perception that the quality effort is not applicable to their business.

Thus, it is incumbent on the organization to prioritize early efforts at driving quality into the organization. The long-term goals of a quality effort must be that everyone in the organization practice the concepts and techniques of quality and see the organization in a business process management mind-set. However, prioritizing the subprocesses for improvement in the early stages of implementation will greatly maximize chances for success. This success will be more effective in neutralizing resistance in an organization.

The methodology for prioritization is relatively simple. The managing team should decide on the selection criteria for an improvement project. It is strongly recommended that the first set of criteria will be the strategic business objectives of the organization.

This will be followed by an additional list of criteria agreed to by the managing team, which should include current performance of the process targeted for improvement. In the latter case, focus on the poorer performing processes will increase the probability that the first projects will "bear fruit" since we are working on the lowest hanging fruit on the tree.

With that in mind, Bill Dougherty, organizational development director, Elizabeth Ruppe, human resource director, Elizabeth Norberg, and I worked out a short but powerful list of project selection criteria focused first on strategic business objectives followed by current performance and rounded out by the following additional criteria:

➤ Strategic Business Objective One—GOPAR.

➤ Strategic Business Objective Two—The AAA Four-Star Rating.

➤ Strategic Business Objective Three—Employee Satisfaction.

➤ Current Performance.

➤ Feasibility (Degree of Difficulty, Use of Resources, Time Commitment).

With these criteria selected, we waited for all process managers to return with a brief data presentation on their dashboards. This occurred on schedule. After the presentations, each subprocess was listed down the left-hand side of a sheet of flip chart paper.

Then the management team and process owners rated each process' impact on each of the project selection criteria using a "fist-to-five" method. I asked each participant to rank each process' impact on each project selection criteria where putting up a hand with five fingers means that process has major impact on that criteria to "fist"—no or little impact.

You can see simulated data of the results for Westin in Exhibit 2.4. Using this data, we chose subprocesses 6, 12, and 3 for the first Westin projects.

Bill Dougherty then did something dramatic. (I now recommend this to each business leader.) He asked each process owner to predict what would be the performance report on each dashboard 90 days from that day. Each process owner signed up for a target and stretch goal. Later, he told me that each process owner's stretch goal was greater than he would have set.

Key Sub/Enabling Process	SBO 1 - Revenue	SBO 2 - Growth	SBO 3 - Emp. Sat.	Feasibility	Current Performance	Sum
1. Subprocess 6	5	5	5	5	5	25
2. Subprocess 12	4	4	5	4	4	21
3. Subprocess 3	5	4	4	3	4	20
4. Enabling-process 2	4	4	4	4	3	19
Nth Process	3	2	4		1	10

Exhibit 2.4   Project prioritization matrix.

Not only did he have owners signing up for more aggressive goals, he also had buy-in and ownership of the projects, as well as some friendly competition knowing reports on progress were due in 90 days.

Dependent on resources available, the strategic team may decide to initiate as many teams as warranted, though use of this methodology usually focuses on just a few of the top processes. The higher rated subprocesses should be targeted for the first projects. This does not mean that those processes not targeted for the first projects should be ignored. As the process owner for any non-targeted project will be quick to tell you, she or he recognizes the importance of managing a process irrespective of whether it is on the "radar screen."

Fortunately, the majority of the first Westin projects proved successful. One of the prioritized projects was to improve the employee acquisition process. The functional area was human resources. By looking at the processes related to this function, the problems associated with acquisition became more apparent. Historically, it would take more than 4 weeks to hire even the simplest position. Through the application of the methods used in future chapters, the team was able to take a process that had 150 process steps and remove over 100 of them that added no value. This process not only improved the efficiency of the process but now the employees that are hired stay longer. Today, the Westin Tabor Center has the lowest turnover rate of any hotel in Denver.

Every ninety days, Bill Dougherty uses the project selection criteria to set in motion another set of projects. The results have been amazing. This hotel facility that once was considered a poor performer is now a consistent top 10 performer in the Westin chain.

KEY LEARNINGS

➤ Any quality improvement effort *must* include management.

➤ To include management, the quality effort must be seen as the vehicle toward achieving the business objectives of the organization.

➤ A quality improvement effort's goal is to improve the effectiveness and efficiency of an organization.

➤ Effectiveness is meeting and exceeding the needs and requirements of the customer.

➤ Efficiency is the time, cost, or value of the activities that lead to customer satisfaction.

➤ Customers travel through an organization through a series of processes, not through the functions or departments of the organization.

➤ Each process must measure its effectiveness and efficiency.

➤ Projects to improve quality should be selected that have the greatest impact on the business objectives of the organization.

Chapter 3

Profits = Customer + Process + Employee

In Chapter 2 we learned about the importance of creating an infrastructure called *Business Process Management* (BPM) that will allow for successful process improvement through project teams. In this chapter, we discuss the different types of methodologies to apply to improve a process.

■ THE HIGH-FUNCTIONING ORGANIZATION

Organizations that have utilized quality principles and methods to achieve improvement have had three major focus areas (Exhibit 3.1). They are strongly focused on the Customer, Process, and Employee.

Sometimes businesses forget why they are in business. While any business (including consulting businesses) exists to achieve and maintain profitability, many organizations do not realize that profitability comes about by satisfying customers. While this does not seem to be a controversial statement, it is always amazing how many organizations lose focus on the customer.

When I was a boy, I was fortunate to have parents who took us on a plane trip from our home in Michigan to visit relatives in New York City. I remember awakening early and dressing in my Sunday best. The trip on the old viscount turbo-prop was amazing. Flight attendants provided us with great food, attention, smiles, and inquiries into whether my brother and I would like to visit the cockpit. All of this for the purchase of a coach class ticket! I was reminded of this trip during a recent airplane trip. After a successful

The High-Functioning Organization

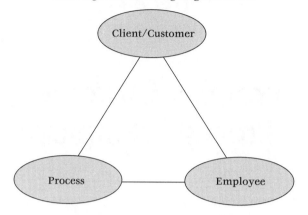

Exhibit 3.1   Major focus areas.

consulting endeavor, I boarded a flight from Buffalo to Chicago with connections back to my home in Denver. Arriving in Chicago, the pilot began to maneuver into what airlines call the "penalty box." Within a few minutes, the pilot informed us that our gate was occupied and we would be there "shortly." From my window seat I could see numerous unoccupied gates and wondered why we couldn't park in one of them. The minutes ticked off slowly and as they did the cabin's mood became more and more anxious. Most of the passengers had connections to make. The customers of this flight were victims of the hub-and-spoke system of most major airlines, where customers are transported from satellite airports to hubs like Chicago to be transferred to flights to their final destination. This approach to flight is more economical (read profitable) to the airlines, but often an inconvenience and anxiety-producing experience to the customer.

Waiting impatiently in the penalty box, all I could hear in my first class seat was the incessant chatter of the two flight attendants. During the 80-minute flight from Buffalo, I had been served a quick snack and a beverage with virtually no communication between the flight attendant and me. But now as we waited to be cleared from the penalty box, the two flight attendants were talking to each other in voices that could be heard in the second row of first class. Their conversation was centered on how hard their jobs were, what schedules they were trying to work out to get the most paid time off, and finally and most amazingly, how rude and discourteous the customers were. I was observing service providers who were not even conscious of whether the people they were criticizing could overhear them. This type of behavior is not atypical. I thought back to my flight as a boy and the special treatment accorded me in coach. Now, when traveling first class, I was considered rude and an inconvenience.

The state of customer service on the airlines is but one example of how organizations do not provide focus on the customer. Being customer focused means knowing what a customer is, who your customers are, and what you provide in terms of product and/or service. Further, it means knowing the customer's requirements of the product and/or service.

But a high-functioning organization that simply focuses on the customer is not enough. Being customer focused without the other two elements of focus—process and employee—often results in customer dissatisfaction. As discussed in Chapter 2, customers pass through an organization through a series of processes. Without control of these processes, even with the greatest of focus on customers, dissatisfaction is soon to follow.

Another example highlights this concept. Recently, a client wanted to continue a discussion with me regarding improvement after a day consulting with his business leaders. He suggested we have dinner at an upscale restaurant. Indeed, this restaurant personified the idea of customer focus. We were immediately greeted by the concierge and taken to our table. The restaurant was immaculately decorated and the surroundings were first class. It soon became apparent, however, that the restaurant was not process focused. Our drink orders were taken almost immediately by a friendly, customer-oriented waiter, however, it took 15 minutes for the drinks to be served. Of course, the waiter apologized. Our orders were taken and my host ordered a steak, medium rare, I ordered chicken. Since I had once consulted for a chicken processor, I always order my chicken well done and jokingly referenced to the waiter why I did this. Our orders seemed to take forever and I apologized to my host since I felt it was my chicken that was taking the extra time. However, when our orders arrived, my chicken was cold and underdone, while my host's steak was medium well, not medium rare.

The restaurant was profusely apologetic. They offered to recook my chicken and provide my host with a new steak. When the orders arrived, they were done to perfection. They agreed to make monetary restitution and even gave us a free bottle of wine. They were highly conscious of being customer focused but it was apparent that at least two key processes at this restaurant were not under control, the food preparation process and the food delivery process.

Without control of processes, it doesn't matter how customer focused you are. The restaurant exists to provide a service that results in a profit to the organization. By having to compensate for poor process control, the monetary restitution and free wine negatively impacts profitability. Actions taken to remedy poor process performance will result either in negative profit impact to the service provider or the service provider going out of business.

Finally, creating a customer- and process-focused organization requires being employee focused. Being employee focused includes such principles as promoting greater employee involvement, developing a culture of support and communication, and managing change in the work environment. Employee-focused organizations don't become that way just to be good social neighbors. Repeated studies have shown that the happier and more satisfied an employee is, the greater the customer satisfaction. Thus, being employee focused makes good business sense.

To become a high-functioning organization through Six Sigma, an organization must take an approach toward improvement that combines customer, process, and employee focus.

■ PROCESS IMPROVEMENT VERSUS PROCESS DESIGN

Once the organization has created the infrastructure for Six Sigma through the concepts of Business Process Management discussed in Chapter 2, the process improvement team has two basic choices. They can identify broken processes that need to be fixed or they can create new processes for their organization to achieve their strategic business objectives. In the first case, they will use *Process Improvement*. To create new processes, they will use *Process Design*.

We'll briefly discuss Process Design, however, our main focus will be on process improvement. Process Design is best used when one or more of three situations exist:

1. *When a new process will assist an organization to achieve a strategic objective.* Perhaps, through Business Process

Management an organization realizes that a strategic business objective is business growth. When they examine their core and key subprocesses, they discover that there is no business development process. In this case, Process Design of the business development process would be an appropriate course of action.

2. *When a current process is irreparably broken.* When processes are considered beyond repair, Process Design should be the option. This is a subjective decision, however, and Process Improvement should be considered first.

3. *When a process has reached "entitlement."* Finally, there are some processes designed to be less than Six Sigma when functioning optimally. That is, after improvement has been successfully implemented, a process may still not achieve a desired level of customer satisfaction. Thus, when a process is optimized at 2 or 3 sigma after successful improvement, it is said to be operating at *entitlement*. When a process is operating at entitlement and when the organization is not satisfied with this performance, Process Design is desirable.

In two of the three previous situations, some process improvement has occurred first. Because the vast majority of processes in an organization will call for improvement, we focus on Process Improvement.

➤ The Scientific Method

Consider the following seven steps and think of their origin:

1. *Observing.* Identify objects and their properties utilizing all five senses, identifying changes in various senses, and making observations.

2. *Classifying.* Sort objects and their properties, match objects by their likenesses and differences, and describe the subcomponents of objects.

3. *Measuring.* Compare two like quantities where one is used as a unit of measure.

4. *Collecting and organizing.* Gather, describe, and record data and then order, classify, and compare data to identify patterns and similarities.

5. *Predicting and inferring.* Suggest explanations for a set of collected data and then form generalizations.

6. *Identifying variables.* Formulate a hypothesis from a set of observations and inferences, and devise a method to verify the hypothesis.

7. *Synthesizing.* Integrate the lower process skills in the design, experimentation, and interpretation of an investigation of an observable phenomena.

The preceding list was a hand-out from my son's fifth grade class. Amazingly, this list (which is the scientific method) is the foundation of Six Sigma improvement.

Listed below is a high level overview of the Six Sigma improvement methodology that GE Capital has used to practice its process improvement.

1. *Define.* Define the customers, their requirements, the team charter, and the key process that affects that customer.

2. *Measure.* Identify the key measures, the Data Collection Plan for the process in question, and execute the plan for data collection.

3. *Analyze.* Analyze the data collected as well as the process to determine the root causes for why the process is not performing as desired.

4. *Improve.* Generate and determine potential solutions and plot them on a small scale to determine if they positively improve process performance.

5. *Control.* Develop, document, and implement a plan to ensure that performance improvement remains at the desired level.

While stated in different terms, the essence of both methods center around identifying problems, determining their root causes, formulating ideas around what would result in improvement, testing those improvements, and maintaining improvement. The scientific method is used in achieving Six Sigma quality.

When asked what Six Sigma is, one of the following explanations is usually given:

➤ A measure of variation that achieves 3.4 defects per million opportunities.

➤ A cultural value or philosophy toward your work.

➤ A measurement system.

➤ A goal.

Let's look at the first two of these more closely.

➤ A Measure of Variation That Achieves 3.4 Defects per Million Opportunities

On a technical level, the concept of Six Sigma is based on the theory of variation. All things that are measured fine enough vary. Assuming this to be true, anything that can be measured on a continuous scale (e.g., weight, height, length) follows a bell-shaped curve (see Exhibit 3.2).

The bell-shaped curve (sometimes called the Gaussian Curve after the German mathematician who empirically determined its characteristics) has the following characteristics:

➤ The curve represents virtually 100 percent of whatever is being measured.

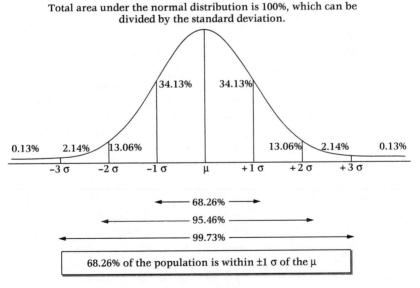

Exhibit 3.2 Segmented bell-shaped curve.

➤ The curve is symmetrical.

➤ The peak of the curve represents the most commonly occurring value or average.

➤ The curve can be divided into a series of segments.

Each segment represents a certain percentage of whatever
is measured. For example, the distance under the curve from the
center line or average out to the first segment line to the left or
right represents approximately 34 percent of whatever is being
measured. The distance under the curve from the first segment
line to the second segment line represents approximately 14 percent of whatever is being measured. (The amount is different because the curve on either side going out into infinity is
curvilinear, not rectangular.) The distance under the curve from
the second segment line out to the third represents approximately
2 percent of whatever is being measured.

The technical name for each segment is the standard deviation
from the mean. The symbol for the standard deviation is the lower
case Greek letter, sigma. As simply put as possible, the technical
concept of Six Sigma is to measure current performance and to determine how many sigmas exist that can be measured from the
current average until customer dissatisfaction occurs. If customer
dissatisfaction is measured as a defect, then Six Sigma indicates
that there would be only 3.4 defects for every million opportunities, or near perfection.

Earlier in our discussion of Business Process Management, we
talked about the room service delivery process. In the eyes of the
customer, room service delivery speed was the most important requirement. It was also stated that any lunch or dinner delivery
past 30 minutes incurred customer dissatisfaction. Thus, a delivery of 31 minutes would be seen as a defect in the eyes of the customer. Since delivery time is a continuous measure, it is possible
to create a hypothetical example of the bell-shaped curve for room
service delivery in Exhibit 3.3.

While it is premature in our discussion to calculate empirically how many sigmas this process is performing at, it is easy to
visualize that the current performance is a little more than three
sigma. We have already indicated that the peak of the curve is
our average and we can count out approximately three "segments" or "sigmas" before we have extended past our customers

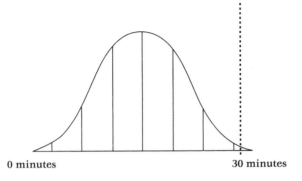

Exhibit 3.3   Bell-shaped curve for room service example.

specification of 30 minutes. If we are to talk in terms of percentages, this hypothetical room service process is operating at greater that 98 percent effectiveness. If historically it had been operating at 75 percent effectiveness, 98 percent would indeed be considered tremendous improvement. However, place yourself in the situations where performance, when measured in percentages, is at a 99.9 percent performance. Would you be happy with any of these examples:

➤ 1 hour of unsafe drinking water every month.

➤ 2 unsafe plane landings per day at O'Hare International Airport in Chicago.

➤ 16,000 pieces of mail lost by the U.S. Postal Service every hour.

➤ 500 incorrect surgical operations each week.

➤ 50 newborn babies dropped at birth by doctors each day.

➤ 22,000 checks deducted from the wrong back accounts each hour.

If you wouldn't accept any of the above, why should your customers accept much worse performance from you? At the most basic, Six Sigma is a way of measuring the variation in a process. It can enable you to determine how close you are to being world class in terms of performance.

➤ A Cultural Value or Philosophy toward Your Work

My clients bring me many issues around the concept of a Six Sigma organization. One of them is the apparent inability to achieve Six Sigma across all processes in an organization. Once they begin to measure sigma within their organizations, they often become discouraged when they see process performance that is two sigma or one sigma or even less than one.

It is demotivating to see Six Sigma as only a technical tool. In reality, the far more potent use of Six Sigma is to achieve understanding of how far you have to go toward achieving Six Sigma. Use Six Sigma to develop a sense of never-ending dissatisfaction with your current performance.

For example, look at what some individuals accomplished by embracing the philosophy of never-ending dissatisfaction with current performance. The year is 1973. Within several months, Bob Fosse, noted theater choreographer, dancer, and director did what no other artist had previously accomplished. In late March, he won the Tony for *Pippin* and two days later, he won an Oscar Award for the movie, *Cabaret* (best director). Later in the same year, he went on to win an Emmy for his direction of Liza Minelli in the television special, *Liza with a Z.* This amazing series of accomplishments has not been duplicated since.

What does Bob Fosse have to do with Six Sigma? It is probably safe to say he never saw a standard deviation in his life. Yet after winning those prestigious awards, *all in the same year,* Bob Fosse almost always talked about how each activity could have been better. Almost 15 years after receiving his Tony, Ben Vareen talked about how Fosse would break into a dance step associated with *Pippin,* showing how the performance could have been better, literally reducing the variation of each dance step around the target of perfection.

This is the ultimate philosophy of Six Sigma. The pursuit of perfection: never-ending dissatisfaction with current performance.

Does your organization embody this philosophical belief, or do they practice the concept of "This is good enough."

While Six Sigma is a technical measure of performance against customer requirements, there is a far more important definition of sigma, that of a cultural philosophy of never-ending dissatisfaction with current performance.

This element of Six Sigma recognizes that whatever current performance is, improvement through never-ending reduction of variation should be the hallmark of every person in the organization.

Defining, measuring, analyzing, improving, and controlling is the method used in never-ending improvement. In the chapters that follow, we address in detail each step in this method, teaching you how to use the method to improve any process you are involved in.

KEY LEARNINGS

➤ For a Quality Initiative in an organization to be successful, there needs to be an overriding focus on the customer.

➤ Being customer focused without being process focused means lost profitability and ultimately lost business.

➤ The scientific method is used to achieve quality improvement.

➤ One definition of Six Sigma is technical—measuring the level of customer satisfaction.

➤ Another definition of Six Sigma is cultural—having everyone in the organization develop and refine the never-ending pursuit of perfection.

Chapter 4

Project Start-Up

Tactical Six Sigma

As a result of the first steps referenced in Chapter 2 in Business Process Management, several formal projects can now be initiated. (We will return to Business Process Management in Chapter 9.) These should be structured to produce quick, dramatic results. There is skepticism in any organization contemplating a quality initiative and quick, dramatic results that impact the organization is an excellent way to build and sustain momentum for a quality initiative. When people inside an organization see the results for themselves, it is a far better motivator than seeing all the organization's other successful efforts.

Successful organizations use a model for improvement. An analogy I use is from the Ed Sullivan show on Sunday nights. Ed Sullivan would introduce a man who would have five sticks measuring approximately six feet each. He would then take out dinner plates and take one and begin spinning it on the top of one of the sticks. He then did that with sticks two and three. Looking back, the man would see that plates 1 and 2 would be wobbly, he would go back and get the plates spinning without wobble. Starting plates 4 and 5, he would check to see plates 2 and 3 starting to wobble and get those plates spinning perfectly again.

When I work with an organization on a quality methodology, I use this analogy to describe how the model should be used. Any model of improvement is not a linear model where the team can finish the elements for a given step in the model and then not return to that step. Like the spinning plate man on the Ed Sullivan show, the model is iterative, and there will be times that a team must loop back to either finish or modify the work done earlier.

Nonetheless, each step in the model must be carefully addressed. In the first step of the model, *Define,* there are three essential elements that the team must address before going on to the second step in the model, *Measure.* Before discussing the three elements of *Define,* we must understand the roles and responsibilities of each team.

■ BUILDING THE TEAM

➤ The Team Sponsor or Champion

Each team must have a sponsor. Typically the sponsor of the team will be the process owner who as a member of the Business Process Management group selected the project.

The sponsor of the team has multiple responsibilities. First, the sponsor will assist in the selection of the team. Second, he creates the strategic direction for the team, showing the team members why this team should be formed and what strategic business objective or objectives the team can potentially impact by successfully completing the project. Third, the sponsor will help describe in general terms what a successful project will accomplish. Next, the sponsor will help establish the general scope of the project, so that the team understands what to work on and, more importantly, what areas are to be avoided.

Once the project is underway, the sponsor has two major responsibilities. He or she must remove obstacles that may prevent the group from achieving success. For example, if a key team member keeps missing meetings because his or her boss does not see the importance of the project, it is the responsibility of the team sponsor to convince the boss of the importance of involvement of this particular person. Another example would be for the sponsor to allocate sufficient resources (e.g., computer time) for the team to achieve its goals.

A final responsibility for the sponsor is to make the major decisions of the group related to the solutions that will be generated during the *Improve* stage of the model. During our discussion of *Improve,* we discuss ideas that will make this decision-making process easier for both the team and the sponsor.

➤ Team Leader (The Black or Green Belt)

GE, like few other organizations has developed a group of future business leaders (what GE calls the Black Belt or Green Belt) whose current responsibility is 100 percent devoted to quality efforts. These future business leaders act in the capacity of full-time team leaders who guide teams through the methodology to achieve project goals. Eventually, these Black Belts will be moved out of the quality effort and into leadership positions with GE.

The Black Belt concept at GE is unusual. Most organizations do not have the staffing or financial resources to devote full-time positions to lead teams. Instead, they establish the need for mid-level management to periodically lead teams on quality projects. When done correctly, it conveys to an organization that quality improvement is part of their job description, not something that a group of specially trained experts is responsible for. At GE, part-time team leaders who have full-time responsibilities elsewhere are called Green Belts.

Whether a Black Belt or Green Belt, the team leader has multiple responsibilities. First, he or she is responsible for the ongoing tactical management of the team's work. He coordinates and runs the meetings, ensures that individual team members complete tasks according to the milestones previously established and keeps an ongoing link to the team sponsor. More successful teams have high levels of communication between the team leader and the sponsor. A formal contact between sponsor and leader a minimum of at least once a week is recommended.

➤ Team Consultant (The Master Black Belt)

At GE, the Master Black Belt is typically not a full-time member of a team. This individual is equivalent to the internal quality consultant, who has the greatest technical skills and will be seen as an ad hoc member of the team. For example, if the team has technical questions about how to calculate the sigma performance, the Master Black Belt can be called in to not only help with the calculation but also provide a mini-tutorial, as needed.

➤ Team Members

Team members are selected on the basis of their technical expertise for the project. Their major responsibility centers on implementing the steps in the quality model.

■ BEGINNING THE WORK OF DEFINING

Once the team sponsor, team leader, team member, and the ad hoc internal quality consultant have been chosen, the work begins. Teams that get off to a poor start often are doomed to failure. Thus, the three major elements of *Define* must be carefully addressed.

Think of the three elements of Define as tollgates on a highway. While we may loop back to finish a particular element of Define, it is essential that the team sponsor puts her or his blessing to these three elements before proceeding to *Measure*.

The three (toll gates) of Define are:

1. Creating the team charter.
2. Identifying the customers of the project, their needs and requirements.
3. Creating a high-level Process Map for the project.

➤ The Team Charter

The team charter is the most important element of any methodology. It is comprised of the following elements:

- ➤ The business case.
- ➤ The problem statement.
- ➤ Project scope.
- ➤ Goals and objectives.
- ➤ Milestones.
- ➤ Roles and responsibilities.

The Business Case

A common problem with many projects, particularly early on, centers on the project's lack of impact to the business. Often well-intentioned groups interested in getting the quality initiative started create the first projects that focus on getting things going, not what is important to the business. No project should be created on this basis alone. If the steps discussed in Chapter 2 are done properly, the projects created will be based on their impact to the business.

As we showed in Chapter 2, each of our first projects were required to go through the project selection criteria. If you look back to Chapter 2, you will see that the three strategic business objectives of the Westin were the major priority of any process selected for improvement.

Without the team sponsor ensuring this link between why the project exists and its impact on some strategic business objective of the organization, not only is the project doomed but the larger issue of the quality initiative succeeding is in jeopardy. Proposed projects that cannot be shown to have an impact on the strategic business objectives should be aborted immediately. Even if they go on to dramatic success, these projects do more harm than good. I have heard people engaged in a quality effort say, "I already have a job and now you are asking me to spend *extra* [my italics] time on a project." This is a red flag to management that they have not exerted effort necessary to establish the business case for a project. When done properly, establishing the business case creates the atmosphere in an organization that quality improvement is part of an individual's job responsibility.

The Problem Statement

While the Business Case creates the strategic purpose for the team, the Problem Statement states the tactical issue that the team wants to improve.

I have always attempted to practice the principles of quality improvement in my own small consulting business. High on my list of strategic business objectives are revenues. (I have yet to see a business where this isn't high on the list of strategic business objectives.)

During a staff meeting several years ago, my chief financial officer reported that while our revenue goal was well within reach, one measurement of our revenues, cash flow, had become a problem because of tardy payments of invoices from one of our primary clients. This problem occurred as a result of poor performance in one of our key subprocesses—Billing and Collections.

Thus, the strategic business objective affected was our revenues (one measure of which was cash flow) and the subprocess affected was Billing and Collections. Our Business Case was alerting Eckes & Associates personnel that revenue (cash flow) was negatively being impacted due to a Billing and Collections process. Having created the Strategic Business Case, we now turned to creating a tactical Problem Statement.

We crafted the following:

➤ Since January 199X, Eckes & Associates' (client) has averaged payment of invoices 96.2 days past due, resulting in additional administrative costs.

While in no way is this Problem Statement perfect, it does have some of the key elements that characterize good problem statements.

First, a good statement describes some time period *(Since January, 199X)*. How long has the problem existed? Problem Statements that describe a time period allow the project team to narrow their later work and thus allow a time frame for teams to focus their later analysis and improvement efforts.

Second, the Problem Statement should be specific and measurable *(has averaged payment of invoices 96.2 days past due)*. Specificity and measurability accomplish two things for the project team. First, it allows the team to see the magnitude of the problem and second it assists the team in thinking of how far improvement must go before the team can consider their project to be successful. For example, in our project we wanted to see a 50 percent improvement, which is a reasonable goal for a first project attempting to be accomplished within 120 to 160 days.

Third, the problem should describe the impact to the business *(resulting in additional administrative costs)*. There should always be a statement of impact that answers tactically the question, "Why should I care about this problem?" In this case, we cared because late payment of invoices increased administrative costs (we could have specified by how much to make this even a better statement).

Fourth, the Problem Statement should either imply or state explicitly the gap between the current state *(96.2 days past due)* and the desired state. In our statement, you do not see the desired state expressed directly but it clearly implies through the term "past due" what the desired state is *(no days past due)*.

Finally, good problem statements are stated in neutral terms. Three conditions typically apply to neutrality. First, there is no jumping to a perceived cause. For example, in working with a travel agency, the team came up with this problem statement:

➤ Due to excessive use of sick time, we have been unable to keep up with demand.

As you can see, this problem statement falls down in several areas. We do not know the time frame for which the travel agency has been unable to keep up with demand. Second, it is not stated specifically what the demand is or the inability to keep up with it. Third, it does not describe the impact and most importantly, they have jumped to a perceived cause *(excessive use of sick time).* The travel agency team may be right but the cause(s) of problems is dealt with during the analysis portion of the project.

The second element of a neutral statement is not jumping to solutions. For the same reason we don't want to jump to perceived causes, we don't want to jump to solutions. There is a separate stage, which we will explore in Chapter 8, that addresses solutions. Now is not the time.

Finally, we don't want to attribute blame with a problem statement.

The Project Scope

Project scope refers to the boundaries of what the team will be working on and more importantly what the team will *not* be working on. Think of the United States' participation in the Vietnam War. Our original goal to provide technical advice to the South Vietnamese in their civil war with the North was laudable. Yet, as we sadly review the history of this conflict, we see that our role gradually and in many ways informally changed. At the time of the Saigon mass exodus in 1975, the scope of the United States' involvement had dramatically changed. Long abandoned was the role of advisor; it was replaced by active combat. Not only did this role go beyond the original mission, the United States invasion of Cambodia and Thailand shows the concept of "scope creep," which in no small part explains the results that ensued.

What I recommend each project team do in one of their first meetings is to create agreement on what the project scope is for their project. The team champion can begin this activity by giving the team leader general ideas of what is inside and outside of the project scope. However, no matter how well the champion has thought through the scope, the team will have additional ideas or concerns. Thus, a simple two-part exercise (page 48) can clear the scope issue and prevent problems later on.

This exercise usually takes little time (less than two hours) and truly proves the adage that an ounce of prevention is worth a pound of cure.

An example may prove illustrative. In 1961, in the face of the Soviet threat to control space. President John F. Kennedy proclaimed in a Congressional speech. "We shall place a man on the

---

EXERCISE TO CLEAR THE SCOPE ISSUE

First, the team leader should create three columns on a wall of the meeting room. At the top of the first column should be a 5 × 7 card that says "In." At the top of the second column should be a 5 × 7 card that says "Out." In the third and final column should be a 5 × 7 card that is labeled, "?." The team leader should then describe the Business Case and present the preliminary Problem Statement using the guidelines described earlier in this chapter. The team leader should then hand out a series of blank 5 × 7 cards. He or she should then instruct each team member to write down on each card what is inside the scope of the project team's activities, what is outside the scope, and what he or she is not certain about.

The team members can then post their cards to the appropriate column. The team leader should review each card in each column clarifying what is written while at the same time looking for duplicate ideas that the team has generated. Most importantly, during this process the team leader should be looking for ideas that appear in more than one column. These cards should be put in the question mark column, along with ideas team members are uncertain about.

It is the responsibility for the team leader to take this work created by the team and immediately report back to the champion. It is then the responsibility of the champion to take this input and create only two columns: what will be inside the scope for the team and what is outside.

---

moon and return him safely by the end of the decade." This proclamation and the ensuing accomplishment of Neil Armstrong's walk on the moon in July 1969 was one of the United States' greatest achievements. NASA's work in the next eight years had to be extremely focused. There had to be a host of activities inside the scope of putting a man on the moon and a host of activities that could have resulted in NASA failing in its mission.

Consider the scope of what NASA had to deal with in the short eight years from the time of President Kennedy's pronouncement to the time Neil Armstrong walked on the moon. Which of the following would you have put inside the scope of putting a man on the moon and which would you have put outside the scope?

Orbiting the earth	Space station	Orbiting the moon
Space walk	creation	Linkage with
Landing a man on	Lunar module	Soviets
Mars	practice	

Inside the Scope	Outside the Scope
Orbiting the earth	Space station creation
Orbiting the moon	Linkage with Soviets
Lunar module practice	Landing a man on Mars
Space walk	

Goals and Objectives

Once the Problem Statement has been created, a set of reasonable Goals and Objectives must be created and agreed to by the team and their champion. It is important for the team to set Goals and Objectives that are achievable within a 120- to 160-day period. A typical rule of thumb is for teams to reduce the problem by 50 percent in the 120- to 160-day window. For example, in the invoice payment project we mentioned earlier, a reasonable but powerful goal would be for invoice payment lateness to go from 96.2 days to 48.

Milestones

While each project varies in terms of completion, first projects should be scoped to be completed in 120 to 160 days. First projects that last longer than 160 days encounter a precipitious decline in the likelihood of goal obtainment. Approximately half of the 160 days should be devoted to the Define-and-Measure portion of the improve methodology with the remainder of the time devoted to analysis and improvement (the bulk of control being implemented after the project team has disbanded). A good champion should provide the project team with project management resources to ensure that the team is on track to meet the 160-day window. Subsequent projects can last longer than 160 days and be successful dependent on factors such as degree of cross-functional impact, business complexity, current performance, and desired improvement.

Roles and Responsibilities

At the beginning of this chapter, we talked of the various Roles and Responsibilities of the project team, from the champion, to the Black Belt or Green Belt, to the team members, and the ad hoc members of the team like the Master Black Belt.

These roles must be carefully chosen, not with those people available and interested in the team but with the individuals *most qualified* to carry out the assignment—those people who most directly impact the strategic goals of the process in question. Many project teams make the mistake of filling positions with those individuals who have interest in improvement. The *most qualified* people must be on the team, particularly team members who have the expertise that will eventually lead to sigma improvement.

➤ Identifying the Customers, Their Needs, and Requirements

Earlier we discussed the three major focus areas of high-functioning organizations; a strong focus on employees, a strong focus on process, and most importantly an overriding focus on the customer. Once the team charter has been validated, the second function of the team is to identify the customer or customers of the project. Many teams make the mistake of assuming that the customer is the external entity that pays the bill. While this could be the case, the customer is the *recipient of the product or service.* It is plausible that a customer of the project could easily be sitting in the cubicle next to you.

In addition, once the team starts brainstorming who the customer or customers of the project are, it is important to stratify or segment the customers, ranking them as primary or secondary (or even tertiary at times). Segmentation is usually based on market segment, revenue impact, geography, business importance, or some other criteria. Segmentation of customers is important for one simple reason: In any process, there is a high probability of multiple customers. In some cases, multiple customers will have complementary needs and requirements. But in other cases, different customers will have different needs and requirements. Segmenting customers into primary, secondary, or even tertiary categories allows the team to make decisions about which customers deserve priority in the case of conflicting needs and requirements. For example, people are always inquiring how I can live with the uncertainty of being a consultant. I tell them that someone who works for someone else is at a much higher risk for he has all his eggs in one basket. If the business takes a downturn and has to downsize, he could be unemployed. Meanwhile, a consultant usually has five or six clients at any one time. If one downsizes Eckes & Associates, I still have four or five other clients, thus I have much more security than someone who has one employer. I also segment my clients. At any one time, I usually have one client I consider my primary client, invariably based on percent of revenue (my most important strategic business objective).

While I have been fortunate to have General Electric as a client since 1991, it has only been since 1995 that I would consider them my primary client. Once a month, we have a consultant conference call. If GE was a secondary or tertiary client, I might not make myself available, but I or someone from my staff will be part of the conference call because of their importance to our business.

Once the project team has established who their customers are and has done some segmentation using appropriate criteria, the team must then move toward determining the customers *Needs and Requirements*.

There are those who believe that I am being redundant by saying needs and requirements. While as a consultant I am guilty of saying too much versus too little, it is not redundant to separate out needs and requirements. The need of a customer is the output or outputs of a process that establishes the relationship between the supplier and customer. Requirements are the characteristics that determine whether the customer is happy with the output provided. For example, in my business, I often must travel from the happy confines of my Denver home, often back to the East Coast or increasingly overseas, primarily to Europe. As I travel east and awaken in the middle of the night Mountain time, I have a "need" for a cup of coffee. There are times when this coffee drinking need turns out to be highly pleasurable and others when I am disappointed. Whether this experience is pleasurable or disappointing is dependent on my requirements.

If you are a coffee drinker, what are your requirements that determine if you are happy or not? For me, early in the morning, my requirements include the following:

Caffeine.
Strength of brew.
Taste (Yes, I love Starbucks. I would give them a great discount if they hired Eckes & Associates.).
Additives (real cream and raw sugar).

Container (cup vs. styrofoam the latter of which should be outlawed).

The Critical-to-Quality Tree

While there are a variety of tools to use to help a team reach requirements, one of my favorites is the critical-to-quality (CTQ) tree. This simple tool helps the team move from general needs of the customer to the more specific, behavioral requirements of the customer. The steps of creating the CTQ tree are:

1. *Identify the customer.* First, the team does a CTQ tree to determine whether the identified customers need to be segmented, since, in some cases, different customers have different requirements. In the example that follows, we use the Westin room service delivery process CTQ tree (Exhibit 4.1). Thus, the customer of room service is the hotel guest requesting a meal. There is no need to segment this customer—the hotel guest requesting room service.

2. *Identify the customer's need.* In Exhibit 4.1, we place the customers need in the level 1 line of the tree: The hotel

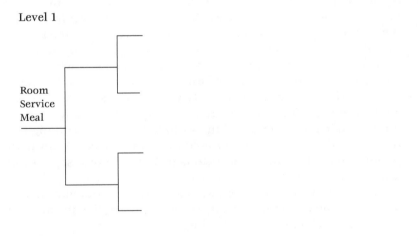

Exhibit 4.1 Beginning CTQ tree.

guest who calls room service is in need of a room service meal.

3. *Identify the first set of requirements for the need.* As we saw in the identification of the process dashboards in Chapter 2, each process should identify 1 to 3 measures of effectiveness and efficiency that help drive the process. We mentioned whether these requirements of the need determine whether the customer of that process is satisfied or not. Thus, it is critical to validate these requirements with the customer. In our Westin case study, we indicated that data brought back by the process owner indicated that speed of delivery, food quality, and menu variety were the three most important requirements of those who were using room service. We then see how the first three "branches" of the CTQ tree are formed (Exhibit 4.2). We see how these elements are placed on the Level 2 area of the CTQ tree.

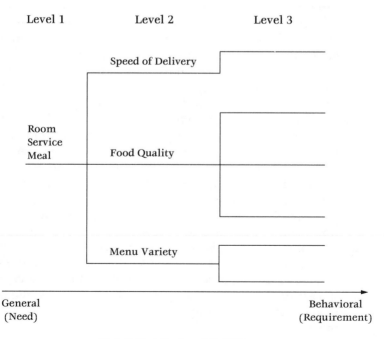

Exhibit 4.2 Level 2 CTQ tree.

4. *Drill down to level 3 if necessary.* In our example, we want to examine if each level 2 element of the CTQ tree can be taken to another level of specificity. At this point, if the additional level produces what we would consider a measurement, we should stop at the second level of the CTQ tree. For example, if the team considers the next level of speed of delivery to be minutes, they have gone too far because minutes is how speed is to be measured and that will be covered in our next chapter (Chapter 5). Thus, our work for speed is complete with the level 2 entry. However, if you asked what about food quality would make the experience enjoyable (as we did in this example), we were told three things. First, the temperature of the food was important. The soup is hot and the ice tea is cold. Note we are not specifying how temperature of the food is measured, thus, this is an area that will go forward. Second, the food service customer indicated to us that the taste of the food was a determinant of food quality: Medium rare or well done, meat lean, fish fresh, and so on. Finally, the third major component of food quality was presentation of the food. These three areas are located on the third level of the CTQ tree as seen in Exhibit 4.3: Likewise, when asked about menu variety, the customers' third most important requirement, two elements were consistently mentioned, quantity of items (number of items), and number of healthy choices (e.g., Heathmark items). These are listed in Exhibit 4.3 under the next branch of items for Menu Variety.

Many project teams fall into the trap of having the tool use them rather than vice versa. The most common problem with the CTQ tree is attempting to create the third level when two levels will suffice. There is no science to this determination, simply common sense. One consideration in determining if you have gone far enough in the CTQ tree is to see if any third level requirement is really how the requirement will be measured. For example, in the case of speed of delivery, if a team tried to create the third level, invariably they would talk about elapsed time measured in minutes to deliver the meal. Minutes is a type of measure. We won't talk about measurement until the next chapter. How something is measured should not be a part of a CTQ tree.

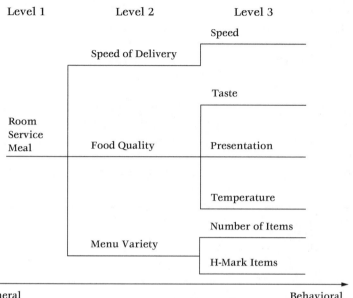

Level 1	Level 2	Level 3

Room Service Meal — Speed of Delivery — Speed

Food Quality — Taste, Presentation, Temperature

Menu Variety — Number of Items, H-Mark Items

General (Need) ⟶ Behavioral (Requirement)

Exhibit 4.3 Level 3 CTQ tree.

5. *Validate the requirements with the customer.* At this point, the CTQ tree is the creation of the project team's brainstorming. While valuable, it needs to be validated with the customer. In many cases, what the team considers important, the customer will see in a different way. There are many ways to validate what the customer considers important. The major ways to validate what the customer's needs and requirements are include:

—Customer one-on-one interviews.
—Surveys.
—Focus groups.
—Being the customer/Observing the customer.
—Customer complaints.

Customer One-on-One Interview. Customer one-on-one interviews involve taking a customer through a series of questions that will validate the CTQ tree. The advantages of the interview include being able to take a response and follow up the answer to get to more detailed answers. The disadvantages includes the cost of interviewing and the need to have the interview be conducted by someone who can supplement prepared questions with spontaneous questions when the need arises.

Surveys. A survey is a set of written questions that is sent to selected customers to obtain standardized answers that will enable determination of which requirements are most important to the customer. A survey one client uses to evaluate my effectiveness and efficiency after teaching one of their quality classes, is:

How would you rate this course in terms of:					
	Excellent		*Fair*		*Poor*
a. Practical value	5	4	3	2	1
b. New ideas	5	4	3	2	1
c. Clarity of how to apply concepts	5	4	3	2	1
d. Understandability of materials	5	4	3	2	1
e. Meeting your expectations	5	4	3	2	1
f. Effectiveness of instructor	5	4	3	2	1

This type of response is called a Likert Scale, so named after the University of Michigan statistician who created it. Likert showed that a scale of 1 to 5 is far better because people given larger scales (1 to 10) rarely use the whole range of choices, instead opting for extremely low numbers (1 or 2) or extremely high numbers (9 or 10).

Among the advantages to surveys are the data created, which leads to little if any need for interpretation in answers, and the ability to prioritize needs and requirements from direct, no nonsense answers. There are two major disadvantages to surveys: First, response rates to surveys are relatively small, thus calling into question what motivates the respondent. Usually, people respond to surveys if they are highly satisfied or highly dissatisfied. Survey return rates that are greater than 10 percent without some incentive are rare. The second disadvantage to surveys is that there is no opportunity for follow-up and the surveyor is at the mercy of how well the questions are created. Significantly different answers can be expected dependent on how a question is asked.

Focus Groups. A focus group is a selected group of customers who are gathered together to answer a set of prepared questions. When in the hands of an able facilitator, focus groups have many advantages: A facilitator who knows what he or she is doing can follow up with additional questions based on the respondents' answers and the ability to read body language. In this way, the customers' needs and requirements can be ascertained in significant detail. There are several disadvantages with focus groups: Often, if there is a dominant personality among those in the focus group, he or she may influence others in the group. Focus groups also can be expensive because bringing people together in one physical location involves a great deal of coordination. There is also the problem of focus groups being run by less than experienced facilitators. Finally, there is the problem of asking the right questions.

The latter problem is not unique to novice organizations. In the mid-1980s, a prominent U.S. company was in a fierce battle with its main competitor. Among other strategies, a focus group was called together to test a new product that more closely paralleled the competition. During the focus group, they concentrated on how the new product compared to the competition and were elated when they found not only similarities between the two, but that the new product was even better than their competitor. With this information in hand, Coca-Cola introduced what many have called the worst new product of the decade. How did this new product for Coca-Cola, "New Coke," end up being such a dud? Among the many mistakes associated with this product was the focus group, which isolated taste as a customer requirement. While taste is a requirement for the need for a cola, it actually is not that high on the list. Instead of letting the focus group bring out what the requirements of the customer are for a cola, Coca-Cola spent the majority of its time with the mistaken impression that taste was a far more important requirement than it really was. They found out the taste of New Coke was very close to Pepsi-Cola but did not inquire about how the image of the cola was a stronger requirement. During the 1980s, Pepsi did an outstanding job of selling their cola as a youth product, having hired then popular Michael Jackson to sell its wares. Thus, the misuse of focus groups led Coca-Cola into a very expensive marketing error.

Being the Customer/Observing the Customer. Several years ago, a well-known restaurant chain (TGIF) was experiencing a sales drop in one of their Midwestern restaurants. The manager of the restaurant indicated poor economic conditions in the town as the reason why they were experiencing difficulty. While this was probably a contributing factor, a regional sales manager came up with an interesting idea. He had staff sit at each table over the course of several weeks and make observations about what it was like to be a customer of that restaurant. While there was no single reason why sales had dropped, taking this approach of being the customer dramatically generated a set of requirements that led to improved sales.

Spending time observing the customer can also be of tremendous benefit in helping an organization determine the requirements of the customer. One European GE Capital business that does this quite well takes the time to have a field engineer spend the entire day after installing the computers at a new site to see how the product is used. As a result, it has been determined that several preconceived notions of what was not important to the customer really are quite important.

Customer Complaints. My friend Bill Dougherty at the Westin has shared many interesting stories with me of the demanding nature of some hotel guests. The focus of some of these demands comes in the package of a complaint. Complaints have the advantage of providing the supplier with an immediate opportunity to right a wrong. In terms of our discussion here, complaints assist in providing specific information about what the customer requires. Unfortunately, there is one major drawback to complaints as a way to learn about customer requirements. I run a simple test in my classes to show what this drawback is: I ask every participant to think of the number of times in the past two weeks they have been dissatisfied when they have been a customer. Amazingly, people raise four or five fingers. Thus, in an average-sized class, I have 50 to 75 opportunities for complaints. Then I ask how many times they formally complained. Universally, less than 10 fingers pop up. Thus, through this test we see that the major disadvantage of determining customer requirements through complaints is that most people don't complain.

Even when a customer complains, you may not be able to right a wrong. Bill Dougherty amused me once with the story of a rock star who stayed at his facility where in the middle of the night he complained that the wind outside was too loud in his high-rise suite. I never did find out how they rectified this problem to entice the rock star to return to the Westin.

➤ Creating the High-Level Process Map

We are now ready to discuss the third and last "tollgate" of Define. In this last step, we create a high-level Map of the process that most directly affects the project we are working on.

There is an old saying, that a picture is worth a thousand words (though I hope this doesn't apply to books on Six Sigma). In earlier chapters, we defined a process as a series of steps or activities that take inputs provided by supplier(s), add value, and produce outputs for customers. What we are trying to accomplish in this last area of Define is to create a high-level picture of how the affected process currently operates. By seeing how the affected process operates, we may be able to determine what in the process in not operating as it should.

When you see how valuable the concepts of Six Sigma are, they come to be a part of your everyday life. The example I have chosen to show the tool of Process Mapping comes from my personal life. Like so many of the tools of Six Sigma there are a series of easy-to-implement steps involved, including:

1. Define the process to be mapped.
2. Establish the start and stop points of the process (boundaries).
3. Determine the output of the process.
4. Determine the customers of the process.
5. Determine the requirements of the customers.
6. Identify the suppliers to the process and obtain agreement on the inputs to the process.
7. Agree on the 5 to 7 high-level steps that occur between the start and stop points of the process.

Define the Process to Be Mapped

Long ago I had promised myself that once I had established my consulting business, I would splurge and buy myself an expensive sports car. Long after I could afford to buy one, I was hesitant. Finally, after my fortieth birthday, I decided to buy the car but I wanted to be as effective and efficient as I could. I soon realized that to be effective and efficient in my car-buying process, I could utilize the same tools that had helped me earn the car.

I set out to practice the concept of Process Mapping to assist me in buying the car. First step, define the process to be mapped. As we discussed in the team chartering section, teams will always be challenged to avoid scope creep. Here we have one of several decisions that could impact scope creep. The process name should include some action verb and, in my case, I defined the process to be mapped: The Car-Buying Process. What if I had named it the Car-Leasing Process? The latter would have been a lengthier process since the process does not end until I return the vehicle. While there is no right or wrong answer to defining the process to be mapped, the team should spend conscious time discussing the impact of their decision. How you define what the process is has impact on the scope of work to be done.

Establish the Start and Stop Points of the Process (Boundaries)

Like our preceding step, there is no right or wrong answer to establishing the start and stop points of the process. However, like the preceding step, the decision made here has impact on our project scope.

In my car buying example, I decided that the start point for buying my car was turning 40. It could have easily been "achieving a certain monetary goal in my business" or having my old car stop running.

I made the determination that driving the car off the lot was the stop point for the process. Think of the implications for project scope if I had made the decision that the last payment for the car was the stop point. If I had decided the latter, the scope of the process would have been much larger. Again, there is no right or wrong answer. Many times, the team will make the decision that the stop point is much later. This is fine as long as the team makes a conscious decision.

Determine the Output of the Process

Our next step was to determine the output of the process. The output of the process should be stated in simple unqualified nouns. Teams often make their work more difficult by getting ahead of themselves by adding adjectives to the output that is the work of later parts of the Process Map. In our car-buying example, the output of the car-buying process is simply a car.

The most common question I receive about the output is whether there can be multiple outputs. The answer is yes. I strongly recommend, however, that the team keep things simple. While any process can have multiple outputs, if the team focuses on the project at hand, they will usually find there is one output.

Determine the Customers of the Process

In the next two steps of Process Mapping, our work should have already been completed. That is, determining our customers and requirements should have taken place earlier in Define. Look back to the CTQ tree. From the tree, we should be able to identify the customers and as we shall see, we should also have their requirements.

In the car-buying example, we have an opportunity to segment our customer base. First, who is the primary customer of the output? Remember that primary customers should have the highest impact on the output, be the most important consideration of the process, and have the greatest interest in the output. Of course, you are probably indicating that the primary customer of this car is me. Thanks, but incorrect. The primary customer is my wife. Always know who your primary customer is. Making such a purchase without naming my wife the primary customer would have been a serious mistake.

If my wife is the primary customer, then is it safe to say I am the secondary customer? Of course not. When you live in a home with two preteenage boys and you are getting an expensive sports car, you would be foolish not to see the two boys, Joe and Temo, as at least the secondary customers.

Can there be tertiary customers? Yes, in this case, it is me.

Determine the Requirements of the Customers

Again, we should already have this work completed. Simply, cut and paste on the Process Map the details of the CTQ tree, either level 2 or level 3 requirements. Fortunately, when I first approached my wife about buying this expensive sports car, she was highly supportive. She said that if I bought this shallow superficial automobile, she would still love me. She would miss me, but she would still love me.

Actually, her only requirement was the color of the car. Easy enough, now on to my secondary customers. They had two requirements. Speed of the car and back seats. The tertiary customer, having just experienced his fortieth birthday, had one simple requirement, status.

You will note in Exhibit 4.4 that we have added an additional column next to the requirements. While not mandatory, at this point we want to ease you into the concept of measurement. Think for a moment how, in this case, the requirements of each of the three major customers could be measured. First, my wife's only requirement was the color of the car. If you met my wife, you would quickly note that her favorite color is black. Her clothes are often black, the dominant color scheme in our home is black, and at the time of our marriage, the color of her husband's hair was black. Thus, the "as measured by" (AMB) for color of car is how dark the color of the car will be.

In the case of my two boys, I learned about the importance of determining the "as measured by" for a requirement. The most important requirement for my two boys was speed. I quickly learned not to assume how the requirement was to be measured. On one of the first days I owned the car, I took my two boys out for a ride and tried to "delight" my secondary customers. Just a half hour north of Denver on the way to Wyoming, the speed limit is 75. As I increased my speed significantly past the 75 limit, I expected to hear the ohhs and ahhs of my two boys. Finally, in the absence of hearing anything from my boys, I inquired if they were happy with the speed. A polite response followed. Ah, boys, I thought to myself, I thought speed was your first requirement of the car?

Where did I go wrong? I found out on the way home. After exiting from the highway and within a mile of our home, I stopped at a light. As the light turned green, I accelerated in what could only be described as a jackrabbit start. As I went through second, third, and fourth gears, I suddenly started to hear the ohhs and ahhs from my boys that I had expected earlier. Suddenly, I realized I had not been practicing what I have preached to so many of my clients. Speed was really acceleration as measured by the time in seconds from 0 to 60 mph.

Finally, how do we determine the "as measured by" for something as subjective as "status," the only requirement of our tertiary customer, me. At first it may seem that measuring something subjective is foolhardy. However, subjective measurements are a daily part of life. In this case, I had many options that would be viable

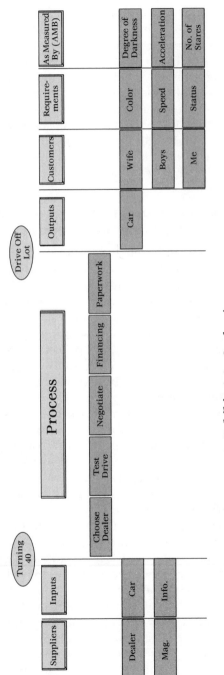

Exhibit 4.4 Car-buying process.

measures of status. The cost of the car would certainly meet the "as measured by" for status. While the car was handcrafted, any fool could certainly see it was overpriced. However, this type of measure is one data point. How could I determine if the car was losing its status? You might say the resale or "blue book" value suffices as a measure of status, but I was interested in some ongoing measure of status. An ongoing measure that would allow for frequent data collection and tell me if the car was losing status was the number of stares I get at stoplights. Since they certainly are not looking at me, this measure would allow me to determine the amount of appeal the car has and when it would wane.

Identify the Suppliers to the Process and Obtain Agreement on the Inputs to the Process

Now we focus on the left-hand side of the Process Map. An often overlooked part of becoming more effective and efficient is recognizing the management of suppliers who provide the inputs to your process. In this case, we first identify the suppliers to the car-buying process. First, we identify the car dealer. What input does the car dealer provide? A car, of course. But wait, how can an output also be an input? Simply put, the process is the steps and activities that take inputs (i.e., the car), add value, and produce an output or outputs. The value add in this case is the transfer of ownership from the dealer to me.

The second supplier I used in this process was *Money* magazine's March issue. The input from this supplier is information. Each March, *Money* magazine has an article on new cars. In this issue, they state the dealer price, the suggested retail price, and your target price when you negotiate the price of your car for over 300 types of cars. This input was used later in the process when I negotiated the price of the vehicle.

In my seminars, some suggest that I should list the car manufacturer as a supplier. I answer this suggestion with the first of my Eckesism's. When creating the high-level Process Map, "Stay as high as you can for as long as you can." Thus, we are only interested in the higher level suppliers and their inputs, not all suppliers and inputs. Of course, this also applies to customers and outputs.

Another problem area when creating the suppliers and their inputs is limiting yourself to only those inputs that occur *before* the process start point. This is incorrect as shown through the car-buying example. The second major input, the information from

Money magazine does not occur until the end of the process, yet we consider this an important input and list it accordingly.

Agree on the 5 to 7 High-Level Steps That Occur between the Start and Stop Points of the Process

We are now ready to complete the Process Map activities with the 5 to 7 high-level steps that occur when buying a car. At this point in creating the map, I encourage the project team to simply brainstorm the higher level steps in buying a car. At a later point, we then will put them in chronological order. As the adage says, there are two uses for a tissue, cleaning your glasses and blowing your nose, but you have to get the order right. However, at this point we just brainstorm the higher level steps in buying the car.

When I use this example in the class, the typical responses for the steps in buying a car are as follows:

➤ Choosing a dealer.
➤ Negotiating a price.
➤ Selecting the option package.
➤ Test driving the vehicle.
➤ Financing.
➤ Completing the paperwork.

In each of the above, the team did a good job with brainstorming the list of high-level process steps. A key to good brainstorming of process steps is making sure that the process step has some action verb associated with it. Note the steps brainstormed above do that. We polish them up and then put them in chronological order:

1. Choosing a dealer (the assumption is that I already know what type of car I want).
2. Test driving.
3. Selecting the option package.
4. Price negotiating.
5. Financing.
6. Completing the paperwork.

Exhibit 4.4 shows the map with all the steps complete. A mnemonic device to assist the project team with creating the Process Map is called SIPOC, which stands for Supplier, Input(s), Process, Output(s), and Customer.

The last step of this section of Define is to validate the process to ensure that the 5 to 7 steps of the process really occur as the team thinks they exist. This is because there are four levels of a process. The first level is what we think the process is. This is the process we create among the team. However, through validating the process, we create the second level, the true, "as is" map. I encourage the team to talk to people who "live" in the process or to walk through the process. The "should be" map is created from the improvements of a project team during the Improve phase of a project. The last and final type of map, the "could be" map comes about from Process Design and will not be addressed in this book.

Last, be wary of a common mistake that teams make when creating this high-level Process Map. Invariably, teams like to create on paper the map they desire the process to look like. This "should be" map will be eventually created but at this point in our project we want the process to look like it does in reality. Thus, the team should be on guard that during this brainstorming process and during the later validation activity, they will be tempted to create the map as they want it to appear. Avoid this temptation.

■ SUMMARY

We have now completed our discussion of the three major tollgates of the Define step of the Quality Improvement methodology of Six Sigma.

First, we discussed the team charter and the five key elements. The team should clearly have the Business Case for the project, which will state the strategic importance of the project. The second major element of the team charter is the preliminary problem statement, which should be a specific measurable statement about the gap between the current state and the desired state, also including the impact of the problem to the business stated in neutral terms.

From the problem statement, a goal statement should be created, one which the first project teams of an organization can achieve in 160 days. After the creation of the goal statement, the team should ensure they have the boundaries of the project, also known as the project scope. While a dynamic element of the project, scope must be managed closely.

A set of milestones for completion of the steps of the project must be established. Finally, roles and responsibilities for the project team must be set. In this chapter, we discussed the various roles and responsibilities of the project team. They include the team leader, the internal consultant who assists the team with the technical elements of the project, and the team members. Supervising the team from afar is the sponsor or champion.

The second of the three elements of the Define step of improvement was determining the customers of the project. We discussed whether it was necessary to segment the customers based on considerations such as market impact, geography, revenue, or some other factor. Once completed, the team must determine the needs and requirements of the customer or customers of the process in question. Reviewed was a popular method to structure the brainstorming of what the needs and requirements of the customer are—the CTQ tree. Discussed were methods to obtain these needs and requirements from one-on-one interviews to focus groups and customer complaints.

The third and final element of the Define step of improvement is the creation of the high-level "as is" Process Map. Using a mnemonic tool called the SIPOC, we created a map of the current process that in later steps in the improvement model we will analyze and improve.

KEY LEARNINGS

➤ The first of the five steps in Six Sigma quality improvement methodology focuses on *Defining* the project team's charter, the needs and requirements of the customer, and creating a map of the process to be improved.

➤ Make sure that a project impacts at least one business objective of the organization.

➤ Every project should have a management sponsor also known as the champion.

➤ Every project should have a team leader, either a Black Belt or a Green Belt.

(Continued)

(Continued)

➤ Project team members should be selected on the basis of their ability to improve the process.

➤ The project team should create a problem statement that is specific, measurable, describes the impact to the business, and does not jump to causes or solutions.

➤ The project team should receive careful guidance from management on the boundaries of what the team should work on, called the project scope.

➤ Successful project teams usually last a finite period of time, usually less than six months.

➤ Project teams need to establish the customers of their project and what customers require of the process targeted for improvement.

➤ A map of the process to be improved should be created that captures how the process operates today.

Chapter 5

Measuring Project Sigma

How Close Are You to Perfection?

What separates Six Sigma initiatives from so many other quality efforts is the emphasis of making decisions on facts and data rather than "seat-of-the-pants" decision making. Decision making based on gut feel or anecdotal information is not how organizations become more effective or efficient.

There are many issues associated with measurement. In my years of consulting I have noticed two major problems. The first major problem I see in organizations is a total lack of measurement. The other problem with measurement is measuring too much and not using what is measured. In the former case, I have observed businesses who have never measured anything going to the other extreme and if it moves, it gets measured.

Think of measurement as an investment. Like any investment, measurement costs time and money. This time and money can produce significant returns but only if the investment is done right. This chapter teaches you how to make a return on your measurement investment.

■ WHY SHOULD YOU MEASURE?

If you have no data, you are just another person with an opinion. There is also this quote attributed to Lord Kelvin (yes, he is the same person whom we associate with one of the temperature scales):

> *I often say that when you can measure what you are speaking about and express it in numbers, you know something about it, but when you cannot measure it, when you cannot express it in numbers, your knowledge is of a meager and unsatisfactory kind.*

> —Lord Kelvin

While these comments highlight the importance of measurement, I was most impressed by the comments my old friend, W. Edwards Deming made to me in the early 1980s.

This is the same Deming who ridiculed me in my first months of consulting. However, almost two years after my first, unpleasant experience with the quality guru, I was in Detroit waiting to put on a seminar at the then Metro Airport Hilton. An early riser, I came down to have breakfast, finding the restaurant nearly vacant. Taking my copy of the newspaper, I began to read the sports section when I heard the sonorous voice of the only other person eating that early. I became aware that the voice ordering breakfast was Deming himself.

Both of us were putting on seminars that week. At that first breakfast I was too timid to approach Deming. On the second day, however, I sheepishly approached Deming as once again, we were the only two eating breakfast. Unlike my first contact with Deming when he unceremoniously walked off after telling me to read some of his books, he was gracious and kind.

"Dr. Deming," I said as I approached his table after he took his order, "my name is George Eckes and . . ." I really don't remember what I said after that. What I do remember is his reaction, "Please, sit down, and have breakfast with me."

I was astounded. This same Deming who had seemed so rude the first time I had met him was now gracious, kind, and considerate. We went on to have breakfast the next four mornings and I only wish in hindsight I could have documented more of what he told me.

There were several gems Deming shared around the topic of measurement. One particular gem Deming shared was this simple fact, "What gets measured, gets done." Simple, direct, and powerful. Later in this chapter we will discuss several other Deming comments on measurement.

■ WHAT YOU SHOULD MEASURE

At the beginning of this book, we described any quality initiative as being an attempt toward becoming more effective and efficient. Thus, what you measure is also focused on these key elements. Exhibit 5.1 outlines the areas that require measurement.

I often talk to my associates about the three levels of mastery of any subject. First, there is memorization. But memorization is only the beginning. The second level of subject mastery is interpretation of what is memorized. Anyone can memorize the sigma formula, but do you know its importance? The final and most important level of subject mastery is assimilation, the ability to tie two or more important subjects together and make sense out of the concepts.

What quality tool from Define does this resemble? If you answered the Process Map, you have just exhibited assimilation. Measurement begins by taking your Process Map and identifying the measures of your effectiveness (output measures of your customer requirements). Then identify the measures of your efficiency (measures of the amount of time, or cost or labor or value steps between the start and stop points in your map). And then what to measure finishes by asking you to identify the measures of your supplier's effectiveness.

Input Measures (Supplier Effectiveness)	Process Measures (Your Efficiency)	Output Measures (Your Effectiveness)
The key quality measures placed on your suppliers.	Measures of your process efficiency: ➤ Cycle time. ➤ Cost. ➤ Value. ➤ Labor.	Measures of how well you are meeting (and hopefully exceeding) your customers' requirements.

Exhibit 5.1 Areas requiring measurement.

■ CREATING A DATA COLLECTION PLAN

The most important tool the project team can utilize in the measurement section of Six Sigma improvement is the Data Collection Plan (Exhibit 5.2). Think of the Data Collection Plan as the who, what, where, when, and how of data collection. Before data is collected, this plan needs to be filled out in detail. The majority of the rest of this chapter is devoted to creating the Data Collection Plan.

➤ Overview

To understand what belongs in each column of the Data Collection Plan, it will be helpful to use an example. Since we have already introduced the Westin Hotel improvement effort, we will use room service as our example.

It is critical that the project team answer the question, "Why am I collecting data?" During that week of breakfasts with Deming, he observed that among the many mistakes teams make in collecting data is not first coming up with the questions that data collection should answer. The questions a team should want answered center around the customer's needs and requirements. Brainstorm with your team to come up with a list of questions you expect to answer with the data you collect.

At the Westin, most of our brainstorming focused on the CTQ tree. The Westin team's main questions were:

➤ What is our current performance relative to room service delivery time?

➤ What does the customer think of our food quality?

➤ Do they like our menu?

The answers to these questions are placed in column 1 of the Data Collection Plan.

➤ The Type of Measure

How many measures are enough? Our second column will answer this for the team. With what has been brainstormed for the first column, we now characterize in the second column what type of measure it is (Exhibit 5.3 on page 74).

The three major types of measures refer to Exhibit 5.1 as to whether something is either an input, process, or output measure. The Process Map can assist the team in determining whether something is a process, output, or input measure.

What to Measure	Type of Measure	Type of Data	Operational Definition	Data Collection Form(s)	Sampling	Baseline Six Sigma

Exhibit 5.2 Data Collection Plan.

What to Measure	Type of Measure	Type of Data	Operational Definition	Data Collection Form(s)	Sampling	Baseline Six Sigma
Room Service Delivery Speed	Output/Process					
Food Quality	Output/Input					
Menu Variety	Output/Input					

Exhibit 5.3 Filling in the columns for Westin room service.

The team takes the Process Map and sees that room service delivery has been rated by customers as their most important requirement (CTQ). It is an output measure. However, look at what constitutes a process measure: It refers to the measure or measures of efficiency of how something is done, either the time it takes, the cost involved, the labor consumed, or the amount of value between the start and stop points in the Process Map.

The amount of time consumed in delivering a room service order is not only an output measure important to the customer, but also can be used as a measure of the efficiency of the process. Thus, one measure (room service delivery time) accomplishes two things for us: it constitutes an output measure *and* a process measure. We call this concept *double-dipping* and the team should always be alert to one measure that can accomplish two things.

The second measure, food quality, is an output measure as constituted by the CTQ tree. Once again, the team examines food quality to see if we can get more out of it. The team examines their Process Map and sees that the primary supplier to the room service delivery process is the food prep process. The input they provide is a room service meal. Thus, the second most important output to the customer (food quality) is dependent on how well we manage the input to our process, the room service meal. Thus, like the car-buying example, where the input can also be an output, we have *double-dipping*.

Finally, we apply the same concept to menu variety. It is the third most important concept as defined by the customer. If we were to go to the Process Map, we would also see this as an input from the supplier of menus, the corporate folks in Seattle.

Let's go back to the question of what is enough measurement. Typically, there should be 2 to 3 output measures and 1 to 2 input measures. Finally, it is rare when you need more than one process measure since most process measures (cost, time, labor, value) are typically strongly correlated. Again, let's use the analogy with the stock market: If the price-to-earnings ratio and the price-to-investment ratio tell you the same thing, why look at both? If cost and time tell you the same thing, why look at both, particularly if one of the measures would take additional time and effort to collect?

➤ The Type of Data

We now move on to the third column, the type of data (Exhibit 5.4). There are two types of data, discrete data and continuous data.

What to Measure	Type of Measure	Type of Data	Operational Definition	Data Collection Form(s)	Sampling	Baseline Six Sigma
Room Service Delivery Speed	Output/Process	Continuous				
Food Quality	Output/Input	Continuous				
Menu Variety	Output/Input	Continuous				

Exhibit 5.4 Type of data.

Discrete data is binary: yes/no, good/bad, on/off, male/female. Continuous data refers to data that exists on a continuum: height, weight, inches, time.

Which is preferred? In most cases, continuous data will tell us more information about the process. Have you ever been awakened by a young child in the middle of the night, complaining that they feel bad? When I ask my class participants what they do in this situation, the answer is almost universal. They indicate that they feel the child's forehead, and then, if warranted, they check their child's temperature with a thermometer. Why this course of action? Because even with the check of the child's forehead (discrete data: hot/normal), they know that the thermometer will indicate the magnitude of the fever.

When possible, continuous data should be collected. In our Westin Hotel example, speed of room service delivery is our most important customer requirement. To determine whether discrete or continuous data will be used for a measure, we need to know what the customer specification for satisfaction is. For room service, it is assumed that once a room service order is phoned in, the quicker it arrives, the happier the customer is. This type of requirement is called a sooner-or-smaller-is-better requirement. Many but not all customer requirements are sooner-or-smaller-is-better. When you order from a catalog, once you place the order, the quicker it comes in the mail, the happier you are. When the customer's requirement is a sooner-or-smaller-is-better characteristic, there will always be a maximum specification. The maximum specification refers to that point when the customer becomes dissatisfied. When the hotel staff asked the customers, they found out that for lunch and dinner, anything greater than 30 minutes incurred dissatisfaction. The customer doesn't expect the room service order to appear instantly, but becomes dissatisfied when the order takes more than 30 minutes.

Knowing the specification for room service delivery time, we are presented with the choice of collecting either discrete or continuous data. The discrete measure of room service delivery is how many room service deliveries were within 30 minutes (good deliveries) and how many room service deliveries were beyond 30 minutes (bad deliveries). The continuous measure for room service delivery is recording the actual delivery time for the delivery, whether it be 23 minutes or 32 minutes or 29 minutes. I recommended the team collect continuous data. As you see in

Exhibit 5.4, for the Type of Data column, we will be collecting continuous data.

Our second requirement is food quality. At first glance it would appear that this requirement would necessitate a discrete measure. You either like the meal or you don't, right? If you cannot generate continuous data, discrete data will suffice. However, remember how we used the Likert scale in the last chapter to evaluate an instructor's effectiveness? We used a 1 to 5 rating scale to evaluate how well an instructor was meeting or exceeding the customer's requirement for transfer of knowledge. We easily could have just asked the class participants whether they liked the course or didn't (discrete data). Offering the customers some options about their degree of happiness results in far more information than a simple yes or no. Therefore, we created a survey for randomly selected customers that evaluated the meal on the three elements the customers indicated were most important to them on the CTQ tree (temperature, taste, presentation). The survey questions were:

	Requirements				
	Exceeded		**Met**		**Did Not Meet**
Temperature of the meal:	5	4	3	2	1
Taste:	5	4	3	2	1
Presentation:	5	4	3	2	1

This type of customer requirement, unlike room service, is what is referred to as a *larger-is-better-quality* characteristic. In some cases, the customer target is 100 percent like a test score. In other cases, like the uptime for your computer, the target is infinity (we want our computers never to fail). In the food quality example, we desire all 5's.

When we have established a *larger-is-better-quality* characteristic, there will always be a minimum specification. Any rating a customer gives which is less than a 3 would indicate they are dissatisfied.

For the last measure listed on our data collection form, menu variety, the project team decided, once again, that a Likert scale should be used and the questions for menu variety are:

	Requirements			
	Exceeded		Met	Did Not Meet
Quantity of offerings:	5	4	3	2	1
Healthmark items:	5	4	3	2	1

Note that the specific questions surrounding menu variety originate from the CTQ tree just as the food quality questions were obtained. There is one final type of quality characteristic that the room service example does not have. This type of characteristic is called *nominal is best*. It occurs when the customers targeted or desired product or service is in the middle and variation on either side of this middle value causes less satisfaction on the part of the customer. For example, when the pilot of the plane I am traveling on lands, I desire him or her to land in the middle of the runway. When I am in the store and buy bananas, assuming I want to eat the bananas the same day, I want yellow bananas. I don't want green bananas and I don't want them to be overripe and be black. Associate salaries is another example of a nominal-is-best characteristic. I don't want to underpay associates and have them go with another consulting firm, but overpaying them results in less profit for the company. Whatever the situation, when you are faced with a nominal-is-best characteristic be aware that you will have a minimum *and* a maximum specification. In manufacturing, this is referred to as a bilateral tolerance. When I order sheet metal and the CTQ is length, I desire it to be a certain length and it cannot be too small or too big.

➤ Operational Definitions

I travel almost every week. Time is of particular importance to me. My usual routine if I am on the East Coast is to take the direct evening flight so that I am back in Denver by 9:00 P.M. or so. Friday evening is date night with my wife. She will pick me up at the airport and we will go out. Therefore, one of my CTQs for Friday evening flights is timely departure. Once I know I am in the air, I start to feel comfortable that I am on my way home.

Attempting to practice what I preach, I recently did some data gathering. During an extended contract with a client located in Manhattan, I researched which evening flight from LaGuardia had the best on-time departures to Denver. I was encouraged to see a 6:50 P.M. flight that arrived in Denver (remember the two-hour time zone difference) at 8:55 P.M. had an 87 percent on-time departure performance.

Using this data to make my airline decision, I took this flight almost weekly for nearly five months. Anxious to see if the historical performance would mirror my actual flights, I collected data on the number of times departure was on time. To my dismay, out of 19 flights, the number of times the flight left on time was zero!

At first, I thought that it was bad luck. Out of curiosity, I checked the official on-time departure for the flights in question and found out that for the 19 flights in question, the on-time departure percentage was 84 percent.

What explains the difference? The Federal Aviation Agency (which publishes the official on-time departures) and I had different operational definitions for what constitutes on-time departure.

An operational definition is a description of something where those affected have a common understanding such that all parties involved experience no ambiguity over what is being described.

It was not until I acquired a Flight Simulator client who trains pilots did I learn what the FAA's definition of departure time was. It was considerably different from mine. A flight's departure time to the FAA is when it pushes back from the gate. Using this definition, 84 percent of the flights I took from LaGuardia to Denver did indeed push back from the gate on the time that was scheduled. The problem was that we would then proceed to get into a queue of planes that did not take off until some time later. As a passenger, my definition of departure was when the plane left the ground.

What is the relevance? In deciding on an operational definition, it is important that there is *agreement* among those involved. While there is no right or wrong answer, the predominant consideration of the customer should always be on the minds of the project team as they determine their operational definitions.

In our room service delivery example, to be sure our operational definitions were clear, I provided the three designated data collectors with stop watches and asked them when they would begin the stop watch for the start of a delivery and when they would stop the watch indicating the end of a delivery. I asked each data collector to write down on a sheet of paper his or her start and stop times (i.e., operational definition of delivery time). Following is what each data collector wrote down:

Data Collector	Start	Stop
1	When the room service phone rings	When the client signs the check
2	After the phone order has been taken	Knock on the door
3	After the phone order has been taken	When the client signs the check

Note the problem we have. If each of the data collectors measures the same room service delivery, we will come back with three different results. What confidence will the project team have in the data if there are three different measures for the same delivery? Each of the three data collectors is conscientious and desire to do a good job, but each has a different operational definition. Before we begin data collection, we must discuss and reach agreement on a common understanding of what room service delivery time is. Reaching agreement may not be simple. In this case, I instructed the team that there is no right or wrong answer but that the requirements of the customer should guide the team toward its definition. The first data collector argued that delivery doesn't end until the check is signed because of his history of believing removing the plastic wrap from the food is important to the customer. After some discussion, the third data collector changed her mind because courtesy is not among the CTQs that were rated high by the customer. Data collector 1 finally relented and we were able to reach agreement on the stop point: When the deliverer knocks on the door. We then move to the start point. Data collector 1 argued for when the room service phone rings. The other collectors successfully argued that many times the customer doesn't know exactly what he or she wants and the time needed to inquire to assist the customer with his or her order should not be included in the data collection. After a lengthy but productive discussion, we had our operational definition: Room service delivery time will be from when the customer hangs up the phone until the time the deliverer knocks on the door.

The same discussion ensued for the other two measures, food quality and menu variety. The discussion to determine the operational definition for these two items was much easier because the decision to create continuous data through a Likert scale goes a long way to the creation of an operational definition. That is, a

rating of 5 for each of the three elements of food quality (temperature, taste, presentation) would mean the customer's requirements
were exceeded, a rating of 3 would mean that the customer's requirement was met, and a rating of 1 would mean that the customer's requirement was not met. The same ratings applied to
menu variety. The finished column for operational definitions is
shown in Exhibit 5.5.

➤ Data Collection Forms

Once the project team knows what to measure and how to measure
it, the question becomes what tools are we going to use to measure.
This is relatively easy in the service arena. One of two data collection forms is used depending on the type of data you are collecting, discrete or continuous.

Discrete Data

When the project team is dealing with discrete data, a form should
be used that categorizes what is collected by the type of defect
that is found (remembering that discrete data is either good/bad,
on/off type data). Among my clients was a grocery chain that
wanted to improve the flow of traffic through their checkout lines.
Despite my suggestion that they should collect continuous data
(i.e., amount of time waiting in line), the chain decided to collect
discrete data. The steps in creating a data collection form for discrete data are as follows:

1. *Determine what is a defect.* In the case of the grocery chain,
   a defect was a wait in line for more than 5 minutes.

2. *Determine categories for the defects.* In the grocery chain,
   defects were categorized into the following:

   —Price check.
   —No money.
   —No Bagger.
   —Register out of tape.
   —Forgot item.
   —Override.
   —Wrong item.

3. *Determine time frame for data to be collected.* The grocery
   chain determined we would collect data over a week.

What to Measure	Type of Measure	Type of Data	Operational Definition	Data Collection Form(s)	Sampling	Baseline Six Sigma
Room Service Delivery Speed	Output/Process	Continuous	From end of phone call to knock on door.			
Food Quality	Output/Input	Continuous	Likert scale for each requirement where 5 = exceeded requirement, 3 = met requirement, 1 = did not meet requirement.			
Menu Variety	Output/Input	Continuous	Same as above.			

Exhibit 5.5 Operational definition.

83

4. *Develop a grid for data to be collected easily.* The grid in Exhibit 5.6 was developed.

The grid that was developed is called a *discrete checksheet*. The discrete checksheet is valuable but not by itself. It can be used to create a *Pareto chart* (Exhibit 5.7). The Pareto chart is named after an economist, Vilfredo Pareto, who mathematically showed that in the sixteenth century, 80 percent of the world's wealth was controlled by 20 percent of the population (today, 99 percent of the world's wealth is controlled by 1 percent of the population). Today, this concept is popularly called the 80–20 rule. Eighty percent of your day is spent on 20 percent of your job description. Eighty percent of manufacturing rework is in 20 percent of floor space. Joseph Juran, an internationally famous quality consultant, made the Pareto principle a popular tool in the quality arena in the 1960s and 1970s.

In the final analysis, my claim to fame may be that the two most prominent names in the field of quality have chastised me. In Chapter 1, I mentioned my infamous run in with Deming. In 1992, I was chosen to present at the annual Juran Institute conference. My topic that day was on supplier management. As my speech was about to begin, from the back of the conference room came the short, owlish-looking octogenarian Juran who took a front row seat. As I discussed the 80–20 rule, I mentioned that the

Item	Frequency	Comments
Price check	142	
No money	14	
No bagger	33	
Register out of tape	44	
Forgot item	12	
Override	86	Manager assistance needed
Wrong item	52	
Miscellaneous	8	

Exhibit 5.6 Data collection grid.

Pareto principle resulted in separating the "vital few elements from the trivial many."

As I uttered those words, I looked down to see Juran jotting down a note. I felt confident that I had made a positive point. At the conclusion of my speech, I saw Juran motioning for me to come to him. He then proceeded to politely correct me on the use of the Pareto principle. "Young man, it is not the vital few versus the trivial many, the Pareto principle separates the vital few from the *useful* many." Wow, I thought, within 10 years I had been corrected on quality by both Deming and Juran.

Juran's correction stuck with me as I went on to coach project teams on the use of this important tool. In the grocery chain example, we took the discrete checksheet results and transformed the data into a Pareto chart which is shown in Exhibit 5.7. We took each category's raw data, turned it into a percentage, and created a bar graph.

What advantage do we receive by placing the data into a Pareto chart? Pareto showed mathematically that it is far easier to reduce a large problem (checkout delays—price checks) by 50 percent than it is to eliminate a small problem (checkout delays—forgot item).

The combination of the discrete checksheet and the Pareto chart are the two most appropriate tools to use with discrete data.

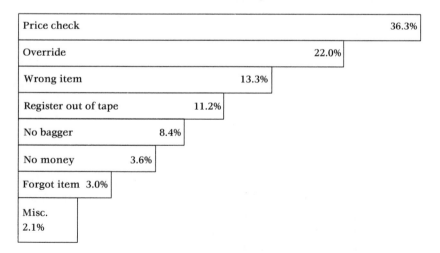

Exhibit 5.7 Pareto chart on data collection.

Continuous Data

When the project team is faced with collecting continuous data, there is one recommended tool, the frequency distribution checksheet. This tool takes the lowest continuous value expected when we collect data and the highest expected value and creates a continuum of values. The Westin room service example gives us an opportunity to see how this is done. When asked about the anticipated lowest value of room service delivery time, the project team thought that 20 minutes would be the lowest value. They anticipated 45 minutes would be the highest level. If the frequency distribution checksheet were to be created using each minute as a measurement cell, it would look like the following:

20 21 22 23 24 25 26 27 28 29 30 31 32 33 34 35 36 37 38 39 40 41 42 43 44 45

Statisticians have recommended that the number of cells be 5 to 7. Thus, in this example when the range is 25 ($45 - 20 = 25$) and we need to include all data points (not just those between 45 and 20), we divide by 5 and create 6 cells of 5 values each:

20–24   25–29   30–34   35–39   40–44   45+

When we collect data for the frequency distribution checksheet, we place tick marks for every time a value within a cell occurs. The actual data for the room service example is proprietary, but a fictional example of data before improvement for room service delivery time might be:

					X
			X	X	X
		X	X	X	X
	X	X	X	X	X
20–24	25–29	30–34	35–39	40–44	45 +

Since food quality and menu variety are also continuous data, we can use the frequency distribution checksheet using the 5 to 1 Likert scale where each of the numbers (1-2-3-4-5) is a cell unto itself. Two examples of frequency distribution checksheets are shown in Exhibits 5.8 and 5.9.

We will revisit the frequency distribution checksheet later in this chapter when we discuss the topic of variation. Exhibit 5.10

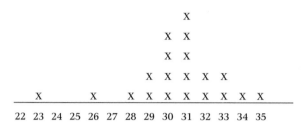

```
                    X
                  X X
                  X X
              X X X X X
   X        X   X X X X X X X X
   22 23 24 25 26 27 28 29 30 31 32 33 34 35
```

Exhibit 5.8   Horizontal frequency plot of room service delivery.

(page 88) shows the continuation of the Data Collection Plan that includes the column for data collection forms.

➤ Sampling

Our penultimate column on the Data Collection Plan is how we will sample. Sampling is the process of taking only a proportion of the total population of available data.

The most common question I am asked about sampling is how much data I should take from the whole population of available data. This is the wrong question to ask first. While how much data to take is important, there are two important considerations to deal with first: ensuring that the sample is representative and random.

Representative Sampling

Representative sampling occurs when the sample is an accurate reflection of the larger population. An example from history will highlight the importance of ensuring that the sample is representative of the larger population. During the Great Depression in 1932, it was time for the presidential election. The Republican incumbent

```
1 | X
2 | X  X
3 | X  X  X  X  X
4 | X  X  X
5 | X  X
```

Exhibit 5.9   Vertical frequency plot of food quality.

What to Measure	Type of Measure	Type of Data	Operational Definition	Data Collection Form(s)	Sampling	Baseline Six Sigma
Room Service Delivery Speed	Output/Process	Continuous	From end of phone call to knock on door.	Frequency distribution checksheets		
Food Quality	Output/Input	Continuous	Likert scale for each requirement where 5 = exceeded requirement, 3 = met requirement, 1 = did not meet requirement.	Frequency distribution checksheets		
Menu Variety	Output/Input	Continuous	Same as above.	Frequency distribution checksheets		

Exhibit 5.10 Data collection form.

was Herbert Hoover and his Democratic challenger was a New Yorker named Franklin Delano Roosevelt. A famed polling firm conducted a telephone poll and asked one simple question, "Whom are you likely to vote for in the election, Herbert Hoover or Franklin Roosevelt?" The results showed that a majority of those polled were going to vote for Hoover. The actual results were an overwhelming victory for Roosevelt. Was the problem in this poll due to not sampling enough voters? No, the actual problem is reflected in the first sentence of this page: The polling firm used a *telephone* poll. In 1932, telephone ownership was rare; they were owned by the affluent. Those who were affluent were (and still are) inclined to vote Republican. Thus, the number of people polled was inconsequential. What was more important was *how representative* the poll was.

How representative the sample is should be the first concern of the project team. What I recommend is to hold a project team meeting and brainstorm a list of issues that the sample should address. This brainstorming session will not produce a sample that will address all issues related to being representative. However, most teams will come up with most of the concerns that will influence the agreed to sample.

For example, in the Westin room service project, the team brainstormed a host of issues. They included:

➤ Making sure the samples of room service deliveries were taken from most of the 19 floors, not just a few.

➤ Ensuring the sample was taken Monday through Friday, since the hotel caters to businesspeople.

➤ Sampling over a series of weeks that did not include a holiday. Further, making sure the sample was taken over a period of time when the hotel occupancy was consistently around its average.

Despite this excellent list, the Westin project team did not think of everything (no team will). One area they did not think of was whether delivery of breakfast orders should be included in the sample. It turned out that breakfast deliveries were excellent. Thus, including breakfast deliveries was really not representative of the overall population of Westin room service orders. This did not reveal itself until later. However, through brainstorming how the sample was to be collected, a much more realistic sample was collected.

Random Sampling

It is also important that the sample be randomly collected. A random sample is one in which each sample has an equal or like chance of occurrence, or putting it another way, a sample taken without bias.

How many of you own a compact disc player with a random button? Think of what this button does and why you use it. Among my hobbies is my music collection. I own thousand of old LP's (albums made of plastic that scratched and popped, to those younger than 30) and hundreds of CD's. One problem with my old albums was that after repeated plays I would anticipate the next song before the end of the current song. This is an example of bias since the second song followed the first, the third song followed the second, and so on. With a CD player with a random button, the first song played may be track 5, followed by 3, followed by 7, and so on. With a CD player with a random button, there is no bias; each song on the CD has an equal or like chance of being played.

Using our example, the selection of room service deliveries must be random. In fact, we must ensure that we take a random selection from *each* floor selected. One way to ensure the sample from each floor is done randomly is to use your CD player's random button, so that if song 9 comes out first, pick the ninth room service order for a given floor. How to pick which floor? Get that CD player plugged in. Hit the random button and if the first pick is 3, then you would pick the third floor. Of course, instead of using a CD player, there is usually a random numbers table in most basic statistics books.

Consider these sampling situations from GE Capital and how the issues of representation and randomness are handled. Several GE Capital businesses have a Call Resolution desk. Customers will call these desks asking for information, clarification of how to use a GE product, or to make a complaint.

Resolution time is an important CTQ. One GE Capital business was interested in studying how many callers had their issues resolved on the first call rather than having to call back. The GE Capital project team created a survey and sent it to approximately 20 percent of their callers. Of those surveys mailed, 10 percent were returned. Under what conditions would this be a representative and random sample?

Answer: Most participants examine this example and immediately discuss the response rate and the 20 percent of questionnaires mailed out. When participants in my classes first see this example they are astounded at the low response rate. However, I tell them that a 10 percent response rate is quite good. If the project team can assure that 20 percent of the population was based on a representative sample, then this sample is adequate.

In another example, an improvement team is interested in improving billing accuracy. They decide to sample every fifteenth bill during the next billing cycle. This type of sampling is called *systematic random sampling*. Novices to the world of sampling believe that sampling every "nth" item is a sign of being statistically oriented in their sampling. This type of sampling can possess bias, however, if there is no evidence of the underlying consistency of the population to be sampled. For example, what if the fifteenth sample is always the same customer. Then, this systematic sampling scheme (sometimes called "skip lot" sampling) would neither be representative nor random at all, since all the samples would be the same customer and not be representative of all customers.

In another example, an improvement team is interested in improving delivery time of leased vehicles which occurs in seven international locations. They sample from their Frankfurt office because it has data readily available.

Answer: I am always leery of taking data from readily available sources unless there is some evidence that the location in question (e.g., Frankfurt) is representative of the other locations. If Frankfurt is similar to the other offices in terms of size, type of customer, and performance, then sampling from that office and inferring to the other offices that don't collect data might work. However, this would be unlikely.

How Much Sampling Is Enough?

Once the practical issues of how representative and random the sample is, the team needs to address the issue of how large the sample should be. There are two formulas used to determine sample size. One addresses sample size when we use continuous data and the other applies when we sample discrete data.

The sampling formula for continuous data is:

$$n = \left(\frac{2s}{\Delta}\right)^2$$

What to Measure	Type of Measure	Type of Data	Operational Definition	Data Collection Form(s)	Sampling	Baseline Six Sigma
Room Service Delivery Speed	Output/Process	Continuous	From end of phone call to knock on door.	Frequency distribution checksheets	100% Sample with assurances that the sample was both random and representative	
Food Quality	Output/Input	Continuous	Likert scale for each requirement where 5 = exceeded requirement, 3 = met requirement, 1 = did not meet requirement.	Frequency distribution checksheets		
Menu Variety	Output/Input	Continuous	Same as above.	Frequency distribution checksheets		

Exhibit 5.11 Data collection sampling.

Where s represents the variability of the data and Δ represents the degree of precision or magnitude of desired change. Suppose we want to determine the sample size of wafer thickness of a silicon chip within plus or minus 1 micron.

Further, suppose we know from previous data that the sample standard deviation is 8. We now solve for n where 2 times $8 = 16$ which is divided by the degree of precision desired (1) and then squared which is 256.

Assuming the issues of representation and randomness have been properly addressed, the desired sample size would be 256.

The sampling formula for discrete data is:

$$n = \left(\frac{2}{\Delta}\right)^2 [P(1-P)]$$

Where Δ represents the degree of precision and P represents the proportion defective. Suppose in the earlier grocery store example, the grocery team wanted to determine how many people they should sample who had waited in line more than 5 minutes (their operational definition of a defect).

They indicate a desire to estimate the defect rate (P) within plus/minus 0.02 (i.e., the degree of precision) and estimate that 5 percent of their customers wait in line more than 5 minutes. Solving for n we would divide 2 by 0.02 and square that number (10,000), then multiply by $[0.05 \times (1 - 0.05)]$ which results in a sample size of 475.

While not always true, here is yet another reason why a team should strive to collect continuous data since in more cases than not, the sample size for discrete data will be significantly larger. In the Westin case study in Exhibit 5.11, the project team took a 100 percent sample after ensuring the sample was random and representative.

■ BASELINE SIX SIGMA

In Chapter 3, we talked about the concept of Six Sigma. We said that sigma is based on the theory of variation. All things that are measured fine enough vary. Assuming this to be true, anything that can be measured on a continuous scale (e.g., weight, height,

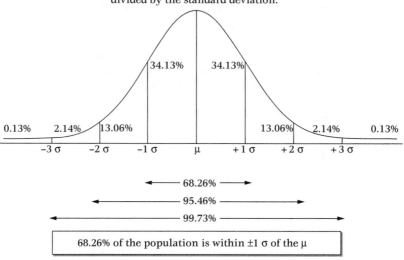

Exhibit 5.12   Segmented bell-shaped curve.

length) follows the bell-shaped curve (Exhibit 5.12). As discussed previously, this curve has the following characteristics:

➤ The curve represents virtually 100 percent of whatever is being measured. Each of the two tails of the curve goes out into infinity.

➤ The curve is symmetrical.

➤ The peak of the curve represents the most commonly occurring value or average.

➤ The curve can be divided into a series of segments as shown in Exhibit 5.12.

To refresh your memory from Chapter 3, each segment's technical name is called the standard deviation from the mean or center line. The symbol for the standard deviation is the lowercase Greek letter, sigma. As simply put as possible, the technical concept of Six Sigma is to measure current performance and to determine how many sigmas exist that can be measured from the current average until customer dissatisfaction occurs. When customer dissatisfaction occurs a defect results. A defect is any event that does not meet the requirements of a customer. Six Sigma is a process that produces no more than 3.4 defects per million opportunities.

Let's return to the example of room service delivery. In the eyes of the customer, room service delivery speed was the most important requirement. It was also stated that any lunch or dinner delivery past 30 minutes incurred customer dissatisfaction. Thus, a delivery of 31 minutes would be seen as a defect in the eyes of the customer. Since delivery time is a continuous measure, it is possible to create a hypothetical example of the bell-shaped curve for room service delivery as shown in Exhibit 5.13.

First, we can see that the deliveries for room service look similar to the bell-shaped curve (only an infinite sample size of room service deliveries will approximate a normal curve). Second, we can see that the peak of the curve (the most frequently occurring values) is centered at 26, so we may conclude that the average room service delivery time is 26. The curve extends out to about 30 which is where the customer has indicated that anything beyond is considered a defect. We can roughly measure that three sigmas of room service occur before the customer's specification of 30 occurs.

One way the sigma of the room service delivery process could be made better is shown in Exhibit 5.14 (page 96). You will notice that the curve looks identical to Exhibit 5.13 except that its center is at 23 instead of 26. The sigma performance is around 4 or a bit higher because there is more distance from the new average until a room service meal would exceed 30 minutes.

Moving the average to a quicker delivery is not the only way to improve the sigma number. The average delivery time could remain at 26 minutes, if the variation of room service deliveries around 26 is less.

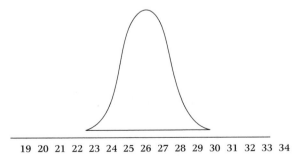

19 20 21 22 23 24 25 26 27 28 29 30 31 32 33 34

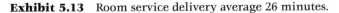

Exhibit 5.13 Room service delivery average 26 minutes.

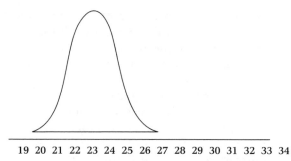

19 20 21 22 23 24 25 26 27 28 29 30 31 32 33 34

Exhibit 5.14 Room service delivery average 23 minutes.

Exhibit 5.15 shows an average room service delivery of 26 minutes but with much tighter and consistent performance around 26. Thus with each sigma smaller, there can be more of them measuring from the average of 26 until a defect occurs with a delivery of greater than 30 minutes. The vertical lines indicate approximately how many sigma exist before the customer specification of 30 is reached (about 4+). By working to both reduce the mean performance (26 minutes), and reducing the variation, sigma can dramatically be improved.

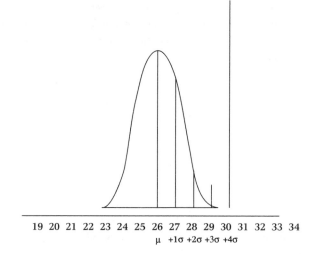

19 20 21 22 23 24 25 26 27 28 29 30 31 32 33 34
μ +1σ +2σ +3σ +4σ

Exhibit 5.15 Sigma specification room service delivery 26 minutes.

Common versus Special Cause Variation

In every process, there are six major components that create the variation we see in a process. These are the machines, materials, methods, measurement systems, the environment (or mother nature), and the people in the process. These six components (5 M's and 1 P) are known as the process component contributors. When there is no undue influence of any one of these six, the variation produced is called *common cause*. For continuous data, this is graphically represented by the preceding examples of room service delivery, where most of the values occur in the middle and fewer tail out in either direction to the left or the right. Other names for common cause variation are:

➤ Normal variation.

➤ Expected variation.

➤ Random variation.

When one or more of the components of variation have an undue influence on the process, *special cause* variation results. This is graphically represented by a distribution that is not bell shaped in nature. Examine the distribution for room service deliveries in Exhibit 5.16.

There appear to be "two" distributions present, what statisticians call a *bimodal distribution*. This bimodal distribution indicates to the project team that there is some special cause to the process, one or more components has an undue influence on the result.

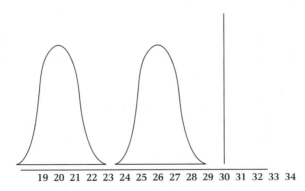

19 20 21 22 23 24 25 26 27 28 29 30 31 32 33 34

Exhibit 5.16 Bimodal distribution room service delivery.

Once again we see the advantage of collecting continuous data in graphical form. Examining just the raw data would indicate no defects. However, by creating a statistical picture, we know something different is happening in the process. This special cause variation is also known by terms such as:

➤ Abnormal variation.

➤ Unexpected variation.

➤ Nonrandom variation.

The importance of knowing whether we are dealing with common or special cause variation is important on several levels. First, knowing what type of variation we are dealing with can determine the kind of problem-solving strategy we will later employ. Common cause variation is variation that is "baked" into the process, where no one component explains the results.

One of the most important things Deming taught me is that management must master the concept of common versus special cause variation.

Imagine the traditional management style of another hotel's room service delivery process (see Exhibit 5.17). The distribution of Exhibit 5.17 shows an average performance of 45-minute delivery time with no deliveries meeting the customer's minimum delivery time of 30 minutes.

Where does traditional management focus its corrective action? Is it on the methods of delivery, the materials in the process, or the machines used in the process? No, history teaches us that traditional management will focus on the people in the process, coaxing, prodding, or more likely yelling or threatening those in the process to work harder or faster to improve room service deliveries.

Yet the distribution of Exhibit 5.17 shows common cause variation which means no one of the 5 M's or 1 P has an undue influence on performance. With common cause variation, there is a systems problem which requires focus on more than just one "M or P." What is the likelihood that subsequent performance will improve by telling the people in the process to work faster or harder? Dropped trays, delivery to wrong rooms, forgotten items, in a few words—performance will worsen.

Even if there is special cause variation occurring in the process, Deming indicated that the probability of people being the main contributors to that variation is between 5 to 15 percent.

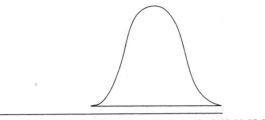

36 37 38 39 40 41 42 43 44 45 46 47 48 49 50 51 52 53

Exhibit 5.17   Performance of another hotel's room
service delivery process.

Therefore, it is critical for management to master the concept of
common versus specific cause variation. This will result in changing the focus of management intervention.

Thus, if you have common cause variation and are not meeting customer requirements, the problem exists with the system of
production, which is controlled by management, not the workers
in that system. We will return to this important topic later.

Calculating Sigma – The Discrete Method

To calculate sigma using the discrete method, you have to know
three items about what you are measuring. They are:

1. *Unit:* The item produced or being serviced.
2. *Defect:* Any event that does not meet the customer's requirements.
3. *Opportunity:* A chance for a defect to occur.

Let's examine the room service example. A unit was defined as
a room service order. The next two definitions were easier. A defect
was any meal delivered beyond 30 minutes or someone who rated
food quality or menu variety less than 3 on the Likert scale.

Finally, since the customer had indicated three major CTQs,
speed of delivery, food quality, and menu variety, there are three
opportunities.

With these three items clearly defined, we are now ready to do
the math. The formula to calculate sigma is as follows:

$$\frac{\text{Number of defects}}{\text{Number of opportunities} \times \text{Number of units}} \times 1,000,000$$

This calculation is called the defects per million opportunities (DPMO). Suppose the Westin measured 520 room service orders and 3 were late and 1 person gave food quality a 2 on the Likert scale. The math would look like this:

$$\frac{4}{3 \times 520} \times 1,000,000 = 2,564.1$$

Now examine the partial sigma chart in Exhibit 5.18. We look at the second column which is the number of defects per million opportunities or DPMO. We can see that 2,550 defects per million is

Long-Term Yield (%)	Defects per Million Opportunities	Sigma
99.99966	3.4	6
99.99995	5	5.9
99.9992	8	5.8
99.999	10	5.7
99.998	20	5.6
99.997	30	5.5
99.996	40	5.4
99.993	70	5.3
99.99	100	5.2
99.985	150	5.1
99.977	230	5.0
99.967	330	4.9
99.952	480	4.8
99.932	680	4.7
99.904	960	4.6
99.865	1,350	4.5
99.814	1,860	4.4
99.745	2,550	4.3
99.654	3,460	4.2
99.534	4,660	4.1
99.379	6,210	4.0
69.20	308,000	2.0
65.60	344,000	1.9

Note: The full chart appears in the appendix on pages 266 to 267.

Exhibit 5.18   Partial Six Sigma chart.

equivalent to a sigma performance of about 4.3. We have slightly more than that in the Westin example (2,564.1), but with rounding we would indicate that this process is performing at a 4.3 sigma level.

DPMO assumes customers give credit to the service or product provider if some of the CTQ's are met even if all are not. What if the room service meal was the best tasting meal you have had from the hotel, taken from a great menu, but it arrives in 45 minutes? According to the DPMO calculation, two-thirds of your requirements were met so that the yield would be 67 percent. That would equate to a sigma of nearly 2.0. To other customers, it is an all or nothing proposition so that defects per unit (DPU) should be calculated. Here a straight yield is calculated and the sigma is looked up on sigma chart. In the DPU for the example in this paragraph, the yield and sigma would be zero. In Exhibit 5.19, we show the full Data Collection Plan.

Using DPMO can provide for a higher sigma performance; however, if your customers are the demanding type, DPU is probably the right metric for you. You will have to decide based on your knowledge of your customers. Surprisingly, in my seminars when I ask about the room service example, they say they prefer the DPMO measure if the meal was really that good.

Calculating Sigma—The Continuous Method

We advocate collecting continuous data for the following reasons:

1. Continuous data tells us the magnitude of the variation in the process.

2. Continuous data can tell us what type of variation exists in the process, common cause or special cause variation, which can dictate the type of problem solving we would attempt.

3. Continuous data results in less data to collect when we sample.

4. Calculating sigma from discrete data, while valid, can be misleading in certain cases.

An example that illustrates this last reason follows. The room service process improvement team had gradually started to improve their sigma performance. While actual data is proprietary, using the discrete method, sigma performance started to creep

What to Measure	Type of Measure	Type of Data	Operational Definition	Data Collection Form(s)	Sampling	Baseline Six Sigma
Room Service Delivery Speed	Output/Process	Continuous	From end of phone call to knock on door	Frequency distribution checksheets	100% Sample with assurances that the sample was both random and representative	DPMO or DPU
Food Quality	Output/Input	Continuous	Likert scale for each requirement where 5 = exceeded requirement, 3 = met requirement, 1 = did not meet requirement	Frequency distribution checksheets		
Menu Variety	Output/Input	Continuous	Same as above	Frequency distribution checksheets		

Exhibit 5.19   Data Collection Plan: baseline Six Sigma.

into the high 3's and even low 4's. Then I received a phone call from the room service process owner.

"George, we just took a sample of room service orders after a new round of improvement and are having trouble calculating sigma. Could I send you the data for some help?"

The data they sent looked as follows:

Room service orders sampled:	506
Number of room service orders delivered late:	0
Number of room service orders with food quality on the Likert scales < 3.00	0
Number of room service orders with menu variety, Likert scales < 3.00	0

You have just learned that to calculate sigma using the discrete method, you need to have *some* defects. When you have no defects as the room service team had now achieved, you have a 100 percent yield. The room service process owner felt his team had achieved Six Sigma. Remember Six Sigma is producing 3.4 defects per million opportunities. Without defects and using the discrete method, they had achieved "infinity" sigma. But had they? One answer for the process owner would have been to dramatically increase the team's sample size to 1,000,000. Obviously, this doesn't make practical sense, but would have seemed the only answer if the team had insisted on using the discrete method to calculate sigma. However, this team had followed my advice on using continuous data to calculate speed of room service delivery. I asked them to send me the *actual* room service deliveries.

When I received the data on delivery, I calculated two statistics on the data. I calculated the average room service delivery time and the standard deviation of the room service delivery for the 506 room service deliveries in the sample.

The average room service delivery time was exactly 22 minutes. This was an amazing improvement in the baseline performance. To calculate this average, I simply added up all 506 room service deliveries and divided by 506. This arithmetic mean is our calculation of the central tendency of the data. I now wanted to calculate the measure of dispersion of deliveries. The standard deviation from the mean is the most accurate measure. The formula is:

$$\sqrt{\frac{\Sigma(X - \overline{X})^2}{n-1}}$$

Most simple calculators can perform this calculation in a matter of seconds. When I calculated the standard deviation, the answer was 2. With this information, we can create a graphical picture of what the process looks like. A process' capability is defined internationally as ± 3 standard deviations from the process' average. Thus, with the information that the room service delivery average is 22, we would expect deliveries that would take as long as 28 (3 standard deviations from the average of 22, 3 × 2 = 6 which is added to 22) and we could expect room service deliveries to take as little as 16 minutes (3 × 2 = 6 which is subtracted from the average of 22). A picture of what this process performance would look like compared to the specification of a 30-minute delivery time is shown in Exhibit 5.20

Knowing the average and standard deviation of a process leads us to a more specific measure of how well the process performs against the specifications. There are several statistics that indicate this measure of capability. We will cover three of them; they are:

1. Capability ratio (CR).
2. Capability index (Cp).
3. Capability index compared to some constant—k (Cpk).

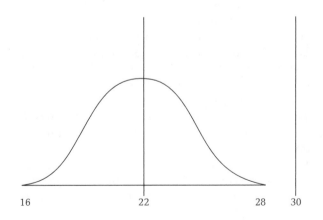

Exhibit 5.20 Room service delivery average 22 minutes.

The capability ratio compares the process performance against the specifications or:

$$\text{Process performance} = \frac{\pm 3 \text{ Standard deviations}}{\text{Customer specifications}}$$

In our room service example, one standard deviation is 2, so multiplying by 6 standard deviations, the process performance is 12 divided by the specification of 0 to 30 minutes. Dividing 12 by 30 equals 0.40. Another way of stating what the capability ratio is telling us is that given the amount of variation in room service delivery, the process is capable of using up only 40 percent of the specification. When using the capability ratio, a smaller number is desired.

Another example may help you understand this concept. Suppose the average of a process equals 100. Suppose the standard deviation of the data equals 1. The process would be expected to produce values as high as 103 and as low as 97 (± 3 standard deviations from the mean). Now let's suppose this is a process with a bilateral tolerance, that is, the process has a lower specification and an upper specification. Let's suppose that the lower specification is 90 and the higher specification is 110. A graph of the process is shown in Exhibit 5.21.

Here, the capability ratio would be:

$$\frac{6 \times 1}{100 - 90} = 0.30$$

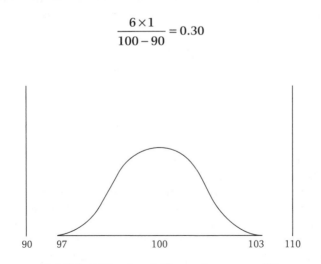

Exhibit 5.21 Capability ratio average 100.

A capability ratio of 0.30 indicates that the process is capable of using up only 30 percent of the customers' specification if the process is properly centered (which it is in this case).

Another statistic popular in the 1980s was the Cp (the capability index), which is simply the inverse of the capability ratio. The operational definition of the Cp is:

$$\frac{\text{Customers specifications}}{\pm 3 \text{ Standard deviations}}$$

In the above bilateral example:

$$\frac{110 - 90}{6 \times 1} = 3.33$$

The limitations of the capability ratio and the Cp is that the statistic produced is only the capability of the process based on the assumption of the process being centered. We know that in reality processes drift from their intended centers. The tool that allows us to calculate capability taking into account the drift tendency of the data is the Cpk (the capability index compared to some constant—k). There are two formulas for Cpk. One formula is used when the center of the distribution is closer to the upper specification; another is used when the center of the distribution is closer to the lower specification and X bar ($\overline{X}$) is the average of the data:

$$\frac{\text{Upper specification} - \overline{X}}{3 \text{ Standard deviations}}$$

or

$$\frac{\overline{X} - \text{ Lower specification}}{3 \text{ Standard deviations}}$$

Which of these formulas do we use? Whichever of the two that produces an average closer to a specification.

For example, suppose in our preceding example the average drifts from 100 to 105. The picture of this drift is shown in Exhibit 5.22. If we were to calculate either the capability ratio or the Cp, the answer doesn't change from when the average was at 100. The capability ratio would remain at 0.3 and the Cp would equal

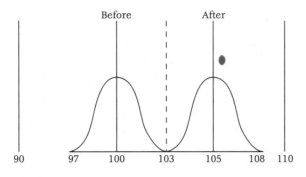

Exhibit 5.22 Capability ratio average shift to 105.

3.33. But, clearly the process has changed through this process drift and we need a formula to capture it. Since the average is closer to the upper specification we will use:

$$\frac{\text{Upper specification} - \overline{X}}{3 \text{ Standard deviations}}$$

In our example, with the upper specification being 110, and the average having drifted to 105, then the Cpk would be calculated as follows:

$$\frac{110 - 105}{3 \times 1} = 1.66$$

If the process had not drifted, the Cpk calculated would have resulted in the same number as the original Cp:

$$\frac{110 - 100}{3 \times 1} = \frac{10}{3} = 3.33$$

This example shows the advantage of the Cpk. It will always take into account the drift in the process average. The mathematicians have taken the Cpk and determined the equivalent sigma performance. The appendix on sigma conversions shows a process capability and sigma conversion table for Cpk from 0.00 through

2.00 which equates to a sigma performance of 6 (3.4 defects per million opportunities).

A Cpk of 1.67 results in a short-term sigma performance of 5. Compare this with the sigma calculation if we had used the discrete method. Since there are no defects present in the data shown, once again we would have produced a calculation with a 100 percent yield. A more accurate picture of what would be expected is shown by calculating a Cpk and seeing the equivalent sigma performance.

Returning to our room service example, with an average delivery time of 22, a standard deviation of 2, and an upper specification of 30, the Cpk would be calculated as follows:

$$\frac{30-22}{3\times 2}=\frac{8}{6}=1.33$$

The Cpk of 1.33 is then converted to a sigma performance. Using the conversation table in the appendix, we can now see the room service delivery sigma performance is 4.00. While impressive, it certainly is not the sigma performance that the discrete method would have us believe. This is yet another example of how continuous data tells us more than discrete data.

➤ Short-Term versus Long-Term Process Performance

A review of the process capability and sigma conversion table will show that there are two sigma equivalencies for a given Cpk. One is the short-term sigma conversion and the other is the long term. These differences are based on the fact that any time we sample our process to calculate performance, we are doing so over a short period of time. Processes, like everything else, vary over time. Mikel Harry, the "Godfather" of Six Sigma claims that there is a 1.5 sigma shift in even the most consistent processes. The long-term sigma column on the conversion chart takes a "worse case" perspective on this typical shift in any process. In reality, keep in mind the short-term sigma conversion may simply be "best case" and don't be surprised if the actual performance is not as good as predicted by this short-term calculation. I don't suggest that my clients use the long-term number because each situation is different. In some cases, where the process is not in statistical control (see Chapter 9), the shift may be worse than 1.5 sigma. In other cases, a 1.5 shift may not actually occur in your process, it may be less. My practical answer to this is for the project team to do a series of Cpk calculations so that their unique shift can be determined.

KEY LEARNINGS

➤ Measure the 2 or 3 most important output measures of the process.

➤ Measure the 1 to 2 most important input measures of your suppliers.

➤ Determine one key measure of your process efficiency: cycle time, cost, labor, or value.

➤ The Data Collection Plan is the who, what, where, and when for the measurement of the project.

➤ Discrete data (yes/no, good/bad) is not as desirable as data that exist on a continuum (time, height, weight, inches, miles).

➤ Spend time agreeing on how the measurement is to be collected (the operational definition).

➤ Use simple collection forms.

➤ Make sure your sampling is representative and random.

➤ Sigma is a measure of the variation from the mean of a distribution to when a customer is dissatisfied (a defect).

➤ The more distance measured in sigma from the mean to the time a defect occurs, the greater the customer satisfaction.

➤ Six Sigma equals 3.4 defects for every million opportunities.

Chapter 6

Data and Process Analysis

The Keys to the Project

The third element of the Process Improvement Model, Analyze, is considered the most important. The true discovery of why the problem exists is uncovered in Analysis. However, many teams have preconceived notions of why the problem exists and go through the motions of analysis to jump ahead to their improvements.

Whenever I think of organizations that ignore analysis or just go through the motions of analysis, I think of my adopted hometown of Denver. I have lived here for over 15 years and I doubt I will relocate. I love the mountains, the climate, the nearly 300 days of sunshine, the Broncos, and the healthy lifestyle of its inhabitants. The one thing that disturbs me about Denver is the new airport. For someone who travels nearly weekly, the extra drive that takes me past the old airport is bad enough. Despite claims that the new airport is only 15 miles from the old one, it takes almost triple the time from the time I leave my house to the time I am in the boarding area. What makes this airport experience even worse is knowing the airport was created because of politicians' ignorance of practicing the Analysis step of process improvement.

Without getting into the messy details, a problem existed with Stapleton airport: delays. These delays contributed to Stapleton airport ranking consistently in the top 5 for delays of domestic airports. While the politicians didn't know it, they had informally addressed the first two steps of DMAIC: defining a problem and measuring how bad it was. But the politicians didn't analyze *why* there were delays, instead they jumped to solutions. Problem: Delays; Solution: New Airport.

Only after investing billions of dollars in this new airport was it reported that the *root cause* of the delays at Stapleton was the proximity of parallel runways that necessitated using single runways during bad weather. If the politicians had focused on addressing the root cause, the ultimate solution would have been far more satisfying to the customer rather than the inefficient and costly solution that Denver International Airport is to the local community.

Many process improvement teams make similar mistakes. One mistake is rushing from the initial problem to a set of preconceived solutions. The other is ignoring the root cause and coming up with solutions to the initial problems that, like the Denver airport, could have been addressed with a more cost effective solution:

The Goal of Analysis — Solving for $Y = f(X_1, X_2, X_3, \ldots X_n)$

You probably were excited that after measurement we were done with math. We almost are. Y is the output measure we calculated sigma on. After calculating sigma, you were probably hoping not to see any more equations.

Y is a reference to the output measure we spent so much time on in Chapter 5. The remainder of the equation is saying that Y (whether it is a high-performing sigma or low-performing sigma) is a function (f) of a series of X's that reference process elements. It is the goal of the Analysis section of our improvement methodology to solve this formula and determine which of the X's in our process are the largest contributors to the performance of Y.

For example, on weekends Temo, Joe, and I experiment with my Italian spaghetti sauce. We have fun altering the taste of the sauce by changing the cooking time, adding more garlic, or using a new cheese we found in the local deli. Each of these changes is examining the process factors (X's like cooking time) to see their affect on the Y (the taste of the sauce). Our method of determining this relationship is crude (it's also most of the fun). If it was our jobs to make spaghetti sauce, then we would have to use the methods we are about to discuss.

■ THE "DOORS" TO ROOT CAUSE ANALYSIS

We expect to leave the analysis section of Six Sigma process improvement methodology with a set of validated X's that explain the current performance of Y. To arrive at these root causes (the X's) we need to do two types of analysis. One type of analysis is to take the data we collect in M and analyze it—data analysis. The second type of analysis is to examine the process—process analysis. Typically, project teams will use a combination of these two types of analysis to arrive at a root cause.

An analogy that is often used is to think of entering the root cause "house" through one of two "doors" (see Exhibit 6.1). If the project team's goals are primarily centered around effectiveness measures, the door of preference will be the data door. If the project team's goals are primarily efficiency measures (e.g., reduce the cycle time of a process), then the process door will be the primary analysis tool. In reality, most teams will use a combination of the two doors to root causation.

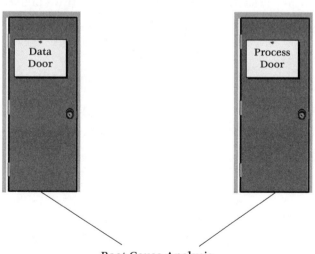

Root Cause Analysis

Exhibit 6.1   Root cause analysis data door/process door.

➤ Data Analysis

The goal of data analysis is to take the data that was collected (in Measurement) and examine it for clues as to what could explain the problem the team is working on.

Joe, Temo, and I love watching *Columbo,* the old detective series starring Peter Falk. Unlike many other mysteries, *Columbo* is not a "whodunit." In the first minutes of the show you see the murder committed and by whom. Why would anyone spend the next one and one-half or two hours watching a show when you know who is the culprit? The fun of the show is watching Columbo see clues that initially passed us by in the first minutes when the murder was committed.

Data analysis is a bit like honing our innate Columbo skills. Through practice, we use data analysis to get the process to talk to us. There are many data analysis tools. Let's look at one that is a natural result of the data collection forms we used for continuous data in Chapter 5. You might remember that for continuous data, the collection form we use is called the frequency distribution checksheet. The room service example from Chapter 5 is shown in Exhibit 6.2.

This frequency distribution tracks the number of times a given event (in this case the number of room service deliveries tracked against time) is seen in a set of observations. If we take the tallies

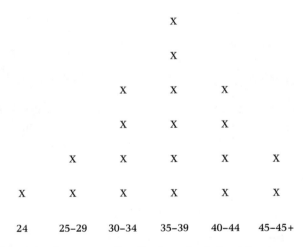

Exhibit 6.2 Frequency distribution checksheet for room service.

and now create a bar graph, the subsequent result is called a *histogram*. (We will use frequency distributions and histograms interchangeably.) The beauty of studying histograms is that often they will tell you more than raw data does. In the next section of this chapter, we will show you how analyzing histograms can help develop the Columbo in you.

➤ Data Analysis Using Histograms

I was fortunate to have an extended contract with a client who was interested in using statistics to track supplier performance. He was amazed at what histogram analysis could do for him.

First, I asked for a supplier they had experienced difficulty with, but who delivered acceptable parts to them. They chose a supplier of castings where length was one of the critical CTQs. They recently had accepted a lot of material that was 100 percent within their customer specifications. The raw data is:

Supplier XYZ/Part # 234-089, Specifications: 0.010–0.020, Target: 0.015

0.017	0.019	0.019	0.018
0.016	0.018	0.019	0.017
0.015	0.020	0.020	0.020
0.015	0.016	0.018	0.020
0.020	0.018	0.020	0.019
0.019	0.014	0.015	0.018
0.019	0.017	0.019	0.020

Examine the data closely. Of the 28 pieces in this lot, not a single piece is outside of the specifications. The customer is legally required to accept this lot since all of the pieces are within the required specification. As soon as I made the histogram I inquired from my client if this supplier was more expensive than competitors and if they had experienced delivery problems.

My client indicated that yes, this supplier was typically more expensive and had had delivery problems in the past but was chosen as the preferred supplier based on historical performance on other similar parts. At this point, the client was intrigued with my analysis of the supplier's performance by looking at a statistical picture. While my credibility increased, all I could think of was Deming and his words of wisdom that variation was the enemy and that it was easier to fight an enemy you could see. Exhibit 6.3 is the histogram that lead to my analysis.

```
                                        X   X

                                        X   X

                                    X   X   X

                                    X   X   X

                                X   X   X   X

                        X   X   X   X   X   X

                    X   X   X   X   X   X   X

  0.010 0.011 0.012 0.013 0.014 0.015 0.016 0.017 0.018 0.019 0.020
```

Exhibit 6.3 Supplier histogram.

You can see from the histogram that the distribution *begins* at the midpoint of the specification. If the supplier was doing a great job, most of the measurements would center around 0.015 and tail off in either direction from 0.015. Instead the distribution is centered around the highest acceptable value (0.020). Distributions do not recognize an upper customer specification and this knowledge leads us to our first clue about the supplier's performance. The performance of this supplier's process produced parts that measured higher than 0.020 which in this lot was successfully sorted from the remaining part of the lot sent to my client. However, this information lead me to conclude that the supplier was more expensive and had delivery problems. Manufacturers rarely include the time it takes to sort a lot (particularly one where virtually half the lot is bad) in calculating delivery dates. Second, the cost of sorting and the price the supplier paid for raw material that is now being scrapped or reworked is rarely included on pricing a part. Putting two and two together, it was easy to take this histogram and conclude that cost and delivery were issues. I could not have concluded this with the raw data alone. Only when I was able to create a statistical picture (a histogram) was I able to exhibit my Columbo skills.

We also should note that in our last chapter we learned that the peak of the curve is where the process is centered. The process we are looking at is centered at 0.019/0.020. All that remained was determining why the supplier would center his process so far away from its desired target. We decided to call the supplier.

Client: "Sam, this is ___ , we just were analyzing your most recent shipment and became aware of your centering toward the upper specification. We were wondering why this occurred?"

Supplier: "What are you talking about? Every part in that lot was within specification. I checked them personally myself."

Client: "Hold on Sam. We are accepting the lot in total. However, we are working with a quality consultant who is teaching us how to use statistics to analyze supplier performance. Based on his analysis, he has indicated that you are centered to the high side of the tolerance and are sorting the lot before you send it to us resulting in higher prices charged to us. This may also explain some of the delivery problems we have experienced."

Supplier: "How can you use statistics to tell what I am doing in my plant when I am over 800 miles from your location?"

George Eckes: "You will have to hire me to find that out" (always alert for a marketing opportunity).

Supplier: "Fat chance of that. But your analysis is correct. But you actually should give me a supplier of the year award. I *do* center to the high side because inspecting and reworking those parts is much cheaper than taking the risk of running to the low side. If I make even one part below the lower specification it costs $2,000 to scrap. So actually I am saving you a lot of money."

All I could think of when I heard this was my days working for General Motors. While I spent most of my time in Saginaw working on steering gears, I was loaned out to the Fisher Body and Assembly Plant for a few weeks. There, GM trucks were assembled. I vividly remember the second to last step in assembly being called the door-hinging process step. There, we attempted to hinge the door on the chassis and close the door. Occasionally, the door would close. If the door did not close, the truck would move into a rework staging area called the door-fitting operation. There, men, built like Arnold Schwarzenegger, used mallets to smash the door frame till the door was able to close.

My client's supplier reminded me of those days. The supplier actually felt he was doing the customer a favor. In reality, rework was built into the processes. After a period of time, these rework activities become so much a part of the process, the supplier believed that value was added. In reality, these rework steps add to costs and impact delivery. Who pays for these rework steps? The customer, of course.

This story had a happy ending. The customer requested the supplier to work with Eckes and Associates to reduce the variation in their process and center the distribution. While initially the supplier showed some resistance, after their improvement they virtually eliminated the rework step in the process and significantly improved delivery times and worked out a price reduction to my initial client while achieving a significant cost savings for themselves.

Another client in Troy, Michigan, called me because of a spate of recent lot rejections from their major customer, Ford. The client was a major supplier of small parts that went into the windshield area. They had recently changed their manufacturing process and had suddenly had problems. When they examined the raw data, they wanted a meeting with Ford because their analysis of the raw data showed the parts were within specification. Ford, on the other hand, was rejecting the parts saying many parts were out of specification.

They called me in to assist with preparation for the meeting. I asked for the data record of the most recent shipment rejected from Ford. My client proudly showed me the following:

Part # 234-AB 3498 Target part 0.65 lower specification 0.60, upper specification 0.70

0.68	0.69	0.70	0.68	0.67	0.67
0.61	0.61	0.62	0.62	0.61	0.65
0.60	0.60	0.60	0.66	0.69	0.67
0.65	0.65	0.65	0.65	0.66	0.69
0.64	0.65	0.63	0.69	0.67	0.69
0.60	0.60	0.60	0.60	0.65	0.62
0.64	0.64	0.64	0.64	0.64	0.66
0.66	0.70	0.70	0.70	0.70	0.70
0.70					

An examination of the raw data showed that no part was out of specification. I created a histogram hoping a graphical picture of variation would lead me to a clue about the windshield wiper clip process. It certainly did. Examine the histogram in Exhibit 6.4 and

X					X					X
X				X	X					X
X			X	X	X				X	X
X			X	X	X	X	X		X	X
X	X	X	X	X	X	X	X		X	X
X	X	X	X	X	X	X	X	X	X	X
X	X	X	X	X	X	X	X	X	X	X
0.60	0.61	0.62	0.63	0.64	0.65	0.66	0.67	0.68	0.69	0.70

Exhibit 6.4 Histogram for windshield wiper clips.

see if you can make a guess as to what was really happening in the plant (the target value is 0.65 with the lowest acceptable value 0.60 and the highest acceptable value 0.70).

I had one question for my client. "Is the person collecting this data also the person doing the sorting of bad parts from good?" The response was affirmative. I wasn't surprised. While the vast majority of assignable cause variation is due to methods, materials, machines, mother nature, or measurement, here we had assignable cause variation that was due to a person. This histogram is affectionately called the "Throwback" effect. Every time the data collector saw a value below 0.60, he or she said, "Oh, close enough," and recorded the value just *inside* the customer's lowest acceptable value and for every value above 0.70 the recorder said, "Oh, close enough" and recorded 0.70. The diagnosis of this "throwback" effect was based on knowledge of the "bell-shaped curve." A distribution doesn't recognize specification limits. Thus, knowing the extreme levels against each specification led to knowing special cause variation was occurring. While many explanations could be possible, the uniformity of the extremes would lead to an explanation of a "people" explanation.

This is yet another example of what Deming called variation through creating pictures of the variation. The beauty of the histogram is that the statistical picture of variation will often tell you more than raw data does.

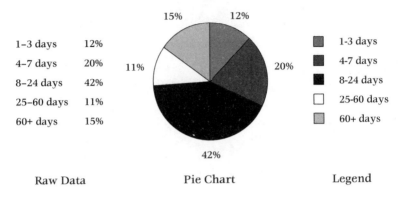

Raw Data		Pie Chart	Legend
1–3 days	12%		1-3 days
4–7 days	20%		4-7 days
8–24 days	42%		8-24 days
25–60 days	11%		25-60 days
60+ days	15%		60+ days

Exhibit 6.5   Percentage of people whose homes remain clean after formal cleaning: raw data versus pie chart.

Histograms are not the only graphical tool that shows variation. A daily review of the newspaper, *USA Today*, shows a variety of graphical tools that exhibit variation. A popular chart used by *USA Today* is the pie chart. In Exhibit 6.5, what draws your attention to the data more—the raw data or the pie chart? Most people would say that the pie chart is easy on the eyes and creates more interest in paying attention to what is presented.

There are many other types of data analysis tools. The use of graphical tools will make your data stand out more and in many cases (like the histogram) tell you more than raw data does.

■ PROCESS ANALYSIS

The other "door" used to continue our path to root causation is the process door. If the goal of the project team is to improve efficiency (e.g., reduce the cycle time of doing something like the Westin Hotel room service project), then it is imperative that the team take the time to conduct process analysis.

➤ Subprocess Mapping

Before we can examine the process for the three types of analysis, the original map we created in the Define stage of improvement should be looked at in more detail. Let's return to my car-buying Process Map to see how it's done.

You may remember that the last step in creating the high-level Process Map was obtaining agreement on the 5 to 7 "as is" steps in the current process, which are:

➤ Choosing a dealer (the assumption is that I already know what type of car I want).

➤ Test driving.

➤ Selecting the option package.

➤ Price negotiating.

➤ Financing.

➤ Completing the paperwork.

We recommend 5 to 7 steps at the high level because less than 5 may indicate we haven't been as thorough as we should be and more than 7 typically indicates we have gotten ahead of ourselves by going into more detail than we should.

However, at this point in the improvement project, the team should take the time to take each of the 5 to 7 steps in the high level "as is" map and drill down 5 to 7 steps for each high-level activity. Performing these activities is called *subprocess mapping*.

We will not create the entire Subprocess Map, but we will take one of the six high-level steps in the car-buying process and show the steps in Exhibit 6.6. As you can see, for the high-level step of negotiation, my first subprocess step was submitting my first offer. I had done my homework and on a brisk Saturday in March I approached Jim, the salesman with my written offer. He quickly looked it over, laughed (that hurt) and rejected my offer. Dejected, I left the showroom which is reflected in my second subprocess step. Jim caught up with me in the parking lot and asked me to resubmit a second offer. Feeling a bit sheepish but desperately wanting the car, I proceeded to rework some numbers and resubmitted my offer which is reflected in the third subprocess step. This leads to the fourth subprocess step, waiting in the showroom while Jim took my resubmission to the manager. Many people overlook steps such as waiting, thinking it really isn't a step. Particularly, if the project team has a goal of reducing cycle time, it is imperative that the team captures steps like waits or moves in the process. This

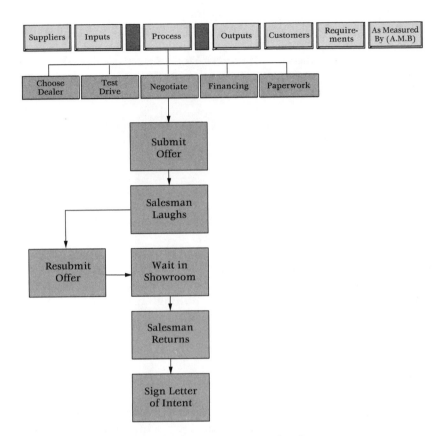

Exhibit 6.6 Subprocess Map: car-buying process.

leads to the fifth subprocess step, Jim's return with a basic acceptance but with the need to renegotiate some of the option package.
At this point, I used the input of the information I obtained by
reading my car magazines. You will note that while an input, it
was used near the end of the process. This leads to the sixth and
final subprocess step for negotiating, signing the preliminary letter of intent.

Subprocess mapping is crucial to later process analysis. A common problem with both high-level "as is" mapping and subprocess
mapping is the tendency for the team to create the "should be"
map. The project team needs to consciously capture all steps in

the subprocess so that later improvement can focus on these areas of inefficiency.

Once the Subprocess Map is created and validated, it is time to move on to Process Analysis. Process analysis is made up of three major steps. First examine and analyze the *moments of truth* in the process. Then analyze the *nature of the work* and finally look at the *cycle time* of work. Each type of analysis is covered in detail next.

➤ Moments of Truth

In many service-related processes, there are those moments between supplier and customer where either a positive or negative impression can be formed. These moments are called moments of truth.

Several years ago, I became deathly ill putting on a seminar in Brussels, Belgium. A rash that had started on my chest began to spread across my arms and legs. I developed a persistent fever. The seminar I was conducting included companies from across Europe and I was highly reluctant to cancel the seminar due to the inconvenience that would be experienced by the participants. However, in the second day, I cancelled the remainder of the seminar and made emergency arrangements to return to Denver. For several years, I have been a 1K (100,000 miles a year) flyer for United Airlines. Less than 1 percent of flyers fly as often in a given year on United. On the phone I had changed my flight for the next morning, flying from Brussels to London, on to Chicago, and then the final leg to Denver, all in first class.

That next morning I arrived early to the airport and attempted to check in with United's affiliate, British Midlands Airlines. They had no record of my changed reservation. It took nearly 30 minutes to get things changed. On the flight from Brussels to London, my fever was uncontrollable and I politely asked for a blanket. Sorry, no blankets on British Midlands flight from Brussels to London.

I later found out I had a severe case of mononucleosis. As I boarded my London to Chicago flight in first class, I was thrilled to find a blanket on my seat. With my incessant fever draining me of fluids, my only remaining requirement was a bottle of water. No, I didn't want a fancy meal, or Godiva chocolates. I didn't want Dom Perigon or first run movies, just a bottle of water. I indicated my requirement to the flight attendant prior to takeoff and was told no. At first, I thought she was joking. After repeating my request, she then told me in a more stern voice that if she gave me a bottle of water she would have to give *everybody* a bottle of water. I cannot tell you how this moment of truth has affected my attitude toward United Airlines to this day. Sadly, any passenger making this simple request should have been treated better. Add to this the fact that I was a first class passenger, was visibly ill, and was one of their frequent passengers, the request was more than reasonable.

This United Airlines employee had an opportunity to increase the loyalty of a frequent passenger and in one moment allowed the opposite to happen. The concept of moments of truth originated from Jan Carlson, the one-time CEO of SAS Airlines. Carlson once said that SAS Airlines used to think of themselves as the aggregate of their aircraft, maintenance facilities, and offices. But he quickly found out that customers focus more on the interactions with a service provider's employees. In a study he conducted, he learned that in one year, the 10 million SAS customers came in contact with an average of five SAS employees lasting an average of 15 seconds at a time. Thus, SAS is "created" 50 million times a year, 15 seconds at a time through these moments of truth. Carlson found that approximately seven criteria are applied by customers that determine whether a given moment will either become a positive moment of truth (and thus increase customer loyalty) or become a negative moment of truth (and thus decrease customer loyalty).

Those seven criteria of a customer-focused company are:

1. Think and talk about their customers a lot.

2. Keep assessing their customers' perceptions.

3. Tend to resolve priority issues in favor of the most profitable impact on the customer.

4. Give in, compromise, or add value for the customer in dispute situations where the value of goodwill exceeds the economic stake.

5. Recover conscientiously from blunders or mishandled moments of truth, make amends to the customer who has received poor treatment.

6. Employ a "whatever it takes" policy in trying to remedy the situation for a dissatisfied customer or one with a special need.

7. Redesign systems, redeploy resources, and turn "sacred cows" out to pasture when they get in the way of service quality.

Look back to my experience with United Airlines. Did the flight attendant resolve an issue in favor of the most profitable impact to the customer? Did the flight attendant compromise, add value, or resolve a dispute situation where the value of goodwill exceed the economic stake? And finally did he or she turn a "sacred cow" out to pasture (the policy of not giving out bottles of water) when the sacred cow gets in the way of service quality?

In my seminars, I challenge the participants to come up with positive and negative moments of truth in the past month and then compare how the service provider failed or succeeded against Carlson's seven criteria. Participants indicate difficulty with coming up with positive moments of truth, and when they do, it's usually when the customer has had a bad moment of truth rectified. Try coming up with a recent moment of truth (positive or negative) and see how the service provider did against the seven criteria.

➤ The Nature of Work

After an analysis of the moments of truth that exist in a process, another area of examination is the *nature of work*. The nature of work deals with making the determination whether the subprocess steps in a process add value or not. The definition of whether a step adds value or not is that it must meet three criteria:

1. The customer must be willing to pay for that step in the process.
2. The step must physically change or transform the product or service.
3. The step must be done right the first time.

Once the project team has completed its subprocess responsibilities, the team must examine its detailed map and determine which of the subprocess steps meet these three criteria. Remember, each step must meet *all* of the three criteria: Failure to meet any one of the three means the step does not add value.

Let's return to the six subprocess steps in my negotiations in the car-buying process:

Subprocess Step	Value (Yes/No)	Reason
1. Submission of offer	Yes	I am willing to pay for that step. The transfer of the offer letter is a change from me to them and I did it right the first time.
2. Leaving the showroom	No	Leaving the showroom as a way to obtain my car did not value add to me, the customer.
3. Resubmitting offer	No	Usually anything that begins with the prefix "re-" is being done for the second time.
4. Waiting for decision	No	No change or transformation in the product or service here.
5. Renegotiation of option package	No	There's that "re-" again.
6. Signing letter of intent	Yes	The customer (me) thought it important. It physically changed something (the letter) and it was done right the first time.

Six subprocess steps and only two of six (33%) added value. The amazing statistic is that for a typical process, this is better than most. The consultant organization, Rath and Strong, claim most subprocesses have a 2 to 8 ratio of value added to nonvalue added.

Once the team has performed the nature of work analysis, it should return to all the nonvalue-added activities and categorize them. Six major categories of nonvalue work are:

1. *Internal failures.* Steps or activities related to correcting errors in the process. Those steps that begin with the word "re-" are usually sure signs of internal failures. Retest, recall, revisit, are all examples of internal failures. Not all words that begin with "re-" are nonvalue added. Reward and recognition are two examples of re's that clearly add value.

2. *External failures.* Steps or activities that are related to re-covering or correcting mistakes discovered by the customer. For example, some larger automobile companies have de-partments exclusively devoted to product recall responsibil-ities. These also can be instances where negative moments of truth are captured.

3. *Control/inspection.* Steps or activities related to inspecting, reviewing, or signing off on previous steps or activities that often add value. This is the most controversial of the steps that are considered nonvalue. Many organizations have en-tire departments devoted to inspection. There is nothing like threatening someone's "rice bowl" to bring out irra-tional thinking. Socializing with some pilot friends one evening, I asked if they had ever found anything important during their "walk-arounds," a part of their checklist prior to take-off. One pilot's answer was both thought provoking and humorous. He said other than an oil leak that later proved not to be serious, he thought it a waste of time but that it probably eased the anxieties of nervous passengers seeing him walking around. Also don't forget our inspection test in Chapter 1 (on page 2): 100 percent inspection is only 80 per-cent effective at best. As you now know, that isn't even two-sigma quality.

4. *Delays.* Long regarded as the most common of nonvalue activities, delays are those waits in a process, whether it be waiting for the car dealer to approve my offer for his car, the wait for a requisition to be signed by your manager, or the wait for a supplier delivery.

5. *Preparation/setup.* Those steps or activities that prepare subsequent activity. One new hobby I have is fantasy sports leagues. Much to the happiness of my wife who knows I pa-trol the sport chat rooms rather than hotel bars, I spend my evenings online checking my league changes. Whenever I boot-up my computer and it takes what I think is forever to come online, I think of how nonvalue added that time is and how this is an example of preparation/setup time.

6. *Moves.* There is a film of the steps that go into manufactur-ing the Mercury Marine outboard motor. There are over one hundred process steps. The filmmaker then sped up the tape to show these process steps in less than a minute. The amazing part of the tape was that a majority of the steps

were moving the parts. Very few of the steps were added value. Most were taking the parts from inventory, returning the parts to inventory, moving the finished parts to the warehouse. In addition to the obvious nonvalue-added moves, these type of steps also contribute to the possibility of damage to the part. I once had a client of metal castings where a majority of their process steps were moves. We later found out that these moves related to the complaint from a customer regarding cracks in the casting. In this later example, we can see how conducting process analysis can affect effectiveness measures considered important to the external customer. The only moves that can be considered value-added are those that directly involve the customer. For example, the last move FedEx makes in delivering a package to the customer would be considered value-added.

Categorizing the type of nonvalue-added activities into the areas listed above is one of the last activities before we get into root cause analysis. Before we show you what to do with the categories of nonvalue-added activity, we will examine the last type of process analysis—flow of work.

➤ Flow of Work

Perhaps there is no more important concern in any business, service or manufacturing, than doing something faster. Thus, when conducting process analysis, one method that can be done concurrent with the other types of analysis is the flow of work. Simply put, the flow of work is calculating the amount of time each subprocess step takes, whether it be value-added or nonvalue-added. Once again, let's return to the six subprocess steps that occurred during the negotiation step of the car-buying process:

		Value	Amount of Time
1.	Submission of offer	Yes	1 minute
2.	Leaving the showroom	No	10 minutes
3.	Resubmitting offer	No	5 minutes
4.	Waiting for decision	No	45 minutes
5.	Renegotiation of option package	No	30 minutes
6.	Signing letter of intent	Yes	15 minutes
		Total	106 minutes

One hundred six minutes to complete the negotiation sub-steps. Examine the balance between the amount of time it took for the value-added steps (16 minutes) versus the amount of time it took for the nonvalue-added steps (90 minutes). Here, the percent of time for value-added activity (15.1%) versus nonvalue-added time (84.9%) is even a worse ratio than the ratio created by analyzing the nature of work (33% versus 67%).

➤ The Summary Analysis Worksheet

Once we have conducted the nature of work and flow of work analysis, we summarize the analysis statistically. A typical tool that I highly recommend is the Summary Analysis worksheet in Exhibit 6.7 as it relates to the negotiation subprocess activities we have discussed. The Summary Analysis worksheet would be created for *all* the subprocess steps that the team has created and validated.

The last line in the Summary Analysis is called *value enabling*. This refers to those steps in the process that are technically nonvalue-adding but are either required by law or unique to the business that are never going to be the target for improvement. For example, if this were an employee acquisition process, drug testing might qualify as a value enabler. For many organizations that are involved in ISO-9000, the process of documentation might not add to the value of the process but would not be a target for improvement because it leads to certification or continued adherence to the ISO standard.

Process Step	1	2	3	4	5	6	Total	%
Time (minutes)	1	10	5	45	30	15	106	100
Value added	X					X	16	15.1
Nonvalue added	—	—	—	—	—	—	—	—
Internal failure			X		X		35	33
External failure		X						9.4
Control/inspection								0
Delay				X				42.5
Preparation/setup								0
Moves								0
Value-enabling								0
Total								

Exhibit 6.7 Summary Analysis worksheet.

By completing the Summary Analysis we can now begin refining the original problem statement. In the car-buying case, if my original concern was the time it takes to buy a new car, I now can focus on the fact that there are too many delays in the car-buying process. After completion of the Summary Analysis worksheet, the project team should examine the original problem statement and attempt to define the specific area of nonvalue-added activity it should focus on. Several original problems from project teams I have worked with and how they entered root cause analysis with a more specific, defined problem to work through are shown next. In each case, after creating the Summary Analysis worksheet, they reconfigured the original problem statement by asking the question "why?"

Before Creating the Summary Analysis	After Creating the Summary Analysis
Since January 1997, Customer XYZ has averaged payment of invoices 22 days past due.	Why are we experiencing so many sign-offs before a bill is paid? (Control/ Inspection)
Customer XYZ has issued 53 complaints in the last 3 months over late deliveries.	Why do we move the finished part 12 times prior to final shipment? (Moves)
It takes three months on average, to obtain a schedule change.	Why are schedules waiting an average of five business days before moving to the next approval? (Delays)
Since September 1990, our competitors have offered quicker, more varied upgrade packages, making us less competitive.	Why do we spend over 50 percent of our time in prep and setup of our new production lines? (Preparation/ Setup)

Once we have created a more detailed statement about a problem formatted into a "why" statement, we are ready to proceed with Root Cause Analysis.

► Root Cause Analysis

Once the project team has completed either data analysis, process analysis, or in all likelihood a combination of both, the team is ready to proceed with root cause analysis.

The project team must travel through three major areas to ensure that root cause analysis is done properly. Initially, the team will go through an open phase of root cause analysis, where any conceivable idea as to the root cause is generated. During the second phase, the larger number of root causes are narrowed down to a more probable list of potential causes and in the last phase, the team closes in on one, two, three, or more root causes. These are the root causes the team must validate before going on to Improvement. A conceptual overview of Open Narrow Close is:

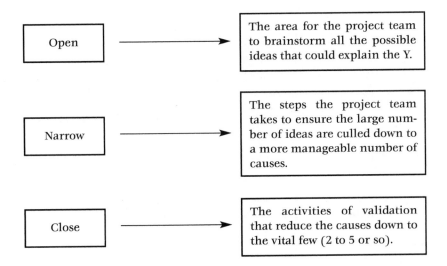

The tools we will cover as they relate to the concept of O-N-C are shown in Exhibit 6.8 (page 132).

Root Cause Analysis—Open

The goal of this first phase of root cause is to generate all potential causes to the detailed problem statement. This phase of the project is devoted to brainstorming. The major rules of brainstorming are:

➤ Document all ideas.
➤ Ensure the team generates ideas, not discussion.
➤ No evaluation of ideas.
➤ Everyone participates.

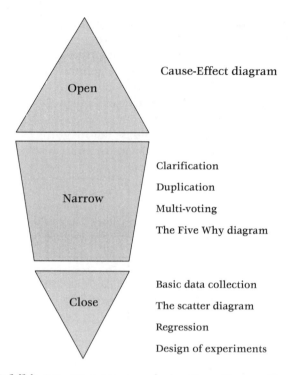

Exhibit 6.8   Root cause analysis—Open-Narrow-Close.

We want to ensure that all these ideas are captured in the Open phase of root cause analysis. However, there is a strong temptation to start debating about these different ideas or go into anecdotal recitations that support an individual's unique idea about the problem. People love talking about their jobs and their associated frustrations with their jobs as much as they enjoy talking about their kids.

To ensure this discipline, particularly at this point in the project, the team should rely on proven tools to assist them. The tool of choice for this phase of the project is the cause-effect diagram, also known as the fishbone diagram or the Ishakawa diagram, so named for the Japanese engineer who popularized the tool in the 1960s and 1970s.

Exhibit 6.9 shows a cause-effect diagram. You will see that to the far right in a box is the effect [or using our formula $Y = f(X_1, X_2 \ldots X_n)$], the Y. Coming out horizontally from the box labeled Y

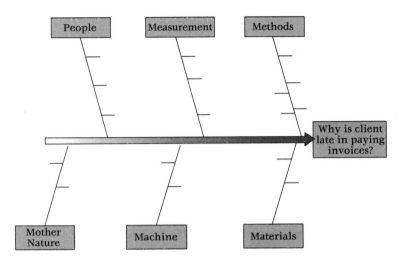

Exhibit 6.9 Cause-effect diagram.

is a line from which six diagonal lines are attached. Each of the six diagonal lines stands for elements of variation that could explain the Y (i.e., the X's). We have previously indicated what these six elements are—the machines, materials, methods, measurement, mother nature (or environment), and people in a process.

These 5 Ms and 1 P become the focus of the team's brainstorming. I usually instruct the team to take some 3 × 5 cards and *silently* write one idea (the X's) per card. They can write as many ideas as they have. After writing these ideas on their cards, they then proceed to the cause-effect diagram which usually is posted across several flip charts on a wall in the project team's work area. As much time as necessary for this activity should be provided because this is the sole activity of the Open stage of root cause analysis.

Stage of Root Cause Analysis	Tool	Goal
Open	Cause-effect diagram	Brainstorm as many X's that could be influencing the Y.

Exhibit 6.10 is an actual example of a project team I once worked with whose original problem was focused around poor

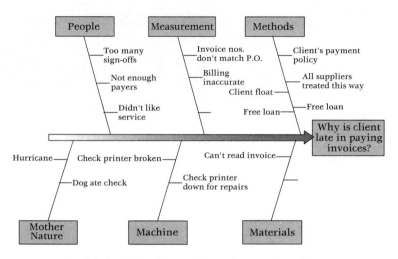

Exhibit 6.10 Cause-effect diagram: invoices.

billings and collections from their major client. This problem was strongly affecting their strategic business objective of revenue and cash flow.

After data and process analysis, they created the following "Why" statement:

Why is our primary client waiting 30 days past our payment terms before initiating payment in their accounts payable department?

In the first activity of the cause-effect diagram, they had generated possibilities shown in Exhibit 6.10.

Root Cause Analysis — Narrow

During this stage of analysis, our goal is to cull or pare down the larger list of items to a more manageable number. This is done by the facilitator practicing C-D-C. No, this is not some type of cardiopulmonary resuscitation; C-D-C stands for:

C Examining the original list of brainstormed ideas for *Clarification* (the consultant word for understanding).

D   Examining the original list for any *Duplicates*.

C   Examining the original list for major *Categories*.

After the team does C-D-C, we reduce the list to a more manageable number. Going back to the cause-effect diagram in Exhibit 6.10, I instructed the team that I was going to read out loud each of the ideas they had posted. I further told the team that if they clearly understood what I had just read out loud, I would continue. However, if the card I had read sounded confusing or they didn't know what was meant, I would then ask the author to clarify or further explain what they had written. To save time, I also asked the billing and collections team to point out duplicates in the cards so we could reduce the overall number. I also stressed to the team that if they understood someone else's idea and *disagreed* we did *not* want to hear from them. Only if there was lack of understanding was discussion allowed.

Clarification of what is written is of vital importance. I have never facilitated a team through this exercise when someone didn't understand what another had written. In the billing and collection's team, client float was not clearly understood by all team members. The author briefly described what he meant by this and it turned out that it was identical to free loan, which had been written by two other people. I took the two free loan cards and client float card and placed them on top of one another. The clarification and duplication steps narrowed the original list of brainstormed items.

Since the cause-effect diagram is already structured into *categories,* it is rare for the third element of narrowing to be seen. When we use the concept of Open-Narrow-Close in Improvement, categorization will occur with greater frequency.

The last step is to multi-vote. Multi-voting is not decision making. It is simply another tool to assist the team to enter the last step of root cause analysis. My approach to multi-voting is subjective. I take out a strip of sticky dots (available in any office supply store) and hand out 3 to 5 dots to each team member based on the number of originally generated root causes. I then instruct the team to carefully review the cause-effect diagram and place up to 5 dots on what they think are the more likely root causes that answer the "Why" question. I also indicate to them that if they feel strongly about any one root cause, they can allocate more than one dot to that root cause. If management is part of the team, I ask that they allocate their votes last, so they don't influence the voting of other team members.

In the billing and collections project team the voting results were:

Free loan	9
Not enough staff	6
Wrong P.O.	5
Sent to wrong address	4
Dissatisfied with performance	3

At this point we can turn the data into one of our data analysis tools. A Pareto chart of the narrowed or prioritized root causes can be made. It is wise to stress to the group that our multi-voting exercise is *not* decision making. So at this point, I ask the team if any root causes on the cause-effect diagram should be added that received few or no votes. The team had a brief discussion and decided no, they did not want to add any additional root causes. The team then made the Pareto chart in Exhibit 6.11.

The Pareto chart is nothing more or less than the opinions of the project team at this point. We need to generate some data to prove or disprove the opinions of the team. These validating activities are the total focus of our next chapter, the Close activity of root cause analysis.

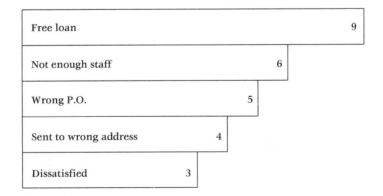

Exhibit 6.11 Invoice Pareto.

KEY LEARNINGS

➤ Analysis is considered by many the most important element in the DMAIC cycle.

➤ The goal of analysis is to determine and validate the root causation of the project team's original problem.

➤ One method to arrive at root causation is through analyzing the data collected during the Measurement phase of the project, particularly if the goal of the team is to improve effectiveness (e.g., improve customer satisfaction).

➤ Another method is to analyze the process itself, particularly if a primary goal of the team is to improve efficiency (e.g., reduce cycle time in a process).

➤ Most teams will use a combination of data analysis and process analysis to arrive at root causation.

➤ Process analysis is based on taking the Process Map we created in Define and determining the next level of activities below the levels we created in Define. This is called subprocess mapping.

➤ One aspect of process analysis is examining those moments between customer and supplier where either a positive or negative impression can be formed, thus named moments of truth.

➤ Another type of process analysis is examining how many of the subprocess steps add value (nature of work).

➤ Value-added steps in a process must meet three criteria: The customer must consider it important, the product or service must change, and the activity must be done right the first time.

➤ The final type of process analysis is examining how long a step in the process takes to complete (flow of work).

➤ Once we complete process analysis, the team should have greater information about the type of problem it needs to fix.

➤ Root cause analysis begins with brainstorming.

➤ Good brainstorming means that each team member has contributed, that all ideas are captured, no idea is a bad one, and that ideas and not debate about ideas occurs.

➤ The most used tool for brainstorming root causes is the cause-effect diagram.

➤ Once brainstorming has been completed, the team needs to clarify all ideas, find duplicates, and narrow the list down through data collection and/or multi-voting.

Chapter

Root Cause Analysis

Never Stop Asking "Why"

In Chapter 6, we learned the importance of analyzing data and process so that we eventually determine the root causes of the project team's initial problem. Good project teams make sure that they analyze data and analyze their processes. We learned the steps of process analysis. First, the team must prepare a Subprocess Map so there is sufficient detail for the team to analyze the process. Covered in detail were the ways a process was analyzed, from moments of truth to the nature of work to the flow of work.

Special focus was placed on the need for the team to conduct sufficient data and process analysis to proceed to the most important element of analysis, *root causation.*

We also discussed two of the three phases of root cause analysis. In the first phase (Open), brainstorming of all possible root causes is completed. In the second phase (Narrow), the team clarifies their ideas, looks for duplicates, and narrows the initial list by multi-voting down to a prioritized list of root causes. Because of the importance of the last phase of root causation (Close), we devote this entire chapter to it.

■ THE FIVE "WHY" DIAGRAM

Once the team has narrowed its list of potential root causes, the act of closing begins with a tool called the five "Why" diagram. This diagram takes one of our narrowed root causes and tries to explain it. In our previous chapter, we created a Pareto chart of the more likely root causes as shown in Exhibit 7.1.

The most likely root cause for the failure of payment was to allow the cash to act as a free loan by accounts payable. The five "Why" diagram attempts to find out why.

The team is asked, "Why does the client use our invoice as a free loan?" Using the concepts of brainstorming, we capture all ideas. One of the project team members says, "Because we don't charge penalty fees."

The question is posed again. Another team member comes up with yet a second idea: "Because it is common practice among large companies."

The question is posed yet a third time. Another team member comes up with yet a third idea. As you've guessed, we want this question answered at least five (5) times. This usually takes no more than a few minutes of the project team's time and this particular team's answers were:

Because we don't charge penalty fees.

Because it's common practice among large companies.

Because it's part of their plan to make financial goals.

The interest they accrue then allows them to pay higher daily rates.

They don't receive complaints about the practice.

While the five why diagram suggests that five responses are recommended for the original question, obviously this should be

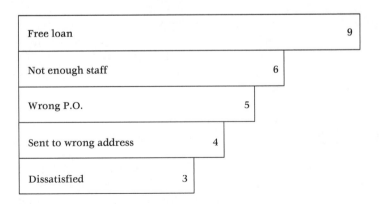

Exhibit 7.1 Invoice Pareto chart.

used only as a guide. Sometimes the team may brainstorm 6 or 7 items, other times only 3 or 4.

At this point, the team should look at the responses and determine if there are any data currently available to eliminate or support the brainstormed ideas. In the invoice project, one of the project team members points out that there are data to support eliminating two of the five items. First, the team member shows that on several occasions the client was charged a penalty fee. Another team member who was responsible for tracking the invoice indicated that the client's accounts payable person said they received repeated complaints about their payment practices.

Therefore, two of the five whys can be eliminated. The three remaining whys are now voted on by the team in a manner similar to multi-voting. With seven people on the team, here's how the voting went on the remaining three items:

Why does the client use our invoice as a "free loan"?	✓✓	Because it's common practice among large companies.
	✓✓✓✓	Because it's part of their plan to meet financial goals.
		The interest they accrue then allows them to pay higher daily rates.

Taking into account this voting, the team started to create a critical path of root causes. This critical path helps to explain why the client uses the invoice as a free loan and ultimately why the project team is waiting 30 days past the payment terms before their client pays them.

The next step in the five why diagram is to move to the next level. The project team takes the element that received the most votes (because it's part of their plan to meet financial goals) and does a five why on this element.

Why does the client meet their financial goals through waiting to pay our invoices?	No consequences to not doing it.
	Other companies do it.
	Always have done it this way.
	Not illegal.

When does the team stop drilling down using the five why diagram? When one of two situations occur. Here, we can see that we are starting to experience repetition. "No consequences to not doing it" is very similar to "Because we don't charge penalty fees." When this repetition occurs, it is a sign the team should stop. The second situation is when the team runs out of ideas.

➤ The Importance of Validating Root Causes

How does Six Sigma differ from other quality efforts? While there can be significant overlap in the methodology of Six Sigma compared to other approaches, there is one key difference: All decisions are based on fact and data. There is no more important application of making decisions based on fact and data than in validating root causation. Our final responsibility in Analysis is to verify the root causes so that our work in Improvement (Chapter 8) attempts to find solutions that reduce the impact or eliminate the root causes. There are three major ways we validate root causes; they are by:

1. Using currently available data.
2. Applying regression methods, the simplest form of which is scatter diagrams.
3. Implementing designed experiments.

Using Currently Available Data

Many times currently available data will verify the root causation. One of my clients in the trucking industry wanted to improve the fuel tank conveyor process. Their initial problem was the massive repair time they spent on replacing fuel tanks. As they moved through analysis, they identified fuel tank rotation and tank transfer issues as two of their potential root causes. We will see shortly that there are times for more intricate root cause validation methods. Here, the team looked at past data and observed that 79 percent of the time the conveyor was down was when the tank was rotated and 20 percent of the time the conveyor was down was when the tank was transferred. All but 1 percent is explained through currently available data. Case closed and it's time to move on to Improvement.

The Scatter Diagram

When the team has one potential root cause that it needs to validate, the quality tool of choice is the *scatter diagram.*

A scatter diagram is a graphic representation of the relationship between two variables. Mathematically, it is a tool to see if a given output variable (Y) is explained in whole or in part by a given process variable (X).

Let's look at a simple scatter diagram. The vast majority of us drive cars. What could explain the speed (Y) of the car? If we went through the initial steps of a cause-effect diagram and the five why diagram, it would be safe to assume that all signs would point to the pressure put on the accelerator pedal. We take a series of measures when X is low (pressure on the accelerator is 0 as measured by pounds per square inch of pressure) and measure Y. Then we gradually increase the pressure on the accelerator and measure the subsequent measure of Y. Each dot on the scatter diagram is a measure of X against Y.

When X is low, Y is low. As X increases, Y increases until X is high, and so is Y. When the dots are aligned in such a way that when X is low, Y is low and in a linear fashion proceed upward from left to right, we say that the relationship demonstrates strong *positive correlation* as shown in Exhibit 7.2.

The steps in creating a scatter diagram are quite easy. The steps are:

➤ Collect raw data for X and Y.
➤ Determine increments for X and Y.
➤ Label X and Y axis.
➤ Interpret the scatter diagram for the pattern, if any.

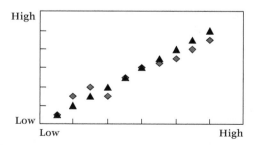

Exhibit 7.2 Scatter diagram: strong positive correlation.

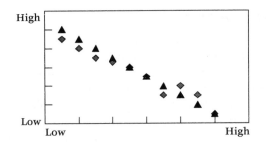

Exhibit 7.3   Scatter diagram: strong negative correlation.

In our first example, we saw the relationship between pressure on the gas pedal (as measured in pounds per square inch) and speed of the car. We described this relationship as a strongly positive correlation. Other typical relationships are shown in Exhibit 7.3 to 7.6.

In Exhibit 7.3, as X moves from low to high, Y *inversely moves* from high to low. A common example of a relationship with strong negative correlation is X being discounts and Y being number of available seats at a concert.

Check the relationship in Exhibit 7.4. Is there any relationship between X and Y? There does not appear to be any relationship. Plot points are scattered whereas X goes from low to high, Y doesn't particularly follow any trend or pattern. Does this mean we failed by doing a scatter diagram? Not at all. Many times, a team may believe that a certain X explains a relationship in Y. By producing a scatter diagram with no correlation, the team now has data to preclude any further investigation of that factor. Having

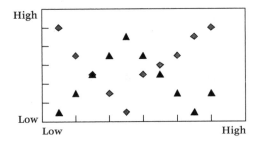

Exhibit 7.4   Scatter diagram: no correlation.

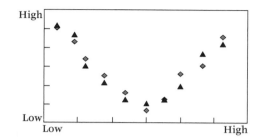

Exhibit 7.5   Scatter diagram: unusual pattern.

data that indicates we no longer have to worry about an X the team previously thought important, makes our jobs of validating root causation easier. When I ask for business examples of the scatter diagram in Exhibit 7.4, I often hear participants indicate X is intelligence, Y is location on the organization chart.

In Exhibit 7.5, we have what is described as an unusual pattern. In this unusual pattern, when X is low, Y is initially high, then as X moves to the right, Y is low, then as X is high, Y is high. The funniest example I have heard from my seminars is X is chronological age and Y is diaper use. On a more serious note, this "bath-tub" curve could represent call resolution time with Y being time and X being experience. Here, calls to newly hired customer representatives take longer. As experience grows, resolution time reduces. It increases once again for the more experienced representatives since, in most call centers, difficult calls are transferred to more experienced customer representatives.

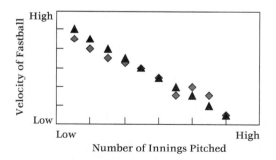

Exhibit 7.6   Scatter diagram: negative correlation.

Common Mistakes in Analyzing Scatter Diagrams

The most common mistake in analyzing scatter diagrams is assuming causation. A scatter diagram only establishes that there is a relationship between X and Y. The relationship could be explained by a third variable that is occurring simultaneously while X and Y are being measured. For example, the scatter diagram in Exhibit 7.2 is a strongly positive correlation. Now, what if I told you that X is ice cream sales and Y is shark attacks. Clearly the scatter diagram would show a strongly positive correlation but there is a "third" variable that explains the relationship; the time of year, where during the summer more people are on the beach (explaining the ice cream sales) and more people are in the water (explaining the shark attacks).

There are many other examples that highlight the *third variable effect*. For example, what if X is number of churches in a square mile area. Now imagine the relationship of X going from low (small number of churches in a square mile area) to high (large number of churches in a square mile area) and its impact on Y, crime. The scatter diagram data would show a strongly positive correlation.

Does anyone think that a higher density of churches causes more crime? Population density is the third variable that churches and crime have in common.

There is no statistical way to discount the third variable effect. Teams need to use their technical expertise in making sure that they draw the right conclusions about what the scatter diagram is exhibiting.

Other Common Mistakes

Most of the other scatter diagram mistakes are technical. Many teams confuse the X and Y. Teams need to keep in mind that Y is the output measure and X is a process factor the team theorizes may impact the output (Y).

Inaccurate data collection methods can lead to improper analysis. If the pairings of X and Y are not accurate, the strength of correlation may not be observed. Improper scaling and incorrect spacing are other problems with scatter diagrams. Improper scaling can occur when computers automatically scale the minimum and maximum ranges and this minimum/maximum do not match the reality of the data. A general guideline is to ensure increments of measure of equal width along the length of the X and Y axes. Analysis that is graphical allows the project team to see clearly the variation that exists. Finally, the scatter diagram is a tool best used with continuous data.

Quantifying the Strength of the Relationship Found in the Scatter Diagram

Up to this point, the strength of the scatter diagram has been evaluated subjectively. We observe the scatter diagram and determine if it is strong or not. There is a way to determine the strength of the relationship statistically.

This statistical concept is called the *correlation coefficient*. This chapter will not cover the mathematics of the correlation coefficient since loading the data into a software program like Mini-tab can do this for you. The correlation coefficient exists on a continuum from –1.00 (which would indicate a perfect negative correlation) to +1.00 (which would indicate a perfect positive correlation). Since this is a continuum, the calculation of a correlation coefficient of zero would mean there is absolutely no correlation between the measured X and the output Y.

What is a "significant" correlation coefficient? There is no such thing as a significant correlation coefficient. The size of the coefficient simply indicates the strength of the relationship between X and Y. By squaring the correlation coefficient and transforming that number (called *r* squared) into a percentage, we get a general indication of the proportion of Y that is explained by that particular X. For example, Exhibit 7.6 is a scatter diagram that is a strongly negative correlated relationship. This means that as X (number of innings pitched) goes from low to high, the Y (velocity of the fastball) goes from high to low. We can see the relationship is strong. To answer the question, How strong? we load the data into Mini-tab and see that the correlation coefficient is –0.88. We then square the coefficient and transform it into a percentage. This percentage, 77.4 percent, means that 77.4 percent of lost velocity is explained by the number of innings pitched. Correlation coefficients are part of regression analysis. While many Six Sigma advocates are strong proponents of regression analysis, I prefer the next tool we will cover, designed experiments.

➤ Verifying Multiple Root Causes— Designed Experiments

It is rare (though desirable) when one factor (X) explains the output measure (Y). It is far more likely that several X's will contribute to explain most of the variation in Y. Thus, a tool is necessary to quickly but thoroughly explain the variation in Y, when faced with multiple X's explaining Y.

That tool is a designed experiment. This is my favorite quality tool because if I look back on the more dramatic successes I have experienced with clients, they almost always involved formal, designed experiments. This tool is so near and dear to me that I published my first book, *Manufacturing Improvement through Design of Experiment* in 1990 (through the consulting organization, Tech Center Courseware).

Many people think designed experimentation is difficult. One possible reason is the emphasis so many practitioners place on statistical analysis. The reason for this emphasis is that many of the practitioners who teach designed experimentation are statisticians. My experience with statisticians is that the question they are most interested in is "Why." The question regarding designed experimentation I will attempt to answer in the next few pages is "How." In other words, I am going to teach you how to drive the car, not why the carburetor works.

We start with a simple question. How many of you reading this book have enjoyed a glass of wine? Do you know the technical definition of wine. Technically, it's the *first* fermentation of some fruit (most notably grapes). How long has humankind enjoyed the fruits of the winemaker's labor? Bible readers know that documented evidence of wine drinking goes back thousands of years.

How many of you have enjoyed a glass of champagne? Many of us enjoy ushering in the New Year by having a glass of the bubbly. Its definition is the *second* fermentation of some fruit (most notably grapes). More specifically, the second fermentation of a certain grape in a specific region of France. How long has humankind enjoyed champagne? Students of sparkling wine will know that the answer to this question is only 300+ years. A French monk named Dom Perignon discovered this second fermentation and mastered this process for millions to enjoy this drink.

What does wine and champagne have to do with experimentation? Fermentation of fruit is a *significant event*. The first fermentation of grapes was documented thousands of years ago. Yet, how many times do you think the second fermentation of grapes occurred (another significant event) and no one was there to document the significant event? In each of our processes significant events that explain variation are occurring all the time and we are not there to document the event. Designed experiments are ways for us to *create* significant events and be there to observe the results. Experiments are ways for the project improvement teams to *actively* create significant events rather than passively and inefficiently hoping they are around when something significant occurs.

For purposes of applying designed experimentation to Six Sigma, we will study several types of experimentation. We will start with an easy example and move forward.

My mother-in-law, Charlotte, is one of the best cooks and bakers I have ever known (quite a compliment coming from someone raised in an Italian home). When Charlotte asked me if I wanted her lasagna, I was skeptical. Asking an Italian if they want a home-cooked Italian meal can be a dangerous challenge. Attempting to be the gracious son-in-law, I indicated how happy I would be to try it out. It turned out to be *the best* lasagna I ever had. It prompted me to ask questions about Charlotte's cooking process. Amazingly, as Charlotte started to talk, she began talking in the language of designed experimentation to explain her masterpiece.

If we think of the equation $Y = f(X_1, X_2, X_3, X \ldots X_n)$ as it applies to Charlotte's lasagna, Y is the taste of the lasagna (as measured in number of portions consumed or the number of compliments received). She began chronicling the various X's:

X_1 = Amount of tomato sauce

X_2 = Amount of garlic

X_3 = Cooking time

X_4 = Cooking method

X_5 = Prep time

X_6 = Secret ingredient

Our definition of an experiment is: *The process of manipulating controllable factors (X's) to see their effect, if any, on some output or outputs (Y's).* Charlotte described her years of experimenting with the X's. She indicated how she would vary the levels of the X's, add new X's, drop out other factors until she had found the right combination of factors and the right levels of those X's.

Of course, Charlotte didn't speak in the language of X's and Y's but the concept was exactly the same. In fact, Charlotte relied heavily on one type of experiment called trial and error. In the next few paragraphs, we will define the four major types of experiments and indicate their various advantages and disadvantages.

Trial and Error

Charlotte told of many trials where she would experiment with her lasagna. As I inquired into her use of the word experiment, it soon became evident that the first and primary form of experimentation she used was *trial and error*. The X's she tested experimentally included:

➤ Amount of garlic.

➤ Cooking time of sauce.

➤ Type of tomatoes.

➤ Secret ingredient.

➤ Amount of brown sugar.

➤ Amount of cheese added to sauce.

➤ Amount of oregano.

➤ Type of olive oil.

➤ Amount of olive oil.

➤ Cooking method.

➤ Cooking time of noodles.

➤ Type of ricotta.

Charlotte had a host of additional factors (X's) she used in making her lasagna but initially she told me she "experimented" on these factors. In fact what Charlotte did was test all of these factors simultaneously without gaining knowledge about which of them potentially improved her lasagna. My first question was whether the lasagna tasted better. She said her husband, Herb, complimented her on the improved taste but she was faced with a dilemma. Which of the factors contributed to the improved taste?

While the experiment was quick and relatively cost efficient, we gained no knowledge of which factors (if any) that we tested improved our Y (in this case the massive compliments Herb bestowed upon Charlotte).

This leads us to one of my favorite "Eckesisms," which is, *Avoid the burnt hut syndrome.* The burnt hut syndrome is based on primitive tribes who lived in huts. In the course of a windy afternoon, fire swept through the village, wiping out all of the villagers' homes. In the coming days as they cleaned up, they found out that pigs had run into the burning huts and the villagers soon discovered the delicacy of baked ham. When they desired baked ham in the future, what was their course of action? Yes, they burned down a hut.

The burnt hut syndrome is very much like trial and error experimentation. We test one or several factors without drawing conclusions about what explains the results. Of course, this assumes the results have moved our Y like it did for Charlotte in her taste tests with Herb. In most cases, trail and error experimentation is error.

One Factor at a Time

A second major type of experimentation is called one factor at a time or OFAT for short. In further discussions with Charlotte, I learned she had tried a simplified type of OFAT. To conduct an OFAT, we hold all things constant and test just one factor to see how manipulating that one factor does against some baseline performance. Charlotte discussed trying an experiment where she isolated three of her lasagna factors she thought were more likely than not to contribute to Herb's compliments. The three factors she focused on were:

1. Sauce cooking time.
2. Amount of secret ingredient.
3. Type of olive oil.

To conduct an OFAT, you need to identify a minimum of two *levels* to test each factor. Charlotte tested sauce cooking time at 1 hour (what she regarded as the low level) and 2 hours (the high level). A minus (−) is the term we use for a low level and a plus (+) is the term we use for the high level of a factor.

For Charlotte's other two factors, she tested them as follows:

Factor (X)	Low Level (−)	High Level (+)
Amount of secret ingredient	No secret ingredient	2 cups of secret ingredient
Type of olive oil	Bertolli	Pompeian

In conducting an OFAT, we must conduct a baseline test. In her first experiment, Charlotte conducted an experiment when all three factors were tested at their low (−) levels. We see that in Exhibit 7.7.

Charlotte went on to discuss how she measured the results of the experiment. Since this experiment was conducted when she had recently married Herb, she thought he might be too liberal with compliments and so made the first batch of lasagna for a group of friends. Since she always made her lasagna in an 8 × 11 pan, she observed how many 3 × 2 inch portions were consumed. This measure became her Y. She noted that 8 portions were consumed among her friends. That data is located in Exhibit 7.8.

Having established a baseline, she now manipulated factor A (cooking time) in a second experiment and once again collected data on how many portions were consumed when the identical number of friends came over for their weekly book club. The results are located in Exhibit 7.9. Unlike trial and error, can you see how some preliminary knowledge is formed doing OFAT that contrasts with no knowledge that is obtained doing trial and error?

In our "second" experiment (but the first testing against the baseline), Charlotte improved her "lasagna yield" from 8 portions to 10 (not counting when Herb snuck into the fridge for a midnight raid on the lasagna pan).

In her third experiment, Charlotte increased her secret ingredient (factor B) from one cup (the low level) to 2 cups. Note the difference in yield again measured in portions consumed (Exhibit 7.10).

Factor A (Cooking Time)	Factor B (Amount of Secret Ingredient)	Factor C (Type of Olive Oil)	Results (Y)
Low (−), 1 hour	Low (−), no secret ingredient	Low (−), Bertolli	

Exhibit 7.7 OFAT three factors—low levels.

Factor A (Cooking Time)	Factor B (Amount of Secret Ingredient)	Factor C (Type of Olive Oil)	Results (Y)
Low (−), 1 hour	Low (−), no secret ingredient	Low (−), Bertolli	8 portions

Exhibit 7.8   OFAT Y results.

For purposes of analysis, this "third" experiment was compared against the results of the baseline. Thus, the use of the higher level of the secret ingredient increased consumption of her lasagna from 8 to 16, a 100 percent improvement in yield (not to mention the two trips to the fridge that Herb made that night).

In the fourth and final experiment, Charlotte returned factor B back to its original level and now just tested factor C, the type of olive oil. The results are shown in Exhibit 7.11.

Again, comparing the last test against the baseline, we see no impact of using Pompeian Olive Oil. In fact, Herb openly wondered when Charlotte was going to make last week's lasagna. Does this mean that the last experiment was a failure? No, because if there is no difference in the use of the type of olive oil against our chosen Y (in this case consumption), then we should use the most inexpensive olive oil. The last experiment helped us gain knowledge.

Through application of OFAT, Charlotte had dramatically improved her lasagna. OFAT is an approach to designed experiment where *some* knowledge can be drawn from the results. An OFAT approach to experimentation has many disadvantages. First and foremost, there is no way to know if there is an interaction between

Factor A (Cooking Time)	Factor B (Amount of Secret Ingredient)	Factor C (Type of Olive Oil)	Results (Y)
High (+), 2 hours	Low (−), no secret ingredient	Low (−), Bertolli	10 portions

Exhibit 7.9   OFAT results—factor A cooking time change.

Factor A (Cooking Time)	Factor B (Amount of Secret Ingredient)	Factor C (Type of Olive Oil)	Results (Y)
Low (−), 1 hour	High (+), 2 cups	Low (−), Bertolli	16 portions

Exhibit 7.10 OFAT results—factor B secret ingredient change.

Charlotte's secret ingredient and another factor, tested or not. An interaction is when a combination of factors produces a result that one factor alone does not produce. Taking our Italian dinner analogy a step forward, when we make our salad for our lasagna dinner, a salad dressing of just olive oil or just vinegar might be acceptable, but there is a clear interaction between olive oil and vinegar.

Look at Exhibit 7.12. This is the design order for an OFAT that tests three factors. Notice that each column is tested three times at the low level (−), and only once at the high level (+). This imbalance precludes us from examining either the average response of each factor at the levels tested or the possible interactions that exist between columns. For us to examine possible interactions, we need columns to be balanced. The fancy name for this is *orthogonality*.

The other major problem with OFAT exists within its definition. We stated earlier that an OFAT is "holding all things constant," while manipulating one factor at a time. When can we create a condition where all things are held constant? In the faster paced environment of the manufacturing or service world, all things cannot be held constant. Thus, an alternative to OFAT that expands its base of gathering knowledge about factors but has orthogonality must be found. There are basically two

Factor A (Cooking Time)	Factor B (Amount of Secret Ingredient)	Factor C (Type of Olive Oil)	Results (Y)
Low (−), 1 hour	Low (−), no secret ingredient	High (+), Pompeian	8 portions

Exhibit 7.11 OFAT results—factor C type of ingredient change.

Factor A (Cooking Time)	Factor B (Amount of Secret Ingredient)	Factor C (Type of Olive Oil)	Results (Y)
–	–	–	
+	–	–	
–	+	–	
–	–	+	

Exhibit 7.12   OFAT three factors—orthogonality.

types of orthogonal designs we will talk about. The first is the *full factorial.*

The Full Factorial

Cooking can be a sensitive subject. I had a proposal for my mother-in-law that I believed could make her lasagna even better. She had produced an Italian masterpiece using OFAT and I knew that application of more sophisticated experimentation could produce even tastier results. Tentatively, I approached Charlotte about trying a different type of experimentation. Her response was encouraging, "I have no idea what you are talking about, but I would love to cook with you."

The type of design I wanted to apply to Charlotte's lasagna was a full factorial. In this type of design, we test every combination of chosen factors at their given levels. In a full factorial, we are afforded the opportunity not only to examine the average affect of each factor, we also get a chance to see the average effect of each factor as all other factors change an equal or like number of times. This can be observed in Exhibit 7.13.

Examine each column. You will see that each column has an equal number of minuses and an equal number of pluses. This indicates that we can mathematically calculate the average effect of factors A, B, and C. Note how the pattern for each column was created. In the first column, where we will place factor A, we start with the low level of the factor and then alternate the high level and then the low level throughout the eight *conditions* or *runs* of the experiment. Note the doubled pattern in the second column for factor B. The first two columns are run at the low level, then twice we run factors at the high level, then repeat low, low, and

Factor A	Factor B	Factor C	Results (Y)
−	−	−	
+	−	−	
−	+	−	
+	+	−	
−	−	+	
+	−	+	
−	+	+	
+	+	+	

Exhibit 7.13 Full factorial design.

then high, high. Finally, for factor C we see the pattern for factor B or the second column doubled yet again, so that the first four experiments are run at the low level and the final four experiments are run at the high level.

How many rows do we need in a full factorial? Mathematically, it is based on calculating the formula 2^k, where the lower case 2 refers to the number of levels tested (for purposes of this book we will only examine 2 level designs so this will always be 2). The k refers to the number of factors desired to be tested in the experiment. Using the factors Charlotte tested in the OFAT we examined 3, so that $2 \times 2 \times 2 = 8$ experiment conditions. If we desired examination of 4 factors, then $2 \times 2 \times 2 \times 2 = 16$. When testing 4 factors at 2 levels we would require 16 experiment conditions. The design created would be alternating minus and plus patterns for the first column (factor A), a pattern of 2 alternating minuses and pluses for the second column (factor B), a pattern of 4 alternating minuses and pluses for the third column (factor C), and finally 8 minuses and then 8 pluses for our fourth and final column (factor D). This is shown in Exhibit 7.14.

I didn't provide this level of detail to my mother-in-law. I asked her to take her secret ingredient and test it against two other factors not previously tested. She indicated she was curious about a new type of tomato and testing two types of ricotta cheese. Since we had obtained information on no secret ingredient versus 2 cups of her secret ingredient, I recommended to her that we try $1\frac{1}{2}$ cups of her secret ingredient (which would now be our low level) versus $2\frac{1}{2}$ cups of her secret ingredient (which would now be our high

Factor A	Factor B	Factor C	Factor D	Result (Y)
−	−	−	−	
+	−	−	−	
−	+	−	−	
+	+	−	−	
−	−	+	−	
+	−	+	−	
−	+	+	−	
+	+	+	−	
−	−	−	+	
+	−	−	+	
−	+	+	+	
+	+	+	+	
−	−	−	+	
+	−	−	+	
−	+	+	+	
+	+	+	+	

Exhibit 7.14   Full factorial design—four factors at two levels.

level of the secret ingredient). For the other two levels, we chose the following:

Factor	Low Level (−)	High Level (+)
Tomato type	Hothouse	Home grown
Ricotta cheese	Merceli's	Merceli's Low Fat

With our factors and levels chosen, we set up the design as shown in Exhibit 7.15. In reality, if one of the factors was more expensive or time consuming to test we would have placed it in the third column because that factor only changes once (between experiments four and five from low to high). In this experiment it didn't matter, but I always tell my clients to take the easiest or most inexpensive factor to test and place that factor in column one because it changes so often. Likewise, the most expensive or most

Factor A (Tomato Type)	Factor B (Ricotta Cheese)	Factor C (Secret Ingredient)	Results (Y)
− (Hothouse)	− (Merceli's)	− ($1\frac{1}{2}$ cups)	
+ (Homegrown)	− (Merceli's)	− ($1\frac{1}{2}$ cups)	
− (Hothouse)	+ (Merceli's Low Fat)	− ($1\frac{1}{2}$ cups)	
+ (Homegrown)	+ (Merceli's Low Fat)	− ($1\frac{1}{2}$ cups)	
− (Hothouse)	− (Merceli's)	+ ($2\frac{1}{2}$ cups)	
+ (Homegrown)	− (Merceli's)	+ ($2\frac{1}{2}$ cups)	
− (Hothouse)	+ (Merceli's Low Fat)	+ ($2\frac{1}{2}$ cups)	
+ (Homegrown)	+ (Merceli's Low Fat)	+ ($2\frac{1}{2}$ cups)	

Exhibit 7.15   Full factorial design lasagna.

time-consuming factor should always be placed in the last column since it changes but once.

Having created this eight-run full factorial, Charlotte went about cooking up the eight batches over the course of two months of book club meetings. The results are noted in Exhibit 7.16. Just as she did in the OFAT example, results are measured in the number of 2 × 3 portions consumed by members of her book club.

Before we began analysis of the data, Charlotte pointed out that during experiment number 4 one of the book club members,

Factor A (Tomato Type)	Factor B (Ricotta Cheese)	Factor C (Secret Ingredient)	Results (Y)
− (Hothouse)	− (Merceli's)	− ($1\frac{1}{2}$ cups)	12
+ (Homegrown)	− (Merceli's)	− ($1\frac{1}{2}$ cups)	13
− (Hothouse)	+ (Merceli's Low Fat)	− ($1\frac{1}{2}$ cups)	12
+ (Homegrown)	+ (Merceli's Low Fat)	− ($1\frac{1}{2}$ cups)	8
− (Hothouse)	− (Merceli's)	+ ($2\frac{1}{2}$ cups)	17
+ (Homegrown)	− (Merceli's)	+ ($2\frac{1}{2}$ cups)	20
− (Hothouse)	+ (Merceli's Low Fat)	+ ($2\frac{1}{2}$ cups)	22
+ (Homegrown)	+ (Merceli's Low Fat)	+ ($2\frac{1}{2}$ cups)	22

Exhibit 7.16   Full factorial design lasagna results.

in what only could be describes as a pique of jealousy, brought over her prized hors d'oeuvres of a wine cheeseball. She also noted that in experiment number 8, one of the club members had called in sick (no doubt from eating too much lasagna).

First of all, I complimented my mother-in-law on making observations about circumstances surrounding the experiment. I am always encouraging my clients to make these types of observations during experiment conditions and many ignore this important advice.

It is usually a good idea to repeat or replicate the experiment. Repetition refers to gathering several observations while running one condition. In our lasagna experiment, an example would be taking a batch of the lasagna made during one of the experiment conditions over to her husband's Thursday night card game. Replication would mean conducting a new set of experiments 1 to 8 again for her book club. In cases where we are interested in greater confidence in the mean value of any condition repetition is recommended. When we are more interested in ascertaining if factors other than those tested explain the results we would replicate. In the case where we have cheeseballs affecting other factors like hunger of the book club, we would replicate. Since at this point I was testing the patience of my mother-in-law I suggested neither.

One of the mistakes many clients make is assuming that analysis has to be sophisticated and complicated. There are three types of analysis I use with my clients, graphical, simple mathematical, and complex mathematical. Complex mathematical refers to tests of statistical significance, analysis of variance, and F tests. These work well, particularly when capital investment is at stake with regard to a factor's significance. My favorite tool is a simple effects table. Here, we calculate the average effect for each factor high and low. For factor A's low level average we would add up the results for the first, third, fifth, and seventh experiments (12 + 12 + 17 + 22 = 63) and then divide by 4 to derive the average of 15.75. For factor A's high level, we would add up the results for the second, fourth, sixth, and eighth experiment (13 + 8 + 20 + 22 = 63) and then divide by 4 to derive the average of 15.75. This also happened to be the average of factor A at the low level as seen in Exhibit 7.17. I take Charlotte's results for factor B and C respectively, by calculating an average for ricotta type at the low level (experiments 1, 2, 5, and 6) and ricotta type at the high level (experiments 3, 4, 7, and 8) and factor C, Charlotte's secret ingredient at the low level (the first 4 experiments) and at the high level (the last 4 experiments).

The effects table in Exhibit 7.17 shows that of the two levels we tested factor A (tomato type), there was no difference between the factors (we use the absolute difference to calculate the effect). In cases like this, it doesn't mean testing the factor was a mistake. As it turns out, Charlotte historically would go out of her way to get homegrown tomatoes thinking they would produce a better sauce. Logically, this makes sense. However, this experiment shows that there is no difference between Hothouse and homegrown. Upon inquiry, between Charlotte's travel to the vegetable market and the higher prices, she could use the cheaper product down the street at the local grocery store. When a client sees results like this on the effects table their immediate reaction is to think they made a mistake in testing that factor. In reality, a factor that has no effect on the response variable (Y) can be evaluated to either reduce costs (as was the case in Charlotte's tomatoes) or to affect production increases. One of my clients hired me to improve the gold plating in a wave solder process. While we tested various factors in an experiment, we tested the spacing of how wafers were processed. As it turns out, wafer spacing produced virtually no effect when analyzed on the effects table. While the team was initially disappointed, it turns out the further distance for wafer spacing was close to the production requirement. The alternative level of wafer spacing placed the wafers closer together. In doing so, production increased 12 percent. Don't immediately think you have wasted time in testing a factor if the effects table shows no effect for that factor.

In Charlotte's experiment, we have gained even further evidence of the importance of her secret ingredient. Factor B, ricotta type seems to have little effect on the tested response variable of taste. For ricotta type, ironically we have learned that there is a slight preference for the low fat type (good news for health nuts).

Factor A (Tomato Type)	Factor B (Ricotta Cheese)	Factor C (Secret Ingredient)
−15.75	−15.5	−11.25
+15.75	+16.0	+20.25
Effect = 0	Effect = 0.5	Effect = 9.00

Exhibit 7.17 Full factorial effects table.

The full factorial is the experiment of choice when factor selection is small or when testing lots of factors is not time consuming or expensive. However, in the early stages of experimentation, this is usually not the case. What if Charlotte had wanted to test 7 or 10 factors. Exhibit 7.18 shows the number of experiment conditions if Charlotte had wanted to test factors beyond the small number she had ultimately agreed to test.

If she wanted to test more than five factors, she couldn't possibly find enough people to eat that amount of lasagna. So what do we do if we want to test more than four or five factors? The type of experiment needed is the fractional factorial which we cover next.

The Fractional Factorial

A fractional factorial tests just a fraction of the possible combinations. This can be done if we allow *confounding*. Confounding is allowing the unique pattern in a column to represent more than one factor or interaction. To understand this concept, let's go back to the full factorial that Charlotte ran.

When Charlotte tested her three factors at two levels, there were 8 conditions or runs ($2 \times 2 \times 2 = 8$). When we have 8 conditions we can estimate $n - 1$ or 7 effects. Obviously we are interested in the three main effects (A, B, and C) which in Charlotte's case were Tomato-type, Ricotta-type, and Charlotte's Secret Ingredient. When we test these three factors, there is the possibility of interactions. Exhibit 7.19 shows the possible interactions in Charlotte's full factorial experiment.

When running the experiment, we follow the pattern of minuses and pluses for the first three columns in the standard order

Levels	Factors	Number of Experiment Conditions
2	5	32
2	7	128
2	10	1,024
2	15	32,768
2	31	2,147,483,648

Exhibit 7.18 Full factorial—more than four factors.

Main Effects	Possible Interactions
A-Tomato type	A × B Tomato type/Ricotta type
B-Ricotta type	A × C Tomato type/Secret ingredient
C-Secret ingredient	B × C Ricotta type/Secret ingredient
	A × B × C Tomato type/Ricotta type/Secret ingredient

Exhibit 7.19 Full factorial interaction.

design. After the experiment, the remaining column patterns created from the first three-column standard order design allows us to mathematically determine the extent of the effect of the four possible interactions. The mathematical determination for an interaction is shown in Exhibit 7.20. We take the pattern of the first two columns (tomato type and ricotta type) and start multiplying the pattern of minuses and pluses. For example, a plus times a plus is obviously a plus, a minus times a plus is a minus, and the old adage of two negatives equals a positive (a minus times a minus equals a plus).

This third column's unique pattern was created by multiplying the minuses and pluses from the main effect columns. Exhibit 7.21 shows the patterns for the remainder of the interactions in a three-factor, two-level design.

A	B	A × B
−	−	+
+	−	−
−	+	−
+	+	+
−	−	+
+	−	−
−	+	−
+	+	+

Exhibit 7.20 Two-factor standard order design with AB interaction.

A	B	C	A × B	A × C	B × C	A × B × C
−	−	−	+	+	+	−
+	−	−	−	−	+	+
−	+	−	−	+	−	+
+	+	−	+	−	−	−
−	−	+	+	−	−	+
+	−	+	−	+	−	−
−	+	+	−	−	+	−
+	+	+	+	+	+	+

Exhibit 7.21 Three-factor standard order design with all interactions.

Again, the A × B interaction pattern was created by multiplying the A and B columns minuses and pluses so that a minus times a plus (or vice versa) would create a minus for that A × B pattern and a minus times a minus and a plus times a plus would equal a plus. The A × B × C column is created by multiplying all three main effect columns together. For example, for the first row A times B (a minus times a minus) equals a plus which is multiplied by Column C (a minus) which equals the minus found in the first row of the A × B × C interaction column.

When running a full factorial if we are interested in these interactions, we run the experiments according to the operating instructions for the first three columns (factors A, B, and C). The creation of an effects table for all seven columns (finding the difference between the highs and lows for each column) would answer the question whether there are any main effects or if there are any interactions that contribute to the results.

If we take Charlotte's last experiment (the full factorial) we can mathematically determine if any interactions explain the results. Exhibit 7.22 shows the results with interaction effects included.

We showed you earlier how to calculate the effects for A, B, and C. While we didn't do anything with the remaining four columns during the running of the experiments, we now use their unique minus/plus pattern to see the effects of interactions (if any) (Exhibit 7.23).

Factor A (tomato type) had no effect on taste (15.75 − 15.75 = 0). Factor B (ricotta type) had virtually no impact (0.5), and factor C

A	B	C	A × B	A × C	B × C	A × B × C	Results
−	−	−	+	+	+	−	12
+	−	−	−	−	+	+	13
−	+	−	−	+	−	+	12
+	+	−	+	−	−	−	8
−	−	+	+	−	−	+	17
+	−	+	−	+	−	−	20
−	+	+	−	−	+	−	22
+	+	+	+	+	+	+	22

Exhibit 7.22 Full factorial with lasagna results.

(Charlotte's secret ingredient) had a huge relative impact on consumption. To calculate the potential impact of the A × B interaction, we take the fourth column's pattern of minuses and pluses and calculate the two averages for the effects table to see the magnitude of difference, or the A × B interaction effect.

We now do the same for columns 5 to 7 to see the effects (if any) of the A × C, B × C, and A × B × C interactions. Looking at the effects table you can see virtually no interactions going on. The A × B effect of 2.0 is larger than A alone or B alone but proportionately it doesn't come close to the impact of Charlotte's secret ingredient. A × C and B × C are at 1.5 and 2.0, respectively. In each case once again, nothing is as close as the secret ingredient (factor C) as a main effect. And in the last column we see the "effect" of A × B × C which checks in at nearly 0 (0.5).

While it is not always the case, the effects table in Exhibit 7.23 is commonplace. A two-way interaction can often explain more than either of the 2 main effects but in setting up experiments,

A	B	C	A × B	A × C	B × C	A × B × C
−15.75	−15.5	−11.25	−16.75	−15.0	−14.75	−15.5
+15.75	+16.0	+20.25	+14.75	+16.5	+16.75	+16.0
0	0.5	9.0	2.0	1.5	2.00	0.5

Exhibit 7.23 Effects: all interactions.

teams often overestimate the potential effects of interactions. One thing is certain, in nearly 20 years of conducting experiments, I have *never* seen a three-way interaction be a large explanation for the variation in experiment results. This knowledge leads us to the creation of our fractional factorial.

Creating the Fractional Factorial

A pharmaceutical client wanted to test four factors to help them determine the potency of a new animal vaccine. The response variable was the impact on pigs and there was the potential of the pigs dying. Because of the likelihood of animals dying in the experiment, my pharmaceutical client was interested in running as few experiments as possible, yet having the ability to determine significant results. The four factors they wanted to test were:

Factor A   Gluten level
Factor B   Sit time
Factor C   Moisture content
Factor D   Catalyst amount

I initially recommended a full factorial. Because of the possibility of other factors affecting our results, I also recommended replicating the experiment so that we could be confident that our results could be attributed to the four factors or their relevant interactions. Replicating a 2×4 full factorial would mean a minimum of 32 experiments—16 experiments replicated a second time.

The client balked, wanting fewer experiments. I indicated to them that if they were willing to compromise on learning about certain interactions, it was possible to do half as many experiments and get essentially the same information. Exhibit 7.24 shows how we were able to do a fractional factorial.

The fractional factorial is examining a fraction of the possible combinations we see in full factorial, where we examine every statistical combination of possible effects. Look at Charlotte's full factorial where testing 3 factors at 2 levels allowed us to estimate $n - 1$ or seven different effects. If the likelihood of an $A \times B \times C$ interaction in virtually nil, why not use that pattern of minuses and pluses for a main effect factor. Exhibit 7.24 is the beginning of the pharmaceutical's fractional factorial where we want to test 4 factors at 2 levels but want to do it in 8 runs instead of 16 which would be required if we did a full factorial.

A Glut Level	B Sit Time	C Moisture Content	A × B	A × C	B × C	A × B × C (D) Catalyst Amount	Results
−	−	−	+	+	+	−	
+	−	−	−	−	+	+	
−	+	−	−	+	−	+	
+	+	−	+	−	−	−	
−	−	+	+	−	−	+	
+	−	+	−	+	−	−	
−	+	+	−	−	+	−	
+	+	+	+	+	+	+	

Exhibit 7.24 Fractional factorial: pharmaceutical company.

We placed factor A (gluten level) in column 1, followed by factor B (sit time) in column two, followed by factor C (moisture content) in column 3. Our remaining factor D (catalyst amount) goes into column 7 where the A × B × C (the gluten level, sit time, and moisture) content interaction would occur.

When we ran the experiment, we followed the operating instructions in the A, B, C, and now the D columns. By putting main effect D (catalyst amount) in the same column with the A × B × C interaction, we confound or alias that column so that whatever results come out of that column could either be due to main effect D (catalyst amount) or the three-way interaction A × B × C. We are willing to take this risk because of the low probability of a three-way interaction. But wait, by putting D (catalyst amount) in column 7 we now set into motion a series of two-way interactions in which we might have interest. For example, the pharmaceutical team mentioned that there might be a sit time and catalyst amount interaction (B × D). Where would this interaction be located? Let's figure it out together. To determine an interaction, we multiply the minus and plus columns together. Thus, we take the second column where factor B (sit time) is located and the seventh column, where we put factor D (catalyst amount). Remember, a minus times a minus is a plus, a minus times a plus is a minus and a plus times a plus is a plus.

Does this pattern formed by multiplying the second and seventh column in Exhibit 7.25 look like any other? Yes, it is the exact

B Sit Time	A × B × C (D) Catalyst Amount	B × D
−	−	+
−	+	−
+	+	+
+	−	−
−	+	−
−	−	+
+	−	−
+	+	+

Exhibit 7.25 Sit time catalyst amount interaction pattern.

pattern found in column 5 where the A × C interaction is located. So the domino effect of confounding or aliasing will continue as it does here in other columns. When I asked the pharmaceutical company if they were concerned about an A × C interaction they said while it was possible it was unlikely, so they were content with taking the risk that the results in column 5 were due to the B × D interaction and not the A × C interaction.

When we completed all the possible patterns, we learned that main effects A, B, C, and D are only confounded with higher order interactions (three-way and higher) while they are not confounded with any two-way interactions. Further, we learned that columns 4, 5, and 6 will hold our two-way interactions as shown in Exhibit 7.26.

The pharmaceutical team is confident that their main two-way interaction to watch for is the B × D interaction. As you can see in Exhibit 7.26, by allowing two-way interactions to confound with other two-way interactions we can now run an 8 run experiment on four factors and complete our work in half the time rather than the 16 experiments it would have taken in the full factorial. The experiment the pharmaceutical company ran is shown in Exhibit 7.27 complete with the two-way interaction confounding that exists. While there are three-way interactions that confound with the main effects, I have removed them from the design even though

Column	Effects Estimated
1	A and higher order interactions
2	B and higher order interactions
3	C and higher order interactions
4	AB and CD interactions
5	AC and BD interactions
6	BC and AD interactions
7	D and higher order interactions

Exhibit 7.26   Effects: pharmaceutical company
higher order interactions.

they technically exist. Remember, the odds of a three-way interaction are slim, so to worry about them is not worth your time.

The pharmaceutical client was thrilled with doing half the
number of experiments. Exhibit 7.28 is the effects table for the experiment after we completed testing glut time, sit time, moisture
content, and catalyst amount.

These results show clearly a catalyst amount effect and sec-
ondarily a glut level effect. Remember, the client had possible concerns about a B × D interaction. There doesn't appear to be any

A Glut Level	B Sit Time	C Moisture Content	A × B C × D	A × C B × D	B × C A × D	(D) Catalyst Amount	Results (Propri-etary)
−	−	−	+	+	+	−	
+	−	−	−	−	+	+	
−	+	−	−	+	−	+	
+	+	−	+	−	−	−	
−	−	+	+	−	−	+	
+	−	+	−	+	−	−	
−	+	+	−	−	+	−	
+	+	+	+	+	+	+	

Note: The response variable has been removed for proprietary reasons.

Exhibit 7.27   Fractional factorial design animal vaccine
experiment confounding alias patterns.

A Glut Level	B Sit Time	C Moisture Content	A × B C × D	A × C B × D	B × C A × D	(D) Catalyst Amount
* * 10.5	2.5	5.0	0.5	2.0	2.0	20.0

* Removed for proprietary reasons.

Exhibit 7.28   Effects: experiment testing three factors.

given the proportionate effect of glut level and catalyst amount. This client went on to use several other experiments to improve the potency of this vaccine.

In this overview of experimentation, I only covered the simple effects table, a simple mathematical approach to analyzing experiment results. The most powerful method of experiment analysis is the Analysis of Variance, a sophisticated tool. Analysis of Variance (ANOVA) is a method to determine the significance of a factor. For example, a simple effects table may show what is a large effect in absolute terms but ANOVA will tell us to what extent and with what statistical significance a factor contributes to the overall variation in our experiment.

■ SUMMARY

Chapter 7 stressed the importance of the last stage of Analysis. Specifically, validating root causation. The concept of Open-Narrow-Close is critical to leading teams to the true root causation of their project. We discussed at the beginning of Chapter 7 the importance of the five why diagram to begin "drilling down" to find the true root causes. Later in Chapter 7, we examined the need to validate root causes. One method is to take current data collection methods to show a before-and-after picture to validate root causes.

In those rare circumstances when one root cause jumps out at the project team, the scatter diagram is a simple tool that can be applied to determine if a given X explains the variation in a given Y. The correlation coefficient statistically tells how much of Y is explained by a given X. We stressed the limitations of the scatter diagram, specifically that it indicates a relationship between an X and a Y but does not prove causation. Often, a third variable will explain the relationship seen in a scatter diagram.

The biggest concern with scatter diagram analysis is that it is rare when one X explains most of Y. Thus, we recommended the use of the designed experiment in those more realistic situations when multiple X's explain a given Y. We discussed multiple types of experiments which included trial and error, one factor at a time, full factorials, and fractional factorials.

KEY LEARNINGS

➤ For any narrowed root cause, drill down to see the true root causes.

➤ The most important step in analysis is validating root causation.

➤ Some root causes can be validated with simple before/after data collection tools.

➤ In those rare situations when one major root cause jumps out at the project team, validate the root cause with a scatter diagram.

➤ Recognize that the scatter diagram can show correlation between an X and a Y.

➤ A common problem in analysis of scatter diagrams is assuming causation.

➤ Many times a third variable effect explains the relationship in a scatter diagram.

➤ The correlation coefficient can explain the magnitude of Y explained by a given X.

➤ Designed experiments are a way for a project team to answer the equation $Y = f(X_1, X_2 \ldots X_n)$ in a short period of time.

➤ Trial-and-error experimentation is a common method of experimentation but is mostly error.

➤ Testing one factor at a time experimentation is a way to gain some knowledge about the equation $Y = f(X_1, X_2 \ldots X_n)$, but will not allow the project team to learn about possible interactions.

➤ Full factorial experiments are used to gain knowledge about main effects and interactions and are best used when examining a small number of main effects.

(Continued)

➤ Fractional factorial experiments are used to gain knowledge about main effects and some interactions when the team is willing to give up some knowledge of some interactions. They are a great type of first experiment.

➤ Creating effects tables is a simple mathematical method to determine which factors are larger contributors to variation.

➤ Analysis of Variance (ANOVA) is a more complex method to analyze results and is not covered in this book.

Chapter 8

Selecting Solutions That Drive Sigma Performance

If the project team has completed the steps discussed in previous chapters, Improve can be the easiest section in the DMAIC methodology. Before a project team enters the Improve stage, they must have documented evidence that root causation (the last stage of the Analysis section of DMAIC) has been validated. With evidence of root causation, the goal of Improve is to select those solutions that impact root causation. Solutions generated and implemented in this section of the DMAIC methodology should attempt to either eliminate the root cause, soften or dampen the effects of the root cause, or neutralize the root causation effects.

Another reason the Improve section should go smoothly for the project team is that we will be using an approach similar to the one mastered in Analysis. By the time the project team reaches Improve, they will have spent several weeks using the Open-Narrow-Close approach we explained in the last two chapters. As a reminder, Exhibit 8.1 is the concept of Open-Narrow-Close as it was applied to Analysis.

Exhibit 8.2 lists the tools associated with Open-Narrow-Close as it applies to Improve. A casual observation shows that while there are differences between Open-Narrow-Close in Analysis and Improve there are distinct similarities. Let's begin with an example.

■ OPEN

Conceptually, the Open phase of Improve attempts to do the same thing that occurs in the Open phase of Analysis. That is, it is a

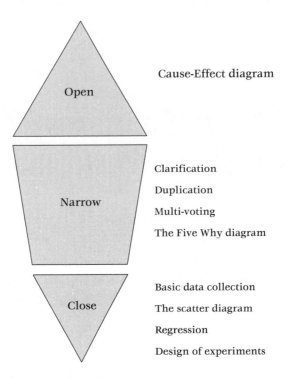

Exhibit 8.1   Root cause analysis: Open-Narrow-Close.

time of brainstorming, gathering all possible ideas that will impact the validated root causes. The use of an affinity diagram is
equivalent to the cause-effect diagram, a tool to gather all the ideas
the project team has on potential solutions. Like any brainstorming session, the following rules apply:

➤ Document all ideas.
➤ Ensure the team generates ideas, not discussion.
➤ No evaluation of ideas.
➤ Everyone participates.

An example will help us with this concept. Each January the
Eckes family holds a family conference. We reaffirm (there is
that re- word, in this context I consider it adds value) our values
and beliefs and Deb, Joe, Temo, and I indicate what our family

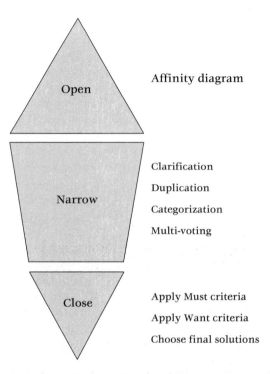

Affinity diagram

Clarification

Duplication

Categorization

Multi-voting

Apply Must criteria

Apply Want criteria

Choose final solutions

Exhibit 8.2   Tools for Open-Narrow-Close root cause analysis.

and individual goals will be. Also at this time, we decide on a summer family vacation spot.

When the agenda turns to the family vacation spot, we begin with the first steps of the affinity diagram. Each of us takes sticky notes and writes as many location areas as each of us individually can possibly see ourselves going to. We write silently and place them on the wall of my office in no particular order or sequence. Below are all the spots we brainstormed in our meeting a year ago:

➤ Disney World, 4 times.

➤ New York, 3 times.

➤ San Francisco, 3 times.

➤ Chicago, 2 times.

➤ London, 2 times.

➤ Camping in the mountains, 2 times.

➤ Boat cruise, 2 times.

➤ Alaska, 2 times.

➤ Rock hunting in the Black Hills.

➤ Africa.

➤ Dallas.

➤ Hockey camp at Notre Dame.

➤ Paris.

➤ Disneyland.

■ NARROW

Allowing as much time as necessary for the brainstorming to be completed, we now move on to narrowing the list. Similarly to the cause-effect diagram, we read out each card. If everyone understands what is written on the card, we move on to the next one. Such cards listed like Disney World, Camping in the mountains, and Hockey camp at Notre Dame pose no problem. When Rock Hunting in the Black Hills was read, Dad asked for clarification, the first step in the narrowing process. My son, Joe, indicates that in his Science class last semester, he took an interest in geology and that one of his classmates had done rock hunting in the Black Hills and had a lot of fun. No discussion of the merits of rock hunting in the Black Hills occurs. No lobbying occurs for or against rock hunting. We only attempt to clarify so that all ideas are understood.

At the same time this clarification activity is going on, we are also on the look out for duplicates. When we see multiple cards for Disney World, New York, San Francisco, Chicago, London, Camping, Boat cruise, and Alaska we place them on top of one another. It is important to note that we only put exact duplicates together. For example, we do not take Disneyland and put it on top of the Disney World cards. We do group these two together for our next step, Categorization.

The cause-effect diagram we used in Analysis has one advantage over the Affinity diagram. It has naturally designed categories so that we can group similar ideas. Whether it was Machines, Methods, Materials, Mother Nature, Measurement, or People, the cause-effect diagram naturally leads us to Categorization. With the affinity diagram, categorization is an additional step we must create from the ideas generated.

In our family vacation example of the affinity diagram, we started grouping our brainstorms into the following groups:

Disney World	London	New York	Camping	Hockey Camp
Disneyland	Paris	San Francisco	Rock hunting	Boat cruise
	Africa	Dallas		
		Chicago		

For each grouping, we now attempt to create a general category and put a different colored card, called a *header card* above it. For example, for Disney World and Disneyland, we label the category *Amusement Parks*. For London, Paris, and Africa, we use the Header, *Foreign Destinations*. For New York, San Francisco, Dallas, and Chicago, we use the category *U.S. Metropolitan Cities*. For Camping and Rock hunting, the family suggests *Outdoor Recreation*. The Hockey camp and Boat cruise are labeled *Miscellaneous*.

The newly arranged vacation spots with appropriate header cards are:

Amusement Parks	Foreign Destinations	U.S. Metropolitan Cities	Outdoor Recreation	Miscellaneous
Disney World	London	New York	Camping	Hockey camp
Disneyland	Paris	San Francisco	Rock hunting	Boat cruise
	Africa	Dallas		
		Chicago		

The last tool we use for Narrow is the multi-vote. In this example, with 13 possible vacation spots, we arbitrarily decide that each of the family members are allocated 5 votes. It is important to note that the votes are placed on the actual locations not on the header cards. The header cards are used as a way for each participant to think about how he or she wants to vote.

Silently, each family member decides on how to vote. In our family, Deb and I decide to vote last so as not to influence the boys. When I facilitate this activity with organizations, I coach the management to vote last so as to not influence those participants with "lesser stripes." Here is how the family allocated their five votes each:

Amusement Parks	Foreign Destinations	U.S. Metropolitan Cities	Outdoor Recreation	Miscellaneous
Disney World	London	New York	Camping	Hockey camp
7	0	6	0	3
Disneyland	Paris	San Francisco	Rock hunting	Boat cruise
0	3	0	0	0
	Africa	Dallas		
	0	0		
		Chicago		
		1		

The beauty of multi-voting is that it results in a Pareto. The Pareto for our selections is:

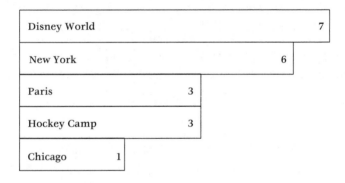

■ CLOSE: APPLYING THE CRITERIA OF "MUSTS/WANTS"

Whether we are talking about the concepts of selecting a vacation spot or selecting solutions, we need to apply a set of criteria. In the example of a vacation spot, we want to apply "Must" and "Want" criteria to select one answer. In the case of a project team, we want to prioritize solutions. Prioritization of solutions is important for two reasons. First, resources to implement even a prioritized list of solutions may be cost prohibitive. Second, we may find that if we propose five or six solutions, by implementing them in waves we may meet our improvement goal after the second or third solution, thus negating the need to implement all of the recommended solutions.

Must criteria are the minimum requirements that a suggestion must meet to be considered. Think of a Must criteria like the old goldminers sieve where they attempted to separate the gold from the dirt or rocks. Must criteria is an either/or decision. Thus, they should be structured as closed-ended questions, not open-ended. While Must criteria are applied in the Improve section of DMAIC to solutions the project team creates, it is wise for Must criteria to be created and communicated to the project team as early as the D phase of the DMAIC application. Must criteria are usually created by the project team's champion. Typical Must criteria include but are not limited to:

- ➤ Must not add to head-count.
- ➤ Must comply with company policy.
- ➤ Must comply with state and federal law.
- ➤ Must be implementable by (date).

In our family vacation example, Deb and I were responsible for creation of the Must criteria. Creation of Must criteria is best when created and communicated as early as possible. Deb and I presented our Must criteria to the boys after our initial brainstorming. We had only two Must criteria:

1. Vacation spot had to be within North America.
2. Vacation spot had to be accessible with frequent flyer miles.

Using the Pareto, we arbitrarily took the top four locations and compared them with each of our two Must criteria.

	Within North America	Accessible with Frequent Flyer Miles
Disney World	yes	yes
New York	yes	yes
Paris	no	yes
Hockey camp	yes	yes

For a solution (or in this case a vacation spot) to be considered further, it must meet *all* the Must criteria. In this case, Paris is not within North America and will no longer be considered any further. Thus, in our use of the vacation spots for application of Must and Want criteria, only three locations remain under consideration:

➤ Disney World.
➤ New York.
➤ Hockey camp.

At this point, Deb and I discuss with the boys the Want criteria. While Must criteria is an either/or test, Want criteria are those criteria that will allow us to compare and judge one solution against another so we can prioritize those solutions.

The reason we discuss with the boys what the Want criteria will be is that while Must criteria usually comes from the champion (and in the vacation example, the parents), Want criteria is usually a joint decision between the project team and the champion. In our selection of a vacation, we as parents have the final decision (just as a champion does), we see that involvement of the boys will make the selection have greater buy-in. This, too, should be a consideration in project teams. There may be great solutions a champion can create, but we want buy-in from the team and those affected by the solutions. Those people who are affected by your solutions or are necessary to implement your solutions are called *stakeholders*. Since Joe and Temo are certainly affected by the choice of a vacation spot, they are considered stakeholders and thus should have a say in the Want criteria. Typically at this point, I encourage the project team to identify potential stakeholders of the prioritized solutions and either bring them into the project on an ad hoc basis or make sure they are involved somehow in the next steps of the Improvement phase of a DMAIC project.

In our vacation example, it was easy to bring the stakeholders into the fray since they were full-time members of our working team (i.e., the family). After I explain how the Want criteria works in our vacation example, I will spend more time on how to deal with stakeholders on a project team.

In our vacation meeting, we brainstormed freely on what the Want criteria should be in the selection of our final vacation spot.

We decided on the following criteria to help prioritize and decide on a location. The remaining locations should be judged against:

➤ Being kid friendly.

➤ Weather conducive.

➤ Learning something.

➤ Access to Major League Baseball.

Once there is agreement on the Want criteria, the team (with the approval of the champion), selects one to be the heaviest weighted and receive a 10 weighting (out of a possible 10). The others are relatively weighted. Since I travel all the time, Deb and I gave the kids the task of picking the heaviest weighted item and they chose "Being kid friendly." We then came to agreement on the other three:

Want Criteria	Weight
Being kid friendly	10
Weather conducive	7
Learning something	8
Access to Major League Baseball	9

You will note that the weighting for the remaining three Want criteria worked out to unique numbers. It would have been possible to have a similar weight for remaining Want criteria. There can only be one Want criteria weighted 10, but other criteria could have been equally weighted. A method I use with project teams is to go around to each project team member and ask how he or she individually would weight that particular Want criteria on a scale of 1 to 9 and take the average. By this point, the team will have already selected the Want criteria with a weight of 10.

With the weights for each Want criteria determined by the project team, we now take the prioritized solutions determined after multi-voting and apply the criteria to these solutions.

In our family vacation spot, there were three locations still under consideration after application of the Must criteria eliminated Paris. The three remaining locations were Disney World (located in Orlando, Florida), New York, and Hockey Camp at Notre Dame (for those who are not Irish fans, Notre Dame is located in South Bend, Indiana, a two-hour drive from Chicago).

The information to make our vacation selection is:

	Weight	Disney World	New York	Notre Dame
Being kid friendly	10			
Weather conducive	7			
Learning something	8			
Access to Major League Baseball	9			

To begin the last phase of selecting our location, we ask the project team members (i.e., the Eckes family) to first rank how "kid friendly" Disney World is on a scale of 1 to 10. The individual scores of the family were:

	Temo	Joe	Mom	Dad
Kid friendly (Disney World)	10	10	10	10

It doesn't take a calculator to know the average rating for how kid friendly Disney World is 10. Since "Being kid friendly" has a weight of 10, we now multiply the weight by the average as determined by the team and we have an overall score of 100.

Next, the family ranks how weather conducive Disney World is during the summer. We have defined our weather conduciveness as twofold. The children want it to be as sunny as possible. Since moving to Denver in 1984, Dad has become spoiled by low humidity, so the higher the humidity, the less weather conducive it is for Dad. With these two elements constituting how we rank weather conduciveness, below are the individual scores of how each team member ranked Disney World on being weather conducive.

	Temo	Joe	Mom	Dad
Weather conducive	7	6	4	3

The average for this criteria is 5. Since the weight is 7, we now multiply 7 by 5 and get an overall score of 35.

Next, we rank whether a trip to the most prominent amusement park in the United States can result in "Learning something," other than how to wait in line. A spirited discussion ensues and I end up doing what I rarely do, admit I am wrong. The boys had come prepared with data. They discussed Epcot Center and the knowledge they would obtain by visiting a host of exhibits. As a result of this data demonstration, I was moved to give it a weight of 7. The rest of the team scores are:

	Temo	Joe	Mom	Dad
Learn something	8	8	7	7

The average of 7.5 is multiplied by its weight of 8 for an overall score of 60.

Finally, the last criteria to determine is how accessible is Disney World to Major League Baseball. Research was required before we voted on this one. The boys and I got out a Florida map and determined that Orlando was approximately two hours from Tampa Bay, where the Devil Rays play.

The team's scores for Disney World being accessible to Major League Baseball are:

	Temo	Joe	Mom	Dad
Access to Major League baseball	6	7	7	5

The average is 6.25 which is multiplied by 9 for an overall score of 56.25. The overall score for Disney World is then calculated by adding all four weighted scores together (100 + 35 + 60 + 56.25) which equals 251.25.

We now move on to scoring New York. Once again, as we did for Disney World, we all rank against the Want criteria. The scores for New York are:

	Temo	Joe	Mom	Dad	Average/ Score
Being kid friendly	9	9	9	9	9/90
Weather conducive	7	7	6	5	6.25/43.75
Learning something	8	8	8	8	8/64
Access to Major League baseball	10	10	10	10	10/90

Again, as we did for the weighted scores for Disney World, we add up the weighted scores for New York and get 289.75.

Finally, we do the scoring for the Hockey Camp at Notre Dame. When we rank the scores for Notre Dame they looked as follows:

	Temo	Joe	Mom	Dad	Average/ Score
Being kid friendly	10	10	10	10	10/100
Weather conducive	7	7	8	7	7.25/50.75
Learning something	10	10	10	10	10/80
Access to Major League baseball	8	7	8	7	7.5/67.5

By adding up the weighted scores for Notre Dame, we got 298.25. Here is the final list showing our results:

	Weight	DisneyWorld Avg./Score	New York Avg./Score	Notre Dame Avg./Score
Being kid friendly	10	10/100	9/90	10/100
Weather conducive	7	5/35	6.25/43.75	7.25/50.75
Learning something	8	7.5/60	8/64	10/80
Major League baseball	9	6.25/56.25	10/90	7.5/67.5
Total		251.25	289.75	298.25

Get out your hockey sticks, boys. Through analysis of the scores, you can see that the hockey camp option with a score of 298.25 beat out New York with a score of 289.75 and Disney World with a score of 251.25.

In the application of Must and Want criteria for the vacation spot, there is one "selection" of a solution for the problem of where to go on vacation. If the budget allowed a second vacation, then our second location would be New York.

In the application of Must and Want criteria on actual improvement projects, the prioritized lists of solutions would not be the either/or choice it was for my family. Instead, it would assist the team in prioritizing the list of solutions.

■ MORE INFORMATION ON CRITERIA FOR SOLUTIONS

I have experienced problems with project teams creating and applying criteria. The most typical problems they encounter are:

➤ Establishing a new set of goals as mistaken criteria.

➤ Structuring Want criteria as Must criteria and vice versa.

➤ Having too many criteria.

The first problem is the most evident. Here, a project team will add a host of new goals. Below are actual brainstormed "criteria":

Actual criteria: The solution must produce improvement.
Comments: Remember that criteria either helps to preclude a possible solution for further consideration (a Must criteria), or helps to sort and prioritize solutions (Want criteria). Saying that a solution must produce improvement is a BGO, (a blazing grasp of the obvious). It is less a criteria than a desired goal. Thus, it does nothing by way of sorting or prioritizing solutions.

Actual criteria: The solution must produce $500,000 worth of cost savings.
Comments: If the solution produces $499,000 worth of cost savings, would it not be under further consideration as a possible solution? Of course, a solution that would produce this type of improvement should be considered further. When I see this type of Must criteria, I encourage the team to phrase a criteria in terms of a Want. Some solutions are more cost effective than others, so I recommend something like, "Impact on Cost Savings." In fact, virtually all Want criteria should be phrased as open-ended questions rather than either/or.

What is a sufficient number of Must and Want criteria? Experience says the more Must criteria, the greater the chances that quality solutions will be filtered out for further consideration. I have always felt that two or three quality Must criteria are better than a larger number that may not help the team. I have seen as many Want criteria as eight or nine, but again, quality is more important than quantity. What I strongly suggest to teams is that they include the following two Want criteria:

1. *Impact on root causation.* Many teams become so wrapped up in Improve, they often forget to link solutions to reducing the effects of the root causes. One way to always have root causation in the project team's thought process is to have this Want criteria so the team will see if their solutions impact root causation.

2. *Impact on stakeholders.* A stakeholder is someone affected by a proposed solution or someone needed to implement the solution. Often teams create great solutions that have significant impact to other groups or individuals. By including

the impact a solution has on key stakeholders, the team may discover that a secondary solution may have greater acceptance by stakeholders and thus, in the long run, have greater impact on the project team's goals. An example of this follows.

Several years ago I had been working with a GE group that was involved in a DMAIC project. Because of the complexity of the problem, they took several months to complete both the Analysis and Improve sections of the project. Several months after I taught them Improve, they called me back to say their project had not achieved the stated goals. They asked me back to do a failure analysis of the project since the group had an unusually high degree of commitment to Six Sigma. They had given up on this particular project but were hoping I had some thoughts on how to make their next project more successful.

I spent time looking through their Improve work and it became apparent why their project failed. I asked them to take their three highest rated solutions and conduct a *Stakeholder Analysis*. This tool is a simple way to graph the acceptance of a given solution among those affected by the solution or those needed to implement it. I asked the team to list the key stakeholders for their project solutions. They listed the following (*Actual names are not used*):

Name	Title
Janice	Manager-Receiving
Joseph	Manager-Fleet Services
Courtney	Associate-Fleet Services transportation
Paul	Associate-Fleet Services transportation
Gerald	Customer
Mary Paula	Customer

The project was to improve delivery time of leased vehicles to customers. The project team (none of whom were stakeholders) came up with three solutions after applying the Must and Want criteria:

1. Have fleet services transportation workers take receipt of leased vehicles earlier in the process. Specifically, have workers deliver vehicles before all paperwork is complete.

2. Have customers fill out paperwork.

3. Have receiving detail vehicles earlier in the process.

Examining these solutions, you may be getting an idea of why the project failed. Let's go back to the two "doors" that project teams enter to arrive at root causation. The data door is used when the primary goal of a project is to improve the effectiveness of some measure (remember, an effectiveness measure is one in which the team is trying to increase satisfaction of some customer need and its associated requirements). The process door is used when we want to improve the efficiency of a process. In the leasing project, the team's primary goal was efficiency based (i.e., improving delivery time). You probably also remember that process analysis focuses on finding nonvalue-added activities in the process and removing them. The aforementioned solutions don't seem remotely to address nonvalue-added activity. In fact, the team unconsciously seems to be improving the delivery time by adding work to areas not originally under consideration during measure (e.g., having the customer fill out the paperwork and thus not include this time in the measure of delivery time).

I asked the project team to consider if their solutions had been successfully implemented what would have happened to delivery time. They responded it would have improved dramatically. Specifically, it would have gone from a 1.7 sigma performance to a 3.9 sigma performance. I diplomatically told them all they were doing was shifting the work to others and scaling back *how* they measured. I then proceeded to conduct a Shareholder Analysis with them. First we listed all the key stakeholders down one line of a flip chart.

I then told them for any proposed solution, there can be five typical responses to the solution. One type of response is called strongly supportive. A person who is strongly supportive will not only do what is asked of them, but they will try to elicit support from others. These people are the "make-it-happen" group. The second category is called moderately supportive. A moderately supportive stakeholder is one who will do what is asked of him. These people are the help-it-happen group, doing what is asked of them but not necessarily going above and beyond the call of duty. The third group is the neutral group. They are not necessarily against the proposed solution but they are not for it either. When I think of someone in this category, I think of someone who will let-it-happen. As such, they are typically stakeholders who are affected by the change, not someone needed to implement the change. The fourth of the five types are those who are moderately against the solution. Here, a request for aid in implementation will be denied or complied with passively, but if you can implement the solution they will not sabotage your overall efforts. The fifth and final category are those who are strongly against the solution. In this category, you find those stakeholders who not only not assist in what is asked of them to implement the solution but also actively try to enlist others to prevent the team from implementing the solution.

With those definitions, the vehicle leasing team was asked to do two things with regard to the stakeholders. First, they were asked to rate where each stakeholder was with regard to the solutions proposed and more importantly where they needed to be in terms of support if the proposed solutions were to be successfully implemented. An x indicates their level of support and an o indicates where we needed them to be if the vehicle leasing team was to be successful with their project. The completed Stakeholder Analysis is shown in Exhibit 8.3.

It now became clear to the vehicle leasing team that without support for the solutions, no actual sigma improvement could be expected. In this example, the project team didn't really create solutions that reduced delivery time, they simply shifted work that would make delivery time look better on their books.

Many project teams have made their solutions more powerful through the use of Stakeholder Analysis. Another example follows.

A client in Silicon Valley had reached solution selection and had recognized that several of their solutions were politically sensitive.

Name	Strongly Against	Moderately Against	Neutral	Moderately Supportive	Strongly Supportive
Janice		x	o		
Joseph		x		o	
Courtney		x		o	
Paul	x			o	
Gerald	x			o	
Mary Paula		x		o	

Exhibit 8.3 Stakeholder analysis completed vehicle leasing.

Specifically, their project focused on reducing the number of incoming defects discovered by their receiving inspection department. The solutions generated and agreed to by the project team would result in fewer jobs needed in receiving inspection. The team created the Stakeholder Analysis shown in Exhibit 8.4.

While the solutions were powerful, if there was no movement from the stakeholders in their current position, the project would fail. At this point, I introduced another tool for this team to use to change the results of the Stakeholder Analysis.

Gathering the team together, I asked the project team members why Dennis, the receiving inspection vice president was strongly against the project? What were the issues that made Dennis resist? What would it take to move Dennis from being strongly against to at least being moderately supportive? The discussion that ensued was lively. The focus of the team's comments was on how bad Dennis was, what an obstacle Dennis was to the project, and how resistant Dennis was to change.

Name	Strongly Against	Moderately Against	Neutral	Moderately Supportive	Strongly Supportive
Dennis (Receiving Inspection Vice President)	x			o	
Toby (Mechanical Inspection Director)		x		o	
Rhonda (Electrical Inspection Director)		x		o	
Paula (Key individual contributor with strong influence with other individual contributors)	x			o	

Exhibit 8.4 Stakeholder analysis Silicon Valley.

All the comments seemed both accurate and understandable. However, they hadn't answered my questions. In response to my questions, the team vented their frustrations but they didn't respond to what they had to do to change Dennis and make their project a success.

I introduced them to a companion tool to the Stakeholder Analysis. It is called a Planning for Influence chart. It is made up of the following columns: Key Stakeholder, Type of Resistance, Issues, and Strategy.

➤ Planning for Influence — Types of Resistance

In this example, the Key Stakeholder is Dennis. The second column is Type of Resistance. People are resistant to change for different reasons. There are four major types of resistance, each having different issues underlying them. Different strategies must be implemented based on the different types of resistance. Further, inaccurate diagnosis of the type of resistance may lead to implementing a strategy that makes things worse in terms of support of their solutions.

Resistance Type 1 — Technical

Many years ago I was computer illiterate. If you heard me back then, you would hear me bashing computers. I was unequivocally resistant to computers. My first book was written long hand. What was the type of resistance I was exhibiting? It was technical resistance. The underlying issue of technical resistance was that computers made me feel stupid. I pride myself on my intelligence and here was this machine that made me feel stupid. Filling out the first columns of the Planning for Influence chart it would look as shown in Exhibit 8.5.

Recognize the underlying work needed by those diagnosing my resistance. Did I come out directly and say computers made me feel stupid? Of course not. Someone had to spend time with me to ascertain what I was saying and what possibly made me feel that way. The project team needs to spend time with those key stakeholders whose support we need to make our solutions work.

The person who spent the most time dealing with my computer resistance was my wife, Debbie. Knowing my need for computer skills, her strategy was to enroll me in a computer class. This

Key Stakeholder	Type of Resistance	Issues	Strategy
George	Technical	The use of computers makes him feel stupid	

Exhibit 8.5 Planning for influence—technical.

class was taught by a computer genius. He knew more about computers than I will ever know. I faithfully attended each and every training session. I attempted all assignments given me. At the completion of the class, I was *more* resistant to the concept of computers.

What went wrong? The most common strategy implemented when someone has diagnosed technical resistance is training. After my training class where I became more resistant, I refused to even try to use the computer. The instructor was a great lecturer but his brilliance reinforced my stupidity. This made my resistance greater. Eventually, I changed.

What eventually reduced my resistance? The change of my approach to computers came from my children. Joe and Temo provided three things that changed my approach to computers:

➤ Information—the advantages of using a computer.

➤ Education.

➤ Involvement.

Notice, training is not in those three elements. Joe and Temo started talking about what they were doing with computers and how they were learning more using the computer (*information*). They showed me some of the preliminary steps in starting and using the computer and did so without putting expectations on me like I had with the computer trainer (*education*). Finally, the boys got me to start using the computer when I asked them to play one of their computer games (*involvement*).

Thus, for the first type of resistance the way to move someone from being either moderately or strongly resistant who is showing technical resistance is information, education, and involvement (Exhibit 8.6).

Key Stakeholder	Type of Resistance	Issues	Strategy
George	Technical	The use of computers makes him feel stupid	Information Education Involvement

Exhibit 8.6 Planning for influence—technical strategy.

Resistance Type 2 — Political

When I teach management of change I have an exercise that proves enlightening to the audience. I ask all the participants to stand and find a partner. I then ask them to face their partner and study them for 15 to 20 seconds. During this period, nervous laughter starts. I then request that they stand back to back with their partner. I instruct them to change three things about their physical appearance. I further instruct them there is but one rule; they cannot create a hostile work environment. After I say go, nervous laughter returns. With those simple instructions, virtually all the participants do the same thing: They start to take off their watches, they loosen and remove their ties, take off their shoes, or unbutton their clothes. After less than a minute, I instruct the participants to face their partner and see if they can find the three things their partner changed. After brief discussion, I tell the pairs to return back to back. In the second round, I instruct them to change *five* additional things about their physical appearance. The only additional rule is that the participants cannot change any of their first three changes.

In the second round, there are far more verbal comments. Among the common ones I hear are:

➤ "I don't have any more clothes to take off."

➤ "I can't change any more things about myself without embarrassing myself."

➤ "I'm starting to look ridiculous."

Once again, I have the participants face their partners to see if they can detect the changes made. Then, I ask them to return back to back for the third round of changes. I ask them if they are ready to change 10 additional things about their physical appearance.

Verbal, overt resistance sets in and rarely do I proceed with round three, fearful of my physical safety.

What does this exercise prove? As a professional instructor I am well aware that the debrief of an exercise can be more important than the exercise itself. I tell everyone to take a seat for the discussion of the process they just experienced. I do not tell them to change back to the way they were originally. As you might expect, though, there is a mad rush to reclothe themselves.

After a discussion of their comments, I collect data. Assuming we have run two rounds and they followed the directions properly, each participant changed eight things about themselves. I ask them to place the eight changes into one of three categories. The first category refers to changes they made that were "losses." For example, removal of their shoes would fit this category. A second category would be neutral changes. For example, switching their wristwatch from one hand to the other would fit this category. Finally, the third and last category are those "additions" they made to change their physical appearance. For example, a participant once took a post it note and put it on her forehead.

I then ask them to show me with fingers raised the numbers in each category. An approximate percentage in the years I have done this exercise is:

Losses	70%
Neutral	25%
Additions	5%

While there are individual differences, a pattern is clearly evident. All I request of participants is to change things about their physical appearance and do so without creating a hostile work environment. The key to the debrief occurs quickly: *People associate the word change with loss.* When we associate change with loss, it is obvious why people are resistant to change. There is even a biological component to this resistance. What does your body do when it receives a heart transplant? Even if this new, healthy heart is the difference between life and death, your body attempts to reject (i.e., resist) this change, opting instead for the status quo that may result in death.

If change is associated with loss, then people will change only if two things are shown to them with regard to the change. One, there must exist a *need* for the change. Second, there needs to be something to be *gained* from the change for the stakeholder affected. In other words, there needs to a WIIFM(What's In It For Me) shown for a stakeholder to buy into the change.

In political resistance, the person exhibiting resistance may not have any technical resistance with the change, but his or her resistance is based on seeing the solution to be implemented as a loss, either real or perceived. Fill out the Planning the Influence chart as shown in Exhibit 8.7.

Type of Resistance 3—Individual

Once I was consulting with a family-owned business in Wisconsin. They had asked me to work with them to install a business-process-oriented approach to their business as they had grown so large, their old family-run approach to business ways had resulted in being on the verge of bankruptcy. Working with the executive staff, work assignments were administered in such a way I initially believed everyone was on board. Soon, it became noticeable that one of their vice presidents was only passively compliant. He had not voiced any overt resistance to the change toward process management, but his work assignments were only half-heartedly completed and after several months working with them I became worried we had what I called a "covert terrorist."

I invited this vice president out to dinner and during drinks I inquired about how he really felt toward the process improvement initiative. Alcohol being the lubricant it can sometimes be, he responded, "Well, now that you asked me, I will tell you. I am in the process of getting a divorce, my mother just died, I have to place my father in a nursing home, and the only time I hear from my

Key Stakeholder	Type of Resistance	Issues	Strategy
Stakeholder	Political	Perceiving the change as a loss, real or imagined	Creating the need for change and then showing how the change can benefit them

Exhibit 8.7 Planning for influence—political.

two children in college is when they call to ask for money. Then, here comes Mr. Hot Shot consultant who comes into the one area of constancy in my life and tries to change that. How do I feel about the change? Well, I just told you."

I resisted the urge to request the check from the waiter. I also resisted the urge to order another bottle of wine knowing that the vice president's acknowledgment was progress. Over this dinner, he had gone from being a covert terrorist to acknowledgment of his resistance. Further, the form of his resistance was not technical. He understood the elements of process management. While the issues behind this individual type of resistance are similar to political resistance (the sense of loss), it goes deeper than that. The vice president's zone of comfort had been threatened by what was happening at work. While loss was a factor in his resistance, with what was going on elsewhere in his life, his stress level for change was at its breaking point. While practicing psychology, I came across a verbal stress test. Highest on the list was the death of a child. The next two were divorce and the death of a parent. When taking into account all that was going on for this man, it was obvious the change at work was pushing him past the point of being able to function. At that level of stress, a person becomes paralyzed to act.

This led me to the strategy we employ with individual resistance. While some of the strategy of combating individual resistance overlaps the strategy of dealing with political resistance, there are significant differences. For example, in our first two types of resistance, we are doing things *to* the resistor, whether it be trying to convince him or her of the need for change or attempting to show him or her what's in it for them. While these factors should also be employed with those who show individual resistance, it also is wise to modify the change elements to match the situation for those already overwhelmed by other issues that prompts the paralysis characterized by this type of resistance.

For example, we had anticipated the vice president having six action items to be completed in three months. Instead we worked out a compromise for him to complete four items in four months. This compromise, worked out with the rest of the executive team, helped the vice president start listening to the other strategies we employed to get greater buy-in (Exhibit 8.8). This included showing how Business Process Management would help sustain the one constant in his life, his work for this family-owned business.

Key Stakeholder	Type of Resistance	Issues	Strategy
Vice President	Individual	High stress Threat to comfort zone General paralysis to activity change	Modifying the action items to reduce the stress experienced by the person showing this type of resistance Creating the need for change and then showing how the change can benefit them

Exhibit 8.8 Planning for Influence—political strategy.

Type of Resistance 4—Organizational

This type of resistance rarely shows itself with one or two people in the organization. Organizational resistance is the resistance shown as the concept of "Not Invented Here." It typically is the type of resistance you see when the entire organization is adverse to change, usually based on seeing messengers of change being shot. For example, at dinner the other night, Debbie and I ordered drinks to celebrate signing a contract with a new client. As the drinks were served, the waitress spilled them significantly. When we requested a replacement not filled as much, the waitress resisted, saying, "I'm sorry, the bar only serves full drinks."

The point of this story is that this resistance to our request was not based on this individual waitress. We are sure we would have gotten a similar answer from any waitress. Organizational resistance occurs when an entire organization is committed to certain beliefs, which are usually instituted and communicated by management. The strategy is to not necessarily deal with the person exhibiting the resistance. In our restaurant example, virtually nothing could be done with the waitress to change her behavior. The resistance is occurring at the management level. Therefore, dealing with organizational resistance is a matter of dealing with management, again, exploring the reasons behind their resistance, dealing with the need for change, and creating the WIIFM. In addition, where organizational resistance is present, it is wise to "share the wealth" and modify the change to accommodate this source of resistance. For example, when I hear someone say "We've tried that before," I will inquire what was tried, find out why it failed, and involve the resistor in the new attempt.

Going back to our Silicon Valley example, I tasked the project team to first reassess the types of resistance their key stakeholders were exhibiting. Their Planning for Influence chart and the issues behind them are shown in Exhibit 8.9.

The last two steps in the Planning for Influence chart are the most important. Once we validate the issues behind the resistance,

Key Stakeholder	Type of Resistance	Issues	Strategy
Dennis (Receiving Inspection Vice President)	Political	Feels solutions would threaten his importance in the organization.	
Toby (Mechanical Inspection Director)	Political	Concerned that implementation of the solutions might mean his position would be eliminated.	
Rhonda (Electrical Inspection Director)	Political	Concerned that implementation of the solutions might mean her position would be eliminated.	
Paula (key individual contributor with strong influence with other individual contributors)	Technical	Doesn't understand the technical issues related to the solution.	

Exhibit 8.9 Planning for Influence—Silicon Valley.

a strategy to overcome the issues becomes the most important element of Improvement. Once the strategy is created and validated with the key stakeholder, creating an implementation plan becomes the next most important step.

In the case of Dennis, the project team created the need for the proposed solutions. Specifically, since their project was to reduce the number of incoming defects sent by suppliers, the project team created the need for their proposed changes. A need for change is created through either communicating what the threats are for the status quo to remain or what the opportunities are to change. The team first brainstormed a list of the threats that faced the Silicon Valley manufacturer of software peripherals. The project team initially fell into the trap of attempting to draw a long laundry list of threats. Some were good, some were valid, but most were not overwhelming. I suggested they practice the concept of Open-Narrow-Close to come up with the top two or three threats that were the most powerful. They used the Open-Narrow-Close concept to generate the following threats:

➤ Continuing at the current incoming defect rate would result in a threat to ongoing profitability to the organization.

➤ Continuing at the current incoming defect rate would result in the need for lay-offs to the organization which would directly affect Dennis' organization.

➤ Continuing at the current incoming defect rate would result in the loss of a new contract with a key customer.

The project team also used the concept of Open-Narrow-Close to create a set of prioritized opportunities that would occur if the project team's solutions are implemented:

➤ Job security would be strengthened.

➤ Profitability would increase.

➤ The role of receiving inspection would focus more on supplier management which would enhance the importance and reputation of those people leading it.

It was this last opportunity that had the greatest leverage with the vice president of inspection. It stressed the WIIFM for the vice president and helped create the need for him to support the solutions proposed by the project team. I always encourage the project team to take either the threat and/or opportunity and personalize the message to the recipient. In addition, when using any threat or opportunity I stress to the team, "If you can't prove it, don't use it." For example, if a continuing defect rate is only rumored to affect a new contract with a key customer, the team is much better off not using it.

The strategy used with the vice president is shown in Exhibit 8.10. In the case of Toby and Rhonda, their strategies are virtually identical to the vice president's strategies as shown in Exhibit 8.10.

Again, we stress the importance of the threats and opportunities that confront this manufacturer and the WIIFM for both of them to support the solutions proposed by the team. An important point in this example is the fact that Rhonda's position was eventually eliminated. Yet, by stressing the different type of job that was eventually created (in supplier improvement management), Rhonda was actually more supportive than Toby. Toby kept his job but it was a job that did not provide the challenge that Rhonda had in her new position.

In Paula's situation, the form of resistance was technical in nature. The traditional approach of dealing with this type of resistance was a training course, but I strongly suggested that information, education, and involvement was the recommended course of action. Since among our solutions was working with suppliers on improvement projects, we included Paula in one of the first projects. By not putting her on the spot, yet giving her responsibilities for the project, she was not only able to become a strongly supportive stakeholder, but had significant influence on other individual contributors who were skeptical about the project team's solutions.

The after picture of the Stakeholder Analysis of the key stakeholders is shown in Exhibit 8.11 (page 201). You can see the before and after picture of the key stakeholder's position toward the project team's solutions. This accurate picture shows the project team was not 100 percent successful (they rarely are), but there was enough significant movement to allow the team to be successful in their project. Paula showed the most change, going from someone who was not only resistant, but was attempting to motivate others against the proposed solutions. Dennis, the vice president, who was targeted to be moderately supportive, only moved as far as neutral. While the project team would have preferred Dennis to be at least moderately supportive, his neutrality ultimately allowed the team to be successful, though because of his neutrality the solutions took

Key Stakeholder	Type of Resistance	Issues	Strategy
Dennis (Receiving Inspection Vice President)	Political	Feels solutions would threaten his importance in the organization.	Stress the threats and opportunities that provide the WIIFM, specifically the role of Receiving Inspection would focus more on supplier management which would enhance the importance and reputation of the vice president.
Toby (Mechanical Inspection Director)	Political	Concerned that implementation of the solutions might mean his position would be eliminated.	Stress the threats and opportunities that provide the WIIFM, specifically the role of Receiving Inspection would focus more on supplier management which would enhance the importance and reputation of the Mechanical Inspector Director.
Rhonda (Electrical Inspection Director)	Political	Concerned that implementation of the solutions might mean her position would be. eliminated.	Stress the threats and opportunities that provide the WIIFM, specifically the role of Receiving Inspection would focus more on supplier management which would enhance the importance and reputation of the Electrical Inpector Director.
Paula (key individual contributor with strong influence with other individual contributors)	Technical	Doesn't understand the technical issues related to the solution.	➤ Information ➤ Education ➤ Involvement in first projects with suppliers

Exhibit 8.10 Planning for Influence—Dennis, Toby, Rhonda, and Paula.

Name	Strongly Against	Moderately Against	Neutral	Moderately Supportive	Strongly Supportive
Dennis (Receiving Inspection Vice President)	X		x	o	
Toby (Mechanical Inspection Director)		X/x		o	
Rhonda (Electrical Inspection Director)		X		x/o	
Paula (key individual contributor with strong influence with other individual contributors)	X			o	x

X—Before influence strategy; o—Target; x—After influence strategy

Exhibit 8.11   Stakeholder Analysis Silicon Valley—after picture.

longer to be implemented. Rhonda became moderately supportive as was targeted and Toby became the only true failure. Due to the success made with other key stakeholders, Toby's resistance did not prove fatal to the project team. In reality, the success of the overall project resulted in Toby making a fatal career choice for himself. As the years progressed, Rhonda became a star player and was considered in the fast track while Toby, through his resistance, protected his turf but rose no further in the organization.

■ PILOTING THE SOLUTIONS

The last step in Improve is development of a pilot to determine if the solution will improve sigma performance. In doing so, we don't make the full commitment that is required for a set of solutions until we see that the solutions improve sigma performance. A pilot is simply taking our solutions and implementing them on a small scale to see their effect on our project goals.

One of GE Capital's first projects came in the group responsible for Six Sigma course delivery. Back in 1996, the Center for Learning and Organizational Excellence (CLOE) created a set of solutions for massive Six Sigma course delivery. They invited a group of consultants to help create the materials and the order of presentation. With many experts preparing the materials and many approaches, it was strongly advised by all parties that we needed to pilot the class rather than go into a full-blown implementation. This pilot proved highly valuable. While there were highlights to the training provided to a select group of GE Capital employees, the feedback was painful to almost all involved. Major restructuring of the course was required based on the feedback of the participants. If there had not been a small scale implementation pilot, a full-blown implementation could have been fatal to the overall instruction provided by CLOE. Instead, the course materials and delivery provided by CLOE ended up being among the most effective put on by General Electric throughout the world.

I always recommend a small-scale pilot to see the results of the team's solutions. No matter how well thought out the solutions for a project may be, there are unanticipated consequences once the solution is actually implemented. A pilot can alert the team to these unanticipated consequences so they may alter, modify or even radically change the solutions to a project.

■ SUMMARY

While most people who have been through projects claim Improve is one of the easier elements in the DMAIC model, it still calls for significant work. The use of the Open-Narrow-Close concept we mastered in Analysis is called on once again to assist the team in going from a large number of possible solutions to a more narrowed list of possible improvements.

The affinity diagram was introduced as the tool of choice to assist the team with brainstorming a potential list of solutions. These solutions are generated, then clarified, duplicated, and categorized so that each set of solutions can more readily be reviewed.

Once the affinity diagram is created, the team applies the Must and Want criteria to make their final decisions surrounding the possible solutions.

Finally, recognition and methods to develop acceptance to the project team's solutions must be addressed.

KEY LEARNINGS

➤ A project team should focus on solutions that eliminate, soften, or dampen the root causes validated at the end of Analysis.

➤ The concept of Open-Narrow-Close applies to Improve just as it did for Analysis.

➤ The Affinity diagram is the primary tool to use to generate and select solutions.

➤ Once a narrowed list of solutions has been determined by the project team, Must and Want criteria determine which solutions should be selected.

➤ Must criteria is usually generated by the team champion and focuses on the minimum requirements that a solution must meet to be considered as a possible solution.

➤ Want criteria are those criteria that will allow us to compare and judge one solution against criteria where one solution will be prioritized against others.

➤ Once a set of solutions has been agreed on, the project team should conduct a Stakeholder Analysis to determine the extent of acceptance of the solutions by those who will be needed to implement the solutions or by those affected by them.

➤ There are different types of resistance and the project team needs to determine what type of resistance exists among key stakeholders and how they can lessen the resistance to their solutions so they are able to meet their project goals.

➤ A Planning for Influence chart can help the team determine the type of resistance exhibited by a key stakeholder, what the issues are that contribute to the resistance, and what strategies are needed to overcome the resistance.

➤ Creating a small scale pilot of the solution(s) can help the team alter, modify, or even radically change the solutions so that they are better able to be implemented.

Holding the Gains

Making Sure Your Solutions Stick

When it comes to the Control element of the DMAIC methodology, I think of my weight fluctuations. I have gone on quick reduction diets, low-fat diets, and high-exercise, vegetarian diets.

In virtually all attempts, I have been initially successful in my weight reduction projects. To relate this to DMAIC terms, I have successfully implemented D, M, A, and I on more than one occasion. In past years, I have defined a problem—excess weight gain. By getting on a scale, I performed measurement. I have analyzed the root cause of this weight gain as too much food. I have developed improvement strategies that, to various levels, have been successful.

Yet my failure to implement control after my initial weight loss projects, my failure to "hold the gains" following D, M, A, and I, shows how this last step may be the most important step in the DMAIC methodology.

We will discuss Control on two levels. First, we will discuss Control at the tactical or project level. We will examine the two major types and four major ways a project team can statistically control a process once the team has reached or exceeded their project goals. We will introduce you to the Control or Response Plan, a method to allow a project team to disband, assured that its improvements will be sustained over time. We then turn our attention to control at the strategic level, returning to Business Process Management and the vehicle for ongoing management of the Six Sigma system, the Business Quality Council.

■ METHODS OF CONTROL

There are two major types of control at the project level. One is qualitative and the other quantitative. Which type of control a team should implement is based on knowing process standardization and process throughput.

Process standardization refers to the stability of the process steps once the project team has completed its improvement work. At the beginning of project work, particularly in a process with high inefficiency, there is almost universal low standardization. Back in Chapter 4, we encourage teams to map the process "as is," warts and all. Once solutions have been implemented, the team should have created the "should be" map—the way the process should run once solutions are implemented.

Once the should be map is completed, steps should be highly repetitive, uniform across employees with stability in each process step. Therefore, if done correctly, most projects should result in high standardization. Take for example the car-buying example from Chapter 4.

Let's return to the six subprocess steps in my negotiations in the car-buying process:

Subprocess Step	Value	Reason
1. Submission of offer	Yes	I am willing to pay for that step. The transfer of the offer letter is a change from me to them, and I did it right the first time.
2. Leaving the showroom	No	As a way to obtain my car, it did not add value to me, the customer.
3. Resubmitting offer	No	Usually anything that begins with the prefix "re-" is being done for the second or more time.
4. Waiting for decision	No	No change or transformation in the product or service here.
5. Renegotiation of option package	No	There's that "re-" again.
6. Signing letter of intent	Yes	The customer (me) thought it was important. It physically changed something (the letter), and it was done right the first time.

Six subprocess steps and only 2 of the 6 (33%) added value. If we had targeted the car-buying process for improvement, our major goal would have been to improve efficiency. By the time we had finished the Improve element of the DMAIC model, we would have created a "should be" map of how the car-buying process should be after improvement. The should-be map of negotiation would look as follows:

Subprocess Step	Value	Reason
1. Submission of offer	Yes	I am willing to pay for that step. The transfer of the offer letter is a change from me to them, and I did it right the first time.
2. Negotiate open package	Yes	I am willing to pay for this step and the changes to the offer sheet are a physical change and it's done right the first time.
3. Car dealer signs offer	Yes	I am willing to pay for this step. The car dealer's signature is the physical change, and it is done right the first time.

Note that the "should be" map has the same steps no matter what car I buy. The biggest mistake teams make is assuming what goes *through* a process is what constitutes standardization. By this inaccurate definition, if I buy a different car each time while using the same process steps, some would think the process is not standardized. In reality, most processes that successfully complete the Improve step of DMAIC will have highly standardized processes. Several examples are listed following:

➤ *The Eckes and Associates Inc. Course Design Process.* My organization has several key processes. One is the Course Design Process. Each time this process is used, a different product is produced. Yet, the steps, from course needs identification to course piloting are essentially the same. Thus, the course design process is highly standardized.

➤ *The Boeing Jet Manufacturing Process.* While Boeing manufacturers all types of jets, the process for making them is remarkably standardized (for those of us who use their products, thank goodness).

The vast majority of processes after Improve are standardized. It is far more difficult to generate examples of nonstandardized processes that exist after improvement. To qualify as a nonstandardized process one or more of the following conditions must exist:

➤ Unpredictable steps in the process.

➤ Highly nonrepetitive steps in the process.

Artwork is the closest thing I can think of to nonstandardized processes. Michelangelo's creation of the Sistine Chapel ceiling and then the Pieta epitomizes nonstandardized processes, but most project teams would not put themselves in that category.

Process throughput is the second element to determine which type of control a project team will implement. Throughput refers to the volume of product or service generated through a given process. The continuum for determining process throughput can exist from 1 through to infinity. Typically, low throughput is measured as less than 10 items produced over the course of the year from the same process. Mid-level throughput usually is estimated as 20 to 50 per year with high throughput as output that exceeds 50 units per year.

It is important to note that output for a given process can have both high or low throughput depending on where the process throughput is measured. For example, when doing business process planning for organizations at the highest level in the process, throughput would be considered low (one strategic plan produced a year) but examining the process in terms of department reviews would make the throughput in the mid-level of the continuum.

Process throughput can also be determined by process elements. For example, what is the most downstream measure of my health? The measure would be whether I am alive or dead. It is first and foremost a discrete measure. Picture me each month placing a tick mark on a discrete checksheet to show I am alive and imagine someone else collecting the data on some sad day when I don't awaken. This type of data would not be collected often nor would it be continuous. But using our weight loss example here, what if my family physician indicates a weight problem. By going into the process, we could examine on a daily basis factors such as caloric intake, fat grams, or amount of time exercised. Each of the preceding are continuous in nature. Due to the frequency of the data when looking at something like caloric intake, throughput would be considered high.

Once the project team makes a decision relative to standardization and throughput, we ask project teams to place an X in the appropriate box of a matrix (the percentages found in Exhibit 9.1 are Eckes and Associates Inc.'s response rate from clients over the years).

High standard Low throughput 15%	High standard High throughput 80%
Low standard Low throughput <1%	Low standard High throughput 5%

Exhibit 9.1   Process throughput—standardization matrix.

Where a project team is located in this matrix determines the type of control tool they will use. Exhibit 9.2 shows the types of tools that the project teams will use based on the matrix. Let's examine some of the particulars of each type of control.

➤ Low Standardization/Low Throughput

In my years of consulting I can only recall an example or two of a process that had low standardization and low throughput. The examples are a process that was used rarely to produce one product. In these situations, the act of control is only used while the process

Nonstatistical controls: ➤ Checklists. ➤ Schedules.	Statistical controls: ➤ X bar and R charts. ➤ Individual and R charts. ➤ X bar and S charts. ➤ Moving X bar and R charts. ➤ Other types of statistical charts.
Nonstatistical controls: ➤ Periodic status reviews.	Other types of statistical controls: ➤ Bar charts. ➤ Pie charts. ➤ Pareto charts.

Exhibit 9.2   Process throughput—standardization matrix tools.

is being implemented and then it's a matter of making sure all work is completed. Going back to Chapter 1, we discussed the concept of craftsmanship in the nineteenth century before the industrial revolution. In essence, the concept of control in those days was equivalent to periodic 100 percent inspection. If you think your project is here, control is periodic status review.

➤ High Standardization/Low Throughput

The best example here is what controls a pilot institutes prior to takeoff. In this situation, we have a highly standardized process with low throughput, if we measure throughput as a single takeoff and landing. To ensure that the process steps are completed, the specific process steps are checked off as they are completed. Another type of control method for this type of situation is the Gantt Chart. For those who haven't had Industrial Engineering 101 an example is shown in Exhibit 9.3.

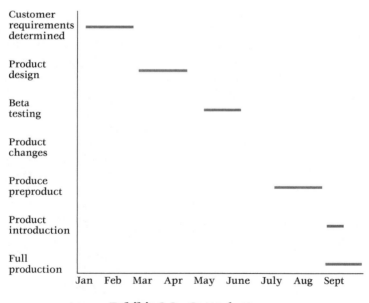

Exhibit 9.3 Gantt chart.

➤ Low Standardization/High Throughput

This is yet another rare situation. By necessity, high throughput that demands high quality output will be dependent on standardizing the process that produces the high number of outputs. The mistake most project teams make by saying they have low standardization and high throughput is making this decision *before* they improve the process. When teams bring to my attention the opinion that they fall in this category, the first thing I do is inquire if they have in fact improved their process. Normally, the answer to this question is no. For those who truly have low standardization and high throughput, after-the-fact static pictures of variation are the control tools of choice. Typical tools such as bar charts, pie charts, and Paretos are used. When a company has a low standardization, high throughput situation, my recommendation is to examine improvement options to standardize rather than focus on control.

➤ High Standardization/High Throughput

When a project team truly has completed Improvement and is ready for Control, the vast majority of projects in virtually any business will have high standardization and high throughput. This allows us to use more powerful statistical tools to control a process rather than control something after the fact. Let's examine a situation that will allow us to learn the concepts of statistical control. I have two friends who are avid golfers. Rhonda and Perry are committed to the game. Last summer, Rhonda had the following scores recorded by month:

Rhonda's Golf Scores May through August

May	June	July	August
83	84	85	86
84	80	86	87
86	85	87	87
89	86	92	85
86	88	88	83
	87	84	82

When Rhonda and Perry came to dinner in the fall, we discussed Rhonda's scores for the summer. An argument soon ensued as Rhonda claimed she was a consistent golfer and Perry demurred. With just the raw data presented, Perry wondered if Rhonda's scores were for 9 holes or 18. After this first round of discussion, I recommended we take a more statistical approach to the determination of whether Rhonda was a consistent golfer or not. Since both Rhonda and Perry had taken my Six Sigma courses, I asked if either of them could generate a statistical tool that could eliminate the subjective "discussion" they were having that would allow us to conclusively answer the question over the consistency of the raw data.

Perry suggested a run chart. We placed the data on a run chart as shown in Exhibit 9.4.

Rhonda looked at the run chart and noted that there were no trends in an upward direction (which would indicate a worsening golf performance) and there were no trends downward (which would indicate a improvement in golf performance). Perry used this primitive run chart to support his claim of inconsistency referring to the many spikes in the data.

I took the data and determined the central tendency of Rhonda's golf scores. Knowing that the middle score is slightly above 85, both of my dinner guests claimed success. Rhonda said approximately half the scores are above and below the middle value and Perry remained adamant that there were too many spikes in the data.

As shown in Exhibit 9.5, I took the data and made a frequency distribution to the right side of the run chart. We could see that the distribution seemed normally distributed. With this knowledge, I took the average and calculated three standard deviations above the average and three standard deviations below the average. These

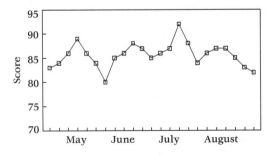

Exhibit 9.4 Rhonda's run chart: golf scores.

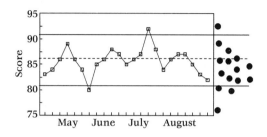

Exhibit 9.5 ➤ Rhonda's individual control
chart: golf scores.

process limits allow us to determine if Rhonda's scores exhibit common cause variation or if a score exceeds the upper or lower limits then special cause would be proven. If there is special cause variation, then Perry would have indisputable proof that Rhonda's golf scores show inconsistency.

Instead of subjective dinner conversation (By the way, can you see how much fun having dinner with me can be?), Perry now had his objective evidence that Rhonda's summer golf scores are not consistent. Her 80 score in late May is *better* than we would expect from chance alone. Could that score in late May have occurred by chance alone? Technically yes, but the odds of this score being a chance occurrence are so low (27 in 10,000) that we treat the score as if something different happened that day in May. Because this dinner was occurring in late September, Rhonda couldn't remember what might have affected her late May score. We brainstormed some of the things that could have happened that day. They included:

➤ Different course.

➤ Tried a different putting style.

➤ Golfed with a pro that day who gave her some pointers.

➤ Tried a new ball.

➤ Tried a new putter or driver.

➤ There was a wind at her back.

➤ Rhonda cheated (that was Perry's brainstorm).

After this brief brainstorming session, we took each item and categorized them as follows:

Item	Category (M or P)
➤ Different course.	Mother Nature
➤ Tried a different putting style.	Method
➤ Golfed with a pro that day who gave her some pointers.	Method
➤ Tried a new ball.	Material
➤ Tried a new putter or driver.	Machine
➤ There was a wind at her back.	Mother Nature
➤ Rhonda cheated (that was Perry's brainstorm).	Measurement/People

Note that each potential cause for the out of control golf score in May is one of the 5 M's or 1 P. By the same token, we examine potential root causes for the special cause golf performance in July that is *worse* than we would expect by chance alone. Again, there is the possibility that this golf score occurred by chance but since the odds are so low (27 in 10,000) we treat the event as if something different happened that day in July. Could it have been?

➤ Different course.

➤ Hit the nineteenth hole before the first hole (this was another Perry idea).

➤ Played with a customer Rhonda wanted to impress.

➤ Tried a new swing.

➤ Had an argument with her new boyfriend (this was Rhonda's idea).

Once again we categorized the ideas into the 5 M's and 1 P:

Item	Category (M or P)
➤ Different course.	Mother Nature
➤ Hit the nineteenth hole before the first hole (this was another Perry idea).	Method
➤ Played with a customer Rhonda wanted to impress.	Method
➤ Tried a new swing.	Method
➤ Had an argument with her new boyfriend (this was Rhonda's idea).	People

The problem with this September dinner conversation is that we were looking back in time and memories become fuzzy, though

Rhonda felt pretty certain about the July score. I proposed what would have happened if Rhonda had been making this type of chart throughout the summer rather than just keeping her raw scores as she did. Perry accurately indicated how Rhonda's performance would have done two things if she were able to create a chart like this on an ongoing basis. First, if she had known she had done something different in her May golf outing, she could have documented what it was while it was still clear in her mind. With this type of special cause variation, she could have further improved her performance since her May score was special in that it was better than we would expect from chance alone.

If the chart had been made before the summer, the July score could have been recorded and corrective action could have been taken. If corrective action on both scores had been done during the fact, two things would have happened. One, Rhonda's average score would have dropped from its overall summer average of 85+. Second, the amount of variation around the lower number would be less.

These last two comments appropriately sum up the importance of the control step in a DMAIC project. First, it is a *preventive* method to ensure that the gains made by the project team hold up after the project team disbands. When a point goes out of control, it indicates that the process has changed, not necessarily that a defect has been made. This process change allows us to react to the process and conduct corrective action sometimes *before* a defect has been made. Second, reacting to special cause variation (particularly when it's like Rhonda's May score) allows a process to improve after a formal DMAIC project team has disbanded. In this way, the philosophy of continuous improvement, a cornerstone of Six Sigma, is achieved.

Think of the possibilities of using this "real time" method of control (for high standardization, high throughput). In our weight loss case, think of me control charting daily caloric intake. Notice I didn't say control charting my weight. Referring back to the equation, $Y = f(X_1, X_2 \ldots X_n)$, it would be fair to say that caloric intake (or fat grams or amount of time exercising) is a major X that contributes to my large Y. Through application of the control chart, special cause variation in the control chart would alert me to conduct corrective action.

On a more serious note, think of someone who would monitor blood pressure with a control chart. Special cause variation could be determined and corrective action (medication or a change in diet) could be implemented before the more serious defect of a heart attack or stroke would debilitate the person.

■ THE FIVE STEPS TO STATISTICAL CONTROL CHARTING

Most software packages can easily calculate virtually any of the myriad types of control charts that exist. We will take the traditional X bar and R chart and examine the five major steps to control charting.

➤ Step 1   Collect Data in Order of Chronological Sequence

When we examine a control chart to determine common cause versus special cause variation, we are using a tool that examines variation over time. Think of the control chart as a snapshot of the process over time. Therefore, it is essential to collect data in order of sequence. Try to remember how the first cartoons were made. In the days of Walt Disney, animators did not have access to computer simulation. Instead, cartoonists would draw out one slide of Mickey Mouse (or Donald Duck or Goofy), then another, then another. Then, Disney would put all the individual pictures in order and create a picture of them so that they "looked" like they were in motion. Imagine if the cartoonist had dropped the thousands of pictures that made up a simple cartoon and then randomly placed them together. The illusion of Mickey's legs moving as if he were walking would be eliminated.

The same is true with control charting. Initially, the project team wants to set up control charting in such a way that it can examine what variation exists in this process over time, like a Disney cartoon. We do not want the sample to be random. A tenet of the Central Limit Theorem from which the control chart is derived states that if we sample a process randomly and create a control chart, nothing would show special cause variation.

There are two phases of control charting. The first step refers to the *study* phase. During the study phase of control charting, we are attempting to find out the expected levels of variation above and below the central tendency of the data. Think of the limits that are generated as the "voice" of the process. On the other hand,

Subgroups	1	2	3	4	5	6	7	8	9	10	11	12
	78	77	74	73	74	75	74	72	73	73	74	75
	70	72	70	72	73	73	73	74	74	74	75	78
	71	73	78	75	76	76	72	76	73	76	73	76
	75	72	74	75	73	75	72	73	72	75	74	72
	73	74	73	73	75	76	76	73	76	75	76	75

Exhibit 9.6   Consecutive measures study phase.

we should not confuse these limits with the specification limits we learned about in Chapter 5 that are the "voice" of the customer, telling us when a defect occurs.

In the study phase of a project, we collect data long enough for the 5 M's and 1 P to exhibit themselves. Exhibit 9.6 is an example of measurements for a project team that collected 60 measures in a row that constituted the study phase of control charting.

You will notice that the entire set of data is organized in 12 subgroups of 5 each. Why 5? Exhibit 9.7 is a chart of subgroup size versus statistical validity. You will note that at a subgroup sample of 5 and beyond there is a plateau effect so that further sampling doesn't show an economic benefit. The slope of the line is still high as it approaches a subgroup size of 5 and then begins its plateau. Thus, the optimum subgroup sample size is 5 for high throughput processes.

In the study phase, we collect all the data in order of sequence. Later, after we have established the inherent limits of variation for the data we will begin sampling the process. In this second or *operational* phase of control charting, we want to sample the process in such a way that the sample is representative of the process at the time the sample is taken. By the same token, when the next

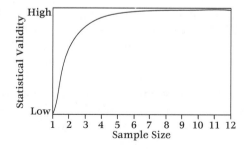

Exhibit 9.7   Subgroup sample size validity chart.

sample is taken in the operational phase, we want to ensure that maximum opportunities for variation have occurred before the next sample will be taken. One maxim to remember at the time of sampling in the operational phase, is to minimize within subgroup variation (i.e., at the time you sample your subgroup) and to maximize between subgroup variation (i.e., allow enough time between subgroup sampling so that variation in the process has had a chance to exhibit itself).

➤ Step 2   Calculate Subgroup Averages (X bar) and Subgroup Ranges

I remember Deming telling me there were two basic ways statistically for a customer to be dissatisfied. One, if the average of the data shifts too much, and second, if there is too much variation around a centered process. Therefore, we want a control chart that monitors both of these important parameters simultaneously. Thus, the average (X bar) and range (a measure of variation) of each subgroup is calculated which, in turn, represents how the process is acting with regard to the two ways a process could change over time.

Exhibit 9.8 shows how we calculated the two parameters for each subgroup. For our first subgroup (for measures 1 to 5 in the study phase of control charting) the summation of the 5 measures equals 367. Dividing by 5, the subgroup average is 73.4. That average is located below the sum. In the first subgroup, the largest value is 78. The lowest value is 70, making the range (calculated by taking the difference of the highest and lowest value) 8 which is then located in the spot just below the subgroup average of 73.4.

➤ Step 3   Calculate the Control Limits

Once we have calculated the 12 subgroup averages and ranges, we are ready to calculate the expected limits of variation in the process, otherwise known as the *control limits*. These limits should be seen as the voice of the process, the inherent limits of variation calculated three standard deviations above and below the central tendency of the data. They have nothing to do with the customer's specifications. To calculate the control limits for the average, we would take all 12 subgroup averages, add those up and divide by 12. This "average average" is at 74.03 or 74.

How far to the high or low side of 74 can this process shift before we would conclude that the shift is special cause variation?

X Bar and R Data

	Sub Gp 1	Sub Gp 2	Sub Gp 3	Sub Gp 4	Sub Gp 5	Sub Gp 6	Sub Gp 7	Sub Gp 8	Sub Gp 9	Sub Gp 10	Sub Gp 11	Sub Gp 12
Sample Measurements	78	77	74	73	74	75	74	72	73	73	74	75
	70	72	70	72	73	73	73	74	74	74	75	78
	71	73	78	75	76	76	72	76	73	76	73	76
	75	72	74	75	73	75	72	73	72	75	74	72
	73	74	73	73	75	76	76	73	76	75	76	75
Sum	367	368	369	368	371	375	367	368	368	373	372	376
Average	73.4	73.6	73.8	73.6	74.2	75	73.4	73.6	73.6	74.6	74.4	75.2
Range	8	5	8	3	3	3	4	4	4	3	3	6

Exhibit 9.8 Subgroup Average and Range Table.

219

Those are our next calculations. There are different types of control charts. If we took the literal upper and lower three standard deviations from 74 (the average of the averages ± 3 standard deviations), the chart would be the X bar and S chart. The X bar and R chart is taking an estimate of the standard deviation, or:

$$\text{Upper control limit} = \overline{\overline{X}} + A2\overline{R}$$

$$\text{Lower Control Limit} = \overline{\overline{X}} - A2\overline{R}$$

$A2\overline{R}$ is taking the average range of the 12 subgroups (4.5) and multiplying this number by the statistical constant A2. Specific A2 numbers are located in the Appendix. All the project team has to know is the number of values in one subgroup. In this example, there are 5 values in each of the 12 subgroups. The corresponding A2 number is 0.58. By multiplying 0.58 times the average range of 4.5 we get 2.6. We then add and subtract 2.6 from 74 to get the expected limits of variation in our process for the averages. Those numbers (76.6 and 71.4) are seen in Exhibit 9.9 as dashed lines.

The area between 76.6 and 71.4 is the expected limits of variation for the averages. In other words, we cannot expect every subgroup average to be 74. Everything varies including subgroup

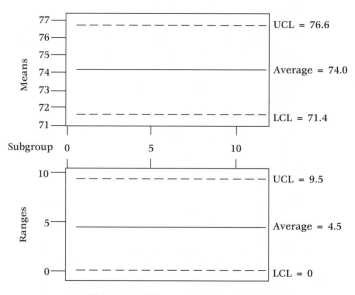

Exhibit 9.9 X bar and R control chart.

averages. As you might expect, when a subgroup average extends beyond 76.6 or goes below 71.4, we no longer can say the variation is common cause. When a sub group average is outside of these control limits, we have evidence that the process has changed because the odds of a subgroup average being above 76.6 or below 71.4 being a chance occurrence are so low (27 in 10,000), we treat it as if something different happened.

We have just calculated the control limits for variation in subgroup averages. Remember, Deming said we need to be concerned not with just shifts in the averages of a process but the variation in the ranges as well. Therefore, we now calculate the expected limits of variation for the ranges. We know already the average range is 4.5. Like subgroup averages, ranges are expected to vary over time. At what point would a subgroup range not be expected to be due to common cause variation? We multiply the average range by another constant located in the Appendix called D4. Like the A2 number for averages, D4 is a constant such that all the project team needs to know is the number of values in one subgroup. Since we already know that the number is 5, looking up the number in the D4 chart for a subgroup size of 5, the number is 1.2. Multiplying the average range of 4.5 times 1.2 we get an upper control limit for the ranges of 9.5. Once again, as it did for the upper control limit for the averages, this upper control limit for the ranges alerts us to when we no longer can accept a subgroup range as being due to common causes. In this case, since we cannot have a fractional subgroup range, if we see a range of 9 or less, we conclude it is due to common cause variation and a range of 10 or greater (since its larger than 9.5) which would have us conclude that we have evidence of special cause variation.

To calculate the lower control limit for ranges, we multiply by the constant D3. You will note that for subgroup sizes of less than 7 our D3 number is always zero. Since most subgroups will be 5 or less you will rarely see a lower control limit for ranges since multiplying zero times anything will always result in a zero. Therefore on a range control chart, you will not usually see a lower control limit.

➤ Step 4 Plot Subgroup Averages and Ranges on the Control Chart

As shown in Exhibit 9.10, we take each of our 12 subgroup averages and subgroup ranges and plot them on the average and range chart area.

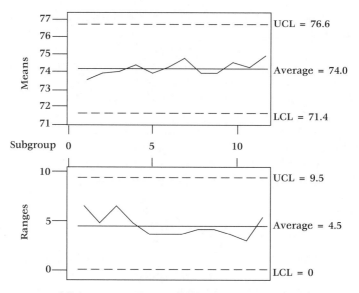

Exhibit 9.10 X bar and R control chart plotted.

➤ Step 5 Analyze, Interpret, and Utilize the Chart to Maintain and Further Improvement

Any software program can perform steps 1 to 4. We showed them to you, not to have you create them manually, but to have you appreciate conceptually what is behind the math. What is imperative is conducting step 5. Conducting Step 5 means that the process will maintain the improvement created by the project team by ensuring that any signs of special cause variation are immediately addressed by way of corrective action by the people who work in the process. At a minimum, this will ensure that the project team's improvements will be maintained. In most cases, not only will the project team's improvements be maintained, proper use of the control chart will result in continual improvement beyond the project team's initial improvements. Let's continue with the example we used for steps 1 through 4.

We now want to examine the chart in Exhibit 9.11 to maintain the improvement this project team created in I of the DMAIC project and possibly further improve the process. The data is taken from a supplier to a computer company that has successfully exceeded project goals in a process improvement project.

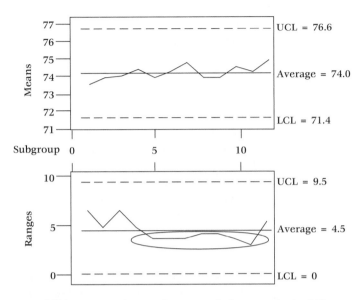

Exhibit 9.11 X bar and R control chart analysis shifts.

This supplier provides a critical part where the outside dimension had caused problems for the computer company. Its target was 0.75 and the supplier had experienced both variation and shift problems. The team had dramatically improved both during the course of the project. Now, during the control phase of the project, the team wanted to ensure consistency in the process and further improvement.

Note that the decimal has been removed from all data points for clarity. To analyze a control chart for consistency, it must be examined for four major elements:

1. *Points out of control.* When analyzing a control chart we first and foremost look for points out of control for either the average or range. There are no points out of control, so we move on to the second of the four analysis elements.

2. *Shifts.* The control chart is now analyzed for shifts, which are defined as 7 points in a row above or below the center or average line. First, we look for shifts on the average chart. Note, the first three measures (73.4, 73.6, 73.8) are all *under* the average of 74. Then, the next two data points are above the average before returning below the average of 74.

These first two patterns called *runs* are not anywhere close to 7 in a row. We continue to look for a run of 7 or more. Examining the rest of the average chart, we see no run of 7. Thus, the average chart doesn't show assignable cause variation for shifts.

We take the same approach to analysis of the range chart. While technically the type of distribution is a binomial rather than gaussian curve, we will still analyze it to see if the range chart has a run of 7 or more. The first run is made up of 8 and 5 and 8. No shift there. Then starting with the fourth subgroup through the eleventh, we see each and every range *below* the average of 4.5. We have a run of 8 values below the average range (indicated by the circled data on Exhibit 9.11). Could this have been a chance occurrence? Yes, but let's figure out the odds of this being a chance occurrence.

What are the odds, if the process is consistent, that a value would be found either above or below the center line? Pay careful attention here. The odds are 50/50 or 50 percent. What are the odds that two consecutive values will be above or below the average range—0.5 × 0.5 or 0.25 or 25 percent? (Note that for the average chart, these calculations are totally accurate, but with a binomial distribution it is not exactly the same. However with increasing sample sizes, the binomial distribution approximates a normal curve so the math I am showing you is for all practical purposes correct.)

Continuing the pattern as shown in the following table, you can see what the odds of 8 ranges being below the average range:

Number of Points in a Row Above or Below the Average Range/Average	Odds
2	25%
3	12.5
4	6.25
5	3.1
6	1.57
7	0.8
8	0.4

The odds of 8 points being below the average range by chance alone is 0.4 percent. Could this be a chance occurrence? There is that possibility but again, as we have been stressing through this chapter and others, the odds are so low that we treat this shift of 8 points below the average range as if something different has happened. For example, what if I told you right now that there was a 99.6 percent chance that your car was being burglarized as you read this. Would you say there was a 0.4 percent chance it's not and ignore the odds? You would probably take some action, such as call the police. The laws of probability determine when we draw the conclusion that special causes are at work. You will note from numbers shown that your threshold of reaction might be sooner than 7 in a row. Maybe 6 in a row would prompt your project team to claim there is special causes influencing the process. In any case, in our diameter example, it's quite clear we can confidently say that between subgroups 4 to 11 there was a special cause of variation going on in the process.

What do we do about it? By control charting on an ongoing basis, we should have some idea what was going on during the time of subgroups 4 to 11 that would explain what M or P that is the special cause. Return to Rhonda's golf score example. Looking back on the summer, we may be fuzzy on some special cause of variation from a golf outing in May, but during the time we are control charting, we should have some idea what was going on. What does the special cause variation imply? Since the run of 8 data points is *below* the average range, we have good news. During that period of time, the computer supplier did something different that *improved* the process. If the process participants can document the special cause and proceduralize the change, the process performance will improve. This is an excellent example of how ongoing control charting can further improve the sigma performance after the project team is disbanded, if those who are responsible for controlling the process practice are using the control chart to achieve never-ending improvement.

3. *Trends.* The control chart could also be analyzed for trends, which are defined as 7 points in a row in an upward direction or downward direction. While we have already shown special cause variation in this example, if we were to examine the data for trends, we don't see any either on the average chart or the range chart. If we had, we again

would be seeing special cause variation, even if the points that constitute the trend never went out of control. Why? Because the odds of 7 points in a row upward or downward being a chance occurrence are so low we draw the conclusion that something different was happening during that period of time.

4. *Unusual patterns.* What if the data had shown two points above the center line (for either the average or range), then two points below, then two above, two below, two above, two below (the latter not to be confused with Elvis' birthplace)? This pattern is so unusual we would draw the conclusion that special causes were in place. Or what if suddenly you got the same measure again and again? If after having common cause measures that were then followed by the same measure again and again you would have evidence of special cause variation. Bonus points to you if you said to yourself the special cause was that the measurement system went haywire and lost its ability to discriminate appropriately.

There are as many different types of charts as there are processes. Reference the American Society for Quality 1-800-248-1946 for the myriad books on specific control chart applications.

■ DOCUMENTATION

We have just seen an application of control charting where improvement can occur after the project team has been disbanded. These improvements can significantly raise sigma performance if done properly. It is essential that the process owner (remember him from Chapter 2?) document improvement as it occurs during the Control phase. Documentation refers to writing down the improvements in a way that everyone involved in that process is doing things the same way. Proper documentation is structured in such a way that:

➤ Employees without formal training can understand and implement the new improvements.

➤ Specificity is emphasized.

➤ Consistency is emphasized. Unrealistic and/or contradictory information must be eliminated from documents.

➤ The Pareto concept of the vital few versus the useful many is implemented. People responsible for documenting the results of ongoing improvements sometimes make the mistake of overdocumenting and lose sight of the key improvements

With regard to the last point remember that documentation can be done too little or too much. Documentation is a nominal-is-best quality characteristic. When too little documentation occurs, the people operating the process may do things in slightly different ways which will ultimately increase variation in that process. When there is too much documentation, creativity is stifled and people ultimately become frustrated which leads to ignoring the improvements that prompted the documentation.

An example might prove illustrative. We live with documentation in various aspects of our lives. Think of driving. If we had no documentation of how this important element of our lives were to be done, we would have everyone driving at the speed of their choice. (Having driven on the German Autobahn, I am not necessarily saying no documentation is a bad thing.) If we had too much documentation, we would have speed laws that dictate driving at 47 miles an hour. This would lead to massive driver frustration or ignoring the law. Knowing that we should drive on the right hand side of the road and driving at a speed limit of 65 miles per hour (with some allowance for measurement error) is proper documentation. This leads to proper adherence to how the process should work.

A business example of the need for appropriate documentation is taken from GE Capital Fleet Services. Ross Gilbert, who was a Master Black Belt at fleet, assisted a project team through a DMAIC project to improve lease efficiency. During the control phase, he coached the team to document time standards for various contracts with flexibility in each time standard.

■ RESPONSE PLANS—THE LAST ACTION ITEM OF DMAIC

Saying a Response Plan is the last action item is a bit misleading. A good Response Plan creates an ongoing action plan for the process participants to follow so that the only change in sigma is positive.

A cursory look at a Response Plan may make one think of the Data Collection Plan. There are similarities. A Response Plan goes further, however. In addition to identifying measures, specifications, and targets of the process, it now includes what types of controls are in place and what process improvements are ongoing or contemplated shortly. Finally, it includes the new improved Process Map (defined in our previous chapter as the "should be" Process Map).

Good Response Plans allow various employees to know how to respond to a process once it has been subjected to DMAIC even if the employee in question was not a member of the project team. Exhibit 9.12 shows what should be in a Response Plan.

While room service would have been a good example, many of the control methods—the process improvements—are proprietary. In fact, most clients are highly sensitive to the proprietary nature of most improvement projects (further evidence that Six Sigma process improvement is a major competitive advantage). I have used one of my businesses key subprocesses, billing and collections to show what a Response Plan should look like. Exhibit 9.13 follows.

From a previous chapter, you learned that Eckes and Associates Inc. has experienced invoice payment problems from a major

Process Map "Should Be"	Measures	Specifications and Targets	Data Collection Methods	Control Methods	Process Improvement

Exhibit 9.12   Response plan table.

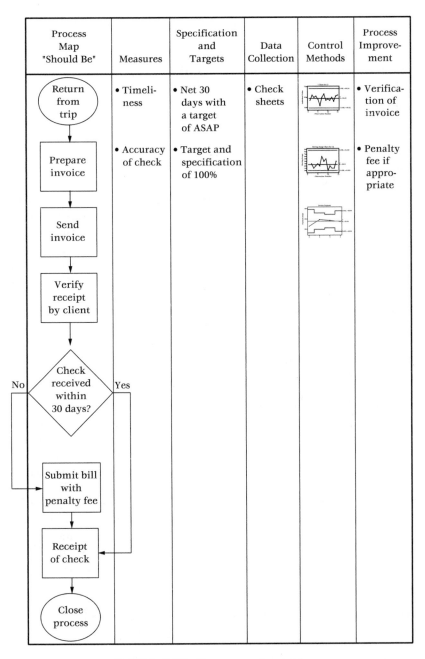

Exhibit 9.13 Response plan table.

client. A DMAIC team at Eckes and Associates Inc. was formed and our project was a partial success. When we reached the control phase of our project we created the following Response Plan. As a result of our improvements, we significantly reduced (though not eliminated) inefficiencies in the process. Our new "should be" map is found in column 1.

In the second column of Exhibit 9.13 we reference the measures for the new process—timeliness of check delivery and accuracy of the check received. Next, we state the specifications and targets for our new measures. For timeliness, our specification is net 30 days with a target of sooner is better. Accuracy is our other key measure with the specification being the same as the target, 100 percent. Our data collection methods were checksheets. After our improvements were implemented, we decided on a control method of a moving X bar and R chart. There are as many types of control charts as there are processes. The moving X bar and R chart has a "smoothing" effect on the data by taking each data point and using it multiple times to get a cumulative average over time. This type of chart is used for processes in which it takes some time to produce a single item and for situations that call for immediate feedback. The advantage of this type of chart is that the most up to date value is plotted (particularly important for processes like billing and collection in which the most recent data is helpful for quicker corrective action should special cause variation exhibit itself).

In the last column, we note any process improvements that have been implemented that assisted the project team in achieving its improvement. This last column should always be referenced when the process goes out of control or when other process related problems are encountered. In the case of our project, verification of invoice receipt and occasional penalty fee attachment has improved our billing and collection process. These two major improvements are referenced when we have an invoice problem. More often than not, when we experience an invoice problem we have failed on one of these two improvements. The finished Response Plan for the Eckes and Associates Inc. Project is shown in Exhibit 9.13.

■ STRATEGIC CONTROL—THE RETURN TO BUSINESS PROCESS MANAGEMENT

At the beginning of this chapter, we stated that control can be focused at the tactical level and the strategic level. To this point we have addressed control at the tactical level. We now move to the strategic aspect of control.

Let's review our discussion of Business Process Management in Chapter 2. You may remember that our introduction of this vital element to the success of your Six Sigma program introduced you to the first seven steps of Business Process Management. Those are:

1. Creation and agreement of strategic business objectives.
2. Creation of core/key sub- and enabling processes.
3. Identification of process owners.
4. Creation and validation of the key measures of effectiveness and efficiency for each process (also known as measurement "dashboards").
5. Collection of data on agreed dashboards.
6. Creation of project selection criteria.
7. Using the project selection criteria for project selection.

These seven steps help establish the process management system and help select the projects for which we apply DMAIC. In Chapter 2, we ended with this seventh step and began our discussion of how to apply DMAIC. Simultaneous to the application of DMAIC on tactical projects, Business Process Management continues with its most important and final step.

➤ Step 8 Continual Management of Processes to Achieve Strategic Objectives of the Organization

This last and most important step of Business Process Management is control at the strategic level. Strategic control is conducted through the Business Quality Council.

The Council is comprised of the business leader and his or her direct reports and any other nonmanagement process owners. After the process management system has been established, it is the job of the Business Quality Council to continually manage progress toward achievement of the business process goals and to maintain the integrity of the Six Sigma initiative. Initially, the Business Quality Council meets twice monthly. Eventually, one of two paths are taken by an organization that is successfully implementing Six Sigma. In the best case scenario, the Business Quality

Council becomes the organization's regular staff meeting. Here, there is no distinction between process management and how the organization manages in a regular fashion. An example of this approach was summed up by Nigel Andrews of GE Capital when he said that his "Quality Plan is the Business Plan, the Business Plan is the Quality Plan." When I hear these types of comments, I know a business is on the way toward integration of process management into how they do business, not something above and beyond their regular job.

In the other scenario, the Business Quality Council is still a separate, stand-alone meeting. What makes this approach successful is that each meeting addresses a multitude of strategic issues whether those issues are done each time the council meets, done only on a monthly basis, or done less frequently. Shown in the following are recommended agenda items for a Business Quality Council meeting, specifically addressing how often an item should be scheduled on the agenda for a council:

Each Time the Council Meets

➤ Report outs on process performance (see balanced scorecards in Exhibit 9.14).

Customer Related	Financial Related
➤ Customer satisfaction ratings (for either internal or external customers, depending on the core or subprocess).	➤ Sales. ➤ Income. ➤ Cost per unit.
Process Related ➤ Effectiveness measures usually expressed in the sigma performance for that process. ➤ Efficiency measures usually measured in value, cycle time, and/or cost.	**Miscellaneous Related** ➤ Systems and structures. ➤ Employee morale. ➤ Competencies required.

Exhibit 9.14 Balanced score card example.

Monthly

➤ Selected project reviews.

Quarterly or As Needed

➤ Review and revision of strategic business objectives.

➤ Review and revision of core, key sub-, and enabling processes.

➤ Reconfirmation of process dashboards (i.e., measures of effectiveness and efficiency for each key subprocess).

➤ Reconfirmation and application of project selection criteria for any Green Belt or Black Belt Project.

➤ Selection of process-related projects that match the project selection criteria.

➤ Continuing education.

➤ Recognize the importance of using the Business Process Council for "Best Practices."

➤ Review of the organization's systems and structures.

Many of the quarterly items should be done on a rotating basis. For example, while project selection should always be addressed quarterly, reviewing the organizations systems and structures and using the Business Quality Council for continuing education can be rotated. We now will address each of the aforementioned.

➤ Every Time the Council Meets

Report Outs on Process Performance

The largest mistake an executive team can make relative to the Business Quality Council is assuming their job is to conduct project reviews. This assumption reflects a tactical bias toward Six Sigma. In reality, its most important job is analysis of process performance report outs that ensure that processes are functioning in a way that support achievement of the organization's business objectives.

An important tool most successful Six Sigma businesses use in the ongoing management of their process systems is the balanced scorecard. The balanced scorecard has four major quadrants. Each of these scorecards is prepared for either a core process or a series of key subprocesses, depending on what makes sense for a given organization. A generic example is shown in Exhibit 9.14.

These scorecards are the responsibility of each process owner. Once the Business Quality Council is up and running, the focus of meetings becomes report outs on these scorecards.

➤ Monthly Activities

Selected Project Reviews

While it is a mistake to assume that project reviews are your sole responsibility, it still is an important activity of the Business Quality Council. Knowing this, virtually every Council fails in conducting a project review. Multiple mistakes occur at this level. I will mention the major ones and how to combat them:

> ➤ *Too much feedback on the content of the project.* Good project reviews are a series of questions about how the project team moved from D to M to A to I. Instead, virtually every team ignores these questions and talks about the proposed solutions spending all of its time on the content of these solutions rather than on how the team arrived at them utilizing the DMAIC methodology. Worse yet is a team presenting its entire work (through Improve) and some executive spends the review suggesting improvements to the project. I thought this was why the Council chartered the team in the first place. When I see this mistake, it is a sure sign that management doesn't want to relinquish its traditional role of providing all the answers. More and more, I provide consulting to Councils. I am always telling them to trust the process and the people in the process. If a team has been chartered, allow them to present the methodology and critique the process of how they arrived at an answer, not just the answers themselves.

> ➤ *Too much negative feedback.* Once an executive hones his or her Six Sigma skills he or she goes through a period where he or she thinks there is only one tool or approach to use to achieve sigma improvement. This is particularly the case when an executive has spent time on a successful project. While I love to see an executive be a part of a successful project team, the old saying, "When your only tool is a hammer, everything looks like a nail" rings true. Whether, it's this cause or just normal management, we tend to focus on the negative. In

my coaching of teams, I stress to management that they should constantly be finding what they like about a project first and foremost. Practice the first rule of marriage counseling, "Catch your spouse doing something right." Even if there are areas of improvement for the project team to work on, find something to compliment first.

➤ *Waiting too long for the formal review.* While I like project teams to report out formally toward the end of the DMAIC cycle, it is wise to have at least your high-profile projects discussed by the Business Quality Council through the champion prior to the project teams presentation to the Council. Midcourse corrections can be made without a lot of investment made by the team prior to formal presentation.

➤ Quarterly or As Needed

There are a series of activities to be done by the Business Quality Council quarterly. Some should be done each quarter and some can be done on a rotating basis. First, those that should be done each quarter:

➤ Review and revision of strategic business objectives.

➤ Review and revision of core, key sub-, and enabling processes.

➤ Reconfirmation of process dashboards (i.e., measures of effectiveness and efficiency for each key subprocess).

➤ Reconfirmation and application of project selection criteria for any Green Belt or Black Belt project.

➤ Selection of process-related projects that match the project selection criteria.

Sometimes the first four can be reviewed in a matter of minutes. In other cases, an entire meeting can focus on any one of them. I am always encouraged when I return to my successful clients and see revised core processes. For example, at the Westin, we spent days coming up with their core processes of Rooms, Events, and Outlets. Today, rooms have been replaced with the Guest Accommodation Process. They have changed the name of the two others as well and, in addition, they have added an Employee Satisfaction Core process.

Each quarter the Business Quality Council should review project selection criteria (see Chapter 2) and formally charter new projects. This is the time that projects that are taking more time than initially thought should be carefully reviewed at the Council level so that mid-course corrections can be made. When projects have extended past their initial milestones, there is a good chance that scope creep is happening.

There are other activities that should be on the quarterly agenda, but can be rotated. They include:

➤ Continuing education.

➤ Recognition of the importance of using the business process council for best practices.

➤ Review of the organizations systems and structures.

Continuing Education

I always stress the importance of the executives in an organization not to treat their quality training as equivalent to an inoculation. Dick Benson, the former operations manager of Fujitsu of America has a plaque on his wall that says it best, "When you are through learning . . . you are through." Assuming you can learn everything you need to learn about Six Sigma, even at an executive level, in a two- or three-day course is absurd. When GE Capital hired me to help create their Six Sigma program, I stressed that they should create a structured course for executives that went beyond just introducing them to the basics. While it did not come about initially, Green Belt for Champions was a course I both helped create and teach that was the highest rated course at GE Capital. This course allowed executives to learn how to coach teams by being in a course that required them to learn the materials through having a project of their own. Once they appreciate how much there is to learn, it becomes easier to schedule time during the council meetings to learn more about a given subject. For example, I encourage a Master Black Belt to circulate among the Business Quality Council members a series of topics that executives may select for a tutorial.

Best Practices

In addition to continuing education, I am a firm believer in Jack Welch's concept of best practices. As a result, the concept of learning from the best—not just within GE—was born. The concept of best practices or benchmarking can allow an organization to learn from the best.

I often would ask Bill Dougherty to come to my GE clients to give testimonials about being a great business leader. Financial Guarantee Insurance Company, a division of GE Capital located in Manhattan is an example. After a less than spectacular beginning, I asked them to have Bill come in and speak to their top level management. The results were amazing. Having heard Bill's personal involvement in process management and improvement did much to mobilize this client toward wanting to be more like the Westin. If it hadn't been for Bill Dougherty and his best practice visit, I doubt seriously whether they would have done as much.

Changing Systems and Structures

Another major responsibility of the Business Quality Council is creating an organization in which Six Sigma thrives. During the Council meetings, the executive team can help create an environment that supports greater process participation. Following are a series of examples of changes made by organizations I have worked with:

➤ *Employee acquisition.* The client I experienced the least resistance with was the Westin Tabor Center in Denver. I once asked Bill Dougherty why this was the case. He had a simple but powerful answer. He hires open-minded, customer-oriented people with a propensity to learn new ideas. This simple concept is the underpinning of this strategic element that Business Quality Councils should work on. Think of how interviews were conducted 10 to 15 years ago. A nearly uniform set of questions were asked about computer skills. These questions were asked because the organization wanted to ensure that those coming on board had these skills rather than hiring someone only to have to train them. Not only were questions asked about computer skills, but it was a factor in the hiring decision. The organization of 10 to 15 years ago was communicating that this was an expectation of the potential hire. Thus, one major structure I strongly recommend to organizations to adopt is to include a set of mandatory questions regarding previous quality experience or aptitude toward quality improvement. Furthermore, quality criteria, like computer skills, should be a consideration in the hiring process. This needs to be done at the strategic level, in coordination with Human Resources.

➤ *Employee development.* Once an employee is on board, there should be the expectation that quality education is an ongoing component of continued employment. Several organizations have adopted a 52/40 policy. What this means is that during a given year, 40 hours of that year should be devoted to quality education. One GE Capital employee has taken my Green Belt for Champions course 3 times over the course of a year and a half and said what was mildly understood in the first class was finally mastered in the third. Having the Business Quality Council build in this structure, and then role model this behavior is another strategic responsibility of management.

➤ *Reward and recognition.* From my psychology days I learned the importance of positive reinforcement. Whether raising children or running a business, the importance of finding and rewarding behavior you desire in the future is critical to the success of a Six Sigma business. Let's discuss reward and recognition separately. Reward refers to financial compensation. At GE, Jack Welch was able to mobilize management commitment by declaring an edict that 40 percent of management's bonus would be calculated based on Six Sigma involvement and results. Another more controversial tact taken by a client was to build in gain-sharing for project results. If there was a $400,000 cost savings documented by the team, the team members shared 5 percent of the savings as their bonus. Recognition refers to nonfinancial benefits. I remember being introduced at a supplier conference by a client's vice president who lauded me for my work with his suppliers. Like any good consultant, I prefer reward to recognition but I remember that introduction more than what I spent my fee on. At that same conference, I remember a printed wiring board supplier who was not involved in process improvement seeing his competitor receive a plaque for the supplier of the year award. No sooner had I left the stage than the supplier approached me to begin work on a quality program. The recognition signified in that plaque triggered his involvement in quality. A year later that supplier won the plaque he desired for the year before. Therefore, it is imperative that there be a combination of reward and recognition in a Six Sigma initiative and it is the work of the Business Quality Council to expedite these important factors.

➤ *Performance measurement.* We have talked in detail about measurement of processes and projects. Another area that has to be measured is performance. Most organizations today have performance appraisals. At least once a year, a manager sits down with his or her direct reports and proceeds to evaluate job performance. This is formally the time that management determines job performance, notes deficiencies in performance, and creates development plans for improvement if necessary. As I noted in a 1994 *Quality Progress* magazine article, these reviews are typically uncomfortable for both reviewer and reviewee. In a Six Sigma culture, the reviews can be made more productive by planning out in detail what will be reviewed at the end of the year before the review. Furthermore, the key to performance appraisals are the informal quarterly reviews that should occur so there are no surprises at the time of the formal review. I remember Deming saying what gets measured gets done. I use this concept in child rearing. If my sons know that I establish a habit of asking about homework or what current book they are reading, then I have established homework completion and book reading as expectations. What if, as a manager, I am starting my informal and formal quarterly reviews with inquiries into their Six Sigma activities, whether it be at the process level or project level. Over time this becomes an expectation of each individual in the organization. Once again, the Business Quality Council plays a strategic role in this endeavor, as human resources should create a standardized performance review form. The Council can also emphasize how important informal reviews are to the success of the Six Sigma initiative.

➤ *Communication.* There is a story told about Bob Galvin, the former CEO of Motorola who was the first business leader to champion Six Sigma. In 1992, we were both speakers at the Annual Juran Institute. He was the keynote speaker and I was giving a tutorial on supplier management; we had a brief time to talk during the speaker's hospitality session. I asked him about a rumor I had heard during the 1980s that he would request that staff meetings begin with an update on Six Sigma implementation and then he would leave. He indicated that he had done that. Moreover, he gave a great reason for it. The reason wasn't just to stress the importance of Six Sigma implementation. It also forced his executives to communicate normal business practices into the Six Sigma methodology. This last point really stuck with me. If the financial officer wanted to communicate financial updates, he had to talk the language of Business Process Management (e.g., dashboards). Another of my clients took my advice to start each "All Manager's" meeting with a Six Sigma update. Soon, he found himself talking the language of Business Process Management, process dashboards, and balanced scorecards in a way that made Six Sigma a "way of doing business," not something he did in his extra time.

■ SUMMARY

This chapter has attempted to address control at two levels. The first level of control occurs at the tactical or project level. Once a project team is ready to control their improvements they need to answer two questions about their process. First, is standardization high or low? High standardization is marked by repetitive steps done each time the process is enacted. Process standardization will usually be high after the Improvement phase of DMAIC is completed. The second element to determine your method of control is process throughput. Throughput refers to the items being processed. Depending on what you have improved, throughput can either be high or low. High throughput and high standardization means statistical forms of control. The control chart and the corresponding Response Plan can alert the people in the process to special cause variation so that the initial improvements the project team created are sustained over time and that never-ending improvement occurs once a project team disbands.

In addition to technical control, we revisited the ongoing work of the executive team relative to sustaining Six Sigma throughout their organization. Strategic Control is the last and most important step of Business Process Management, the topic we began to discuss in Chapter 2. We discussed the various responsibilities required of management from project reviews to dashboard report outs. Finally we talked of the Business Quality Council's periodic responsibilities that include continuing education, best practice learning, project selection, and perhaps the most important of responsibilities—creation and maintenance of the systems and structures in an organization that support Six Sigma as a philosophy of business management.

KEY LEARNINGS

➤ Control must occur at both the tactical level (i.e., the project team level) and the strategic level.

➤ The type of tactical control chosen is based on the extent of standardization of the new process and the throughput rate of the new process.

➤ The vast majority of processes will have high throughput and high standardization that leads to statistical control charting as the preferred method of tactical control.

➤ Statistical control charts can alert the members of the process when the process has changed irrespective of whether defects have been made or not.

➤ Becoming aware of assignable causes to the process can act as prevention to defects occurring and also assist the project team improve sigma performance after a project team has officially disbanded.

➤ Strategic Control is the last element of Business Process Management which was introduced in Chapter 2.

➤ Strategic Control is managed by the Business Quality Council.

➤ Business Quality Councils should meet at a minimum monthly.

➤ Ideally, the Business Quality Council and the executive staff meeting should become one and the same.

➤ Some of the items that a Business Quality Council should do each time it meets is review process dashboards and review high-profile projects.

➤ Some of the items a Business Quality Council does periodically are new project selection, continuing education, benchmarking other organization efforts, and review and revision of the organization's systems and structures.

Chapter 10

How Six Sigma Initiatives Fail and How to Avoid Mistakes

In our final chapter, I plan to address how Six Sigma can fail in an organization. Over the course of almost 20 years of consulting, I have attempted to be even keel in my client work, not promising a nirvana by implementing Six Sigma or other data-oriented approaches to improvement. As we enter a new millennium, I peruse business bookshelves and the advertisements of magazines now touting Six Sigma as the "most powerful breakthrough management tool ever devised" (actual quote from a new Six Sigma book).

This marketing of an otherwise superb approach to managing business makes Six Sigma appear like the latest fad diet. Like most approaches to weight loss, any sensible methodology that is used as a discipline will work. The same can be said for Six Sigma. The problem with Six Sigma is that it is prone to abuse like many other approaches. This is because of the degree of rigor, discipline, and statistics that are used.

In this chapter, we will examine several key points that may help you avoid the mistakes that several organizations have made. My purpose in this chapter is self-serving. I have for many years made a good living teaching the use of statistical tools to organizations. In the past several years, Six Sigma has exploded in terms of popularity. I should be ecstatic. I actually have more concerns than happiness with this explosion. My concerns center on what I call the "meteor effect" of a quality initiative. In my field, I have seen over and over an initiative become a fad. Usually these fads have not been focused in my area of expertise and I have breathed a sigh of relief. Now, the fad has reached me. My biggest worry is that like a meteor, Six Sigma will be explosive in growth for a few years. If the fears covered in this chapter actualize, then companies in the coming years will be turned off as much by Six Sigma as they are turned on currently.

■ CONCERN 1—THE KEY TO SIX SIGMA IS STATISTICS, STATISTICS, STATISTICS

The key that makes Six Sigma work is two-fold. First, in our approach the technical tools of process improvement are merged with strategic thinking and action. Without effective business process management (the strategic piece), the process improvement methodology will only result in tactical cost savings results.

Second, both at the strategic and project level, Six Sigma works because of its rigor and discipline. Rigor and discipline to me is basing decisions on data and the structured "Ready-Aim-Fire" approach that seems missing from so many organizations. Rigor and discipline *is not* throwing more and more statistical tools at a problem. An example will highlight the growing danger of associating more and complex statistics with the concept of rigor and discipline.

I have been contacted by clients who have attended Six Sigma conferences or have made an attempt at Six Sigma and seem more confused than enlightened. During a champions training with a non-GE client, I had just reviewed sigma conceptually and was ready for a break. A hand was furiously waving and it looked like a comment in the form of a question was coming. "Wait a minute, are you done with sigma?" came the comment phrased as a question. "What about the 1.5 sigma shift?"

This question indicated he had either done some reading or had attended some seminar from another Six Sigma consultant. Mikel Harry, the undisputed Six Sigma guru, claims that for a typical process there will be a 1.5 sigma shift in even the most consistent process. In other words, over an extended period of time, any process (even a consistent one) will shift 1.5 sigma from its desired target. That would mean that a three sigma process measure may be as bad as 1.5. Do processes, even consistent ones, vary over time so that the "snapshot" at the time sigma is calculated may be overestimated? Of course I would agree with this common sense analysis that a process varies over time. Yes, a worse case situation means that a 3 sigma process may be 1.5 sigma over time. It would also mean for certain quality characteristics sigma could be *better* than the sigma calculated in the short term. While I always mention process drift, I don't dwell on the 1.5 sigma shift. I rarely talk in those detailed terms for two reasons. For one, even after talking to Mikel Harry in the 1980s, I never was convinced of the exactness of 1.5 as the number. If don't understand the details of the 1.5 sigma shift, I don't believe it's as critical as some of the statisticians make it out to be. While I strongly support teaching the concept of variation in the process, putting so much focus on underestimating the sigma calculated by such a detailed number is detrimental to a project team.

This example highlights the problem that I anticipate for Six Sigma in the future. Many Six Sigma consultants are statisticians. To hear them in a seminar is to believe better quality is the result of more complex statistics. This creates the impression that you must turn your organization over to statisticians, believing that greater profits comes from implementing something you are not smart enough to do yourself.

It's like creating a Rasputin in your organization, thinking that greater profitability comes from turning your business over to consultants who know something you don't. I am proud to be a consultant, but not one that has all the answers. Like the psychologist I once was, improvement in either a person, a family, or an organization comes from getting help at times, but not turning yourself over to someone who claims to have all the answers.

A recent client of mine picked me to help them implement Six Sigma. They indicated a key reason they hired me was that I answered a question honestly. They had almost hired a company to implement Six Sigma until their quality director asked the other consultant the following question:

"How many times have you failed in implementing Six Sigma?"

My competitors for the contract, a noted consultant (who will remain unnamed), said the following:

"When the client does exactly what we tell them, we have never failed."

When the client asked me the same question, I responded by saying:

> *"About 30 percent of my clients have had a true Six Sigma cultural transformation, about 50 percent of my clients have obtained tactical results that justified their investment in paying my outrageous fees. And about 20 percent of clients have totally wasted their money."*

Let's look at some of the other concerns that you need to be aware of so you don't fail.

■ CONCERN 2—OVEREMPHASIS ON COSTS

In 1996, I was fortunate to be selected as one of the course designers for GE Capital's Six Sigma initiative. During the discussions between the internal course developers of GE and the external consultants, the topic of quantifying costs came up. Quantifying the opportunity refers to performing analysis of the costs associated with ineffectiveness and inefficiency in a process targeted for improvement.

While I had taken a flexible approach to the course materials to this point, I was responsible for a heated discussion on whether teams should calculate the costs associated with ineffectiveness and inefficiency. Costs associated with ineffectiveness include:

➤ Warranty claims.

➤ Insurance.

➤ Costs associated with recalls or returns.

➤ Lost business due to poor quality reputation.

➤ Contract losses due to not meeting quality obligations.

➤ Premium freight costs.

➤ Re-issues.

Costs associated with inefficiency include:

➤ Rework.

➤ Scrap.

➤ Machine down-time.

➤ Excessive inventory.

➤ Redo's or other nonvalue added process steps.

The majority of course design participants argued for inclusion of the project team calculating costs associated with the project. I argued the other way. If you examine the above categories, you can see that it is easier to calculate the costs associated with rework but much harder if not impossible to calculate the costs associated with lost customers.

My point of view was heavily influenced by my discussions with Deming in years past. He had once told me that when you calculate costs you tend to gravitate to known costs and ignore the costs that are hard or even impossible to track. In a reference to what he called his theory of profound knowledge, he cited the example of the business that wants to reduce travel expenses. It is easy to track the price of a plane ticket. So when an employee goes to the company's travel service and says they have to go from Denver to New York, the travel agency pulls up several options, which are shown in Exhibit 10.1.

The company's travel agent wants the employee to take the last option. It stresses the nearly 50 percent cost savings by taking the connecting trip to Newark. But the focus of the travel agency is price, not cost. Price is easier to calculate than cost. Price is the known cost. What the travel agency sees is the price of the ticket and they believe they are doing the right thing. But what is the cost of:

➤ The lost time the employee would incur by having to leave the office in the morning and spend more of the day traveling through connecting cities and waiting in airports versus working in the office in the morning and catching his afternoon flight.

➤ Arriving later in the evening.

➤ The stress of having the possibilities of two flights be late rather than one.

➤ The strain of having to worry about whether his or her baggage will make the connection.

➤ The strain of having to worry whether he or she will make their connection.

Destination	Route Options	Departure/ Arrival Time	Ticket Price
Denver to New York which is 45 minutes from Stamford, CT, where the employee is to work the next day	Direct from Denver International Airport to New York LaGuardia	1:08 P.M. (MST)/ 6:15 P.M. (EST)	$1,400
Denver to New York which is 45 minutes from Stamford, CT, where the employee is to work the next day	Connecting flight Denver to Chicago O'Hare and on to LaGuardia	11:30 A.M. (MST)/ 7:00 P.M. (EST)	990
Denver to New York which is 45 minutes from Stamford, CT, where the employee is to work the next day	Connecting flight Denver to Cleveland and on to Newark International Airport	11:20 A.M. (MST)/ 6:55 P.M. (EST)	775

Exhibit 10.1 Travel itinerary.

➤ Last, and certainly not least, by arriving in Newark, he will have all that extra time traveling from New Jersey, the stress of more traffic, the cost of additional tolls and arriving much later in Connecticut. Let's not forget the purpose of the trip. This employee is to work the next day in Stamford. How do we calculate the cost of road-weariness? In this example, how do we calculate the effects on the customer?

The easiest measure to examine in this example is the efficiency measure, the cost of the ticket. This is true in most processes. Therefore, my argument against calculating costs associated with projects in any kind of detailed way is that they are biased toward the "known" costs, while the more important costs are usually more difficult or impossible to calculate. I predicted to my new GE friends that emphasis on cost analysis would result in many projects aimed at improving process efficiency while projects aimed at improving customer effectiveness would be de-emphasized since it would be harder or impossible to calculate the costs of effectiveness.

I lost my battle to exclude cost analysis as part of the curriculum. It was included in the course material and I dutifully taught it, following the letter, if not the spirit of the law. In the first two years of GE reporting Six Sigma results, there were significant cost savings and I was frequently reminded of my "mistake."

It was with some amusement that I received word in 1999 that Jack Welch had presented an edict at his annual management meeting that he had been receiving too many customer calls saying that they were reading about all the internal success of Six Sigma at GE but many were not seeing Six Sigma results as the customer. He exhorted his troops to refocus on customer projects which they dutifully did that year. Virtually all of my GE work in 1999 was customer focus with less emphasis on cost measures. While I felt I lost the "cost" battle, I felt I won the war.

The bigger concern is when management thinks that Six Sigma is exclusively a cost-reduction program. When this happens, the best that can be expected in an organization is tactical results. Further, it excludes management involvement that to me is a cornerstone of a cultural transformation for an organization.

■ CONCERN 3—FAILURE TO ADDRESS IMPROVEMENT AS PART OF THE JOB DESCRIPTION

I have learned patience being a Six Sigma consultant. Despite this claim, there is one question I hear that both frustrates me and alerts me to trouble on the horizon for the client:

> "I just don't have time to do Six Sigma. I already work an 11-hour day and now management wants me to spend all this extra time doing Six Sigma projects."

I hear this comment more often than I would like. At the beginning of each of my seminars, I administer a subjective test of the effectiveness and efficiency of the participants. From over 10 years of test administration, I have accumulated data that indicates that, on average, a person wastes almost 50 percent of their time each day. Many times this is due to working in inefficient, ineffective processes. However, my point in bringing up this statistic is that after awhile, the employee who exists in this atmosphere comes to see this as normal.

Moreover, and far more dangerous, they begin to see the inefficiencies as part of their job unaware of the cost of being inefficient, either in terms of job satisfaction or contributions to the
organization that exist. When I hear the above refrain of not having time to do Six Sigma, I know I am in an environment where
improvement and betterment, whether of a process or person is
not encouraged or rewarded.

Early in my consulting career, I attended a conference where
Genichi Taguchi, the noted Japanese design of experiments expert,
was giving a speech. He received a question about how improvement in his area might cost he and coworkers their jobs, which
were receiving inspection. I often admired his response:

*"You sir, are worse than a thief. A thief makes no pretense of
creating value. He wants what is yours and is willing to steal.
You are a thief. You steal from your employer, but unlike a
thief, you pretend you earn your wages."*

While I was bemused at such directness, I also tried to determine its root cause. Among the many legitimate root causes that I
encounter is a business environment that doesn't encourage improvement in either their people or processes. To expect an organization to implement Six Sigma without the expectation they will
have time to learn and implement it is foolhardy. By the same
token, recognize that the person who claims not to have time to
implement Six Sigma doesn't spend much time talking about all
the wasted time having to do something for the second, third, or
fourth time. They see inefficiency as part of the job. As the old
adage says, "We always seem to have time to do it over again and
again, we never seem to have the time to improve a process enough
to do it right the first time." Organizations need to establish improvement activity as part of the job.

Far too many organizations and people within organizations
expect the forest to be cleared without time spent sharpening the
ax. Six sigma implementation is sharpening the ax. Management
needs to set a tone for this to happen. They can accomplish this
task in many ways, one of which is exemplified by GE's Green Belt
for Champion's course where each executive in the organization
learns the DMAIC methodology by applying the tools to an actual
executive project.

Failure to role model the behaviors associated with Six Sigma
is a sure death knell for improvements in effectiveness and

efficiency. Executives need to strategically address the issue of "ax sharpening."

Finally, those in management who articulate the concern about not having time to implement Six Sigma are those who don't believe in even its short-term benefits. Think of a doctor telling you to exercise or it could affect your life span. There are many who ignore this advice and indicate (at least to themselves) that they don't have time to exercise. Those that heed the physician's advice—*make the time.*

■ CONCERN 4—IGNORING TEAM DYNAMICS AS A ROOT CAUSE OF PROJECT FAILURES

As we indicated earlier in this chapter, I have been associated with abject failures in Six Sigma implementation. I have tried to conduct failure analysis with regard to why an organization wasted valuable resources to implement Six Sigma. Among its failures were projects that did not bare fruit. I have collected informal data that show the following:

> ➤ *20 percent—Poor project selection.* In some cases, before a client has established their Business Process Management system, projects have been selected for improvement that eventually show little impact on the strategic objectives of the organization. Even when these projects show improvement, the results at best show some tactical improvement and don't move the "dials" on the higher level process dashboards. To combat this problem, refer to the implementation of process management (Chapter 2) and specifically the segments on project selection.

> ➤ *20 percent—Misuse of the methodology.* Earlier in this chapter, I indicated that there is too much emphasis on the statistics associated with Six Sigma. That being the case, teams still encounter failure when they don't use the DMAIC methodology properly. The biggest technical issues with projects I encounter are when a project team begins a project with predetermined solutions in their heads during the D phase. These project teams go through the steps of D, M and A but don't really apply the tools. For example, during a cause-effect

diagram (the Open phase of analysis) you see these teams using phrases like, "lack of _____" or "no _____." These teams are not really using analysis; they are going through the motions. The most egregious error technically is failure to validate root causes. It's like the old adage, "Let's not have data interfere with a great opinion." My litmus test for these teams is to examine the last and most important step of A, validating root causes. If I suspect that a project team is married to predetermined solutions, I ask to see their validation of root causes. In more cases than not, the team has either done a substandard job or not done validation at all. In addition to this technical problem, there are teams that are poorly chartered. The champion has not communicated why this project is necessary, why the project has priority over other projects, or why this project should be done now rather than later. As we discussed in our Define chapter, scope creep is an ever-present danger that contributes to project failure.

By far the greatest source of team failures is poor team dynamics and poor facilitative leadership behaviors. Approximately 60 percent of teams that fail have these as their major reasons. I am reminded of an old adage spoken by some of my organizational friends. "The hard stuff is the easy stuff; the easy stuff is the hard stuff." The most common problem areas we have encountered are:

➤ *Meeting skills.* Meeting skills refers to those tools and techniques that make for effectiveness and efficiency in how a project team conducts its business each time they meet. How many of you have attended a meeting where at the end of the scheduled time you feel that a lot of discussion has transpired but not much work has occurred? Many of my clients see meetings as among their largest areas of inefficiency. Six Sigma project meetings are rarely different. In the early stages of working with a project team, it is critical for the project team to begin practicing the skills necessary to achieve its goals. Among the meeting skills that need to become a part of the project teams work are:

➤ *Setting agendas.* Good meetings start with agendas. Good agendas are marked by what the team's desired outcomes are for that meeting, a list of the topics to be covered, the method to be used, and the targeted time allotted for the task. Exhibit 10.2

is an example of an agenda used by the Customer Aftermarket improvement team at Volvo Trucks North America.

➤ *Determining the meeting's roles and responsibilities.* From the example of the team's agendas, we have highlighted the most important role in a meeting, the *facilitator.* The facilitator runs the meeting. He or she will write the agenda on a flip chart, assign the other roles; assist the team with policing ground rules (see discussion following) and document the work done during that specific meeting. In addition to the facilitator, there should be a *timekeeper* assigned. His or her responsibilities includes both tracking the time allotted for each item on the agenda and giving periodic updates when time is running out. The biggest mistake a timekeeper makes is just saying "times up," at the end of the assigned time. The best timekeepers I have seen will give time warnings when 50 percent and 25 percent of time remains for a given item to be completed, and again when 10 minutes remain, and when time has expired. Teams then have the option of going forward, borrowing from another item on the agenda, or modifying the agenda altogether. Another typical role in a meeting is the *scribe.* The scribe should not be confused with the facilitator. Scribes are responsible for documentation of all pertinent information derived during the meeting. Typically, they either keep their own notes or they are responsible for flip chart notes if the facilitator prefers not to be the "keeper of the pen."

➤ *Setting and keeping ground rules.* Ground rules refer to the "operating agreements" for behaviors in the meeting. I typically

Topic	Goal	Method Used	Time	Facilitator
Review cause-effect diagram	Narrow list of potential root causes to the "vital few"	Clarification, duplication and multi-voting	90 minutes	Bill Brubaker
Determine criteria for solutions	Obtain agreement on criteria for final solution selection	Affinity diagram	90 minutes	Jim Talatzko

Exhibit 10.2 Agenda Volvo customer aftermarket project.

start any seminar asking for input about what we can all agree on and how we will operate as a group. I usually start by asking project teams to agree to start on time and to adhere to scheduled breaks. Then I promise that with their cooperation I will always let them out a few minutes early. In addition to this ground rule (i.e., timeliness), other typical ground rules are:

—Discussions should focus on the idea, not the person.
—Confidentiality: Nothing discussed in the meeting can be attributable later.
—Participation: which is operationally defined as talking, note taking, and so forth.
—No rank: which is defined as positions and titles are left at the door.
—One person talks at a time: no sidebar discussions.

These ground rules are posted on a flip chart for each meeting. A good facilitator will not only get agreement to the ground rules but also will ensure that enforcement is a shared responsibility.

➤ *Facilitative behaviors.* Mastery of good meeting skills focuses in on prevention behaviors. The adage of an ounce of prevention being worth a pound of intervention has been documented in meeting after meeting. However, despite the most conscientious of efforts, there will be times when the focus of improving team dynamics will move from "preventions to "interventions." Once there is a need for interventions, good facilitative behaviors are a must.

Good facilitative intervention behaviors exist on a continuum from low-level interventions to high-level interventions. Low-level interventions should be attempted first. This is both least distractive to the team's work and is least embarrassing to the target offender.

For example, suppose we have established a ground rule of no sidebar discussions. This means only one person talks at a time. If I am the facilitator and I see two people talking to each other while another person is trying to say something, a ground rule is being broken. Ignoring this behavior only encourages further behavior of this kind and eventually behavior worsens. While I, as the facilitator, don't have exclusive enforcement responsibility, there is a special expectation that a facilitator has to rectify nonproductive behaviors. If I stop the project team's work and admonish the two talking, I may stop the behavior but the potential level of embarrassment may result in different, more maladaptive behavior. The admonishment of the behavior is considered a high-level intervention. One type of low-level intervention would be to simply make eye contact with the two who are talking. Another low-level interaction would also be to walk in the direction of the participants who are talking. A mid-level interaction, if these first two didn't work, would be to stop talking and if that didn't work to stop talking as you walk in the direction of the talking participants.

In other cases, team dynamics can be affected by behaviors that call for mid-level to higher-level interactions. If I have a team member who repeatedly is late or a no-show for meetings, a meeting "offline" (i.e., just he or she alone) would be a high level intervention. The final and highest intervention is either confrontation of the behavior in the meeting or asking the team to intervene in open session.

While this section of the chapter is not meant to be an exhaustive review of facilitative behaviors, it is intended to stress the importance of managing team dynamics in the Six Sigma project work. Invariably, it is these "easy" elements that, left unmanaged, result in Six Sigma failures—not failure to apply additional statistical tools.

■ CONCERN 5—RELIANCE ON THE BLACK BELT

As we discussed in Chapter 3, there are various roles and responsibilities in implementing Six Sigma. We defined a Black Belt as a full time team leader, a person trained in the tools and techniques of improvement who leads three to four teams a year. At General Electric, Jack Welch has identified Black Belts as the future business leaders of the organization. The goal is to move the Black Belt out of their quality responsibilities within three to five years into line positions in management. The concept of the Green Belt is identical to that of the Black Belt with one difference. The Green Belt is a project leader who also maintains a "real" job in the organization and is leading a team while holding down responsibilities elsewhere.

In my years working with GE in their Six Sigma initiative I have seen firsthand the successful transition of Black Belts to line positions elsewhere in the organization. Ruth Fattori, GE Capital's first Quality Leader, transitioned into a European line management position. Her successor, Dan Henson, has taken on a management position after his quality stint.

The problem with the Black Belt concept in many other organizations is two-fold. First, it is one thing for GE with their vast resources to allocate such massive resources measured in terms of monetary investment and staffing. Most organizations are both philosophically opposed to adding such a layer of people to their organization not to mention the fiscal investment needed.

My biggest concern seen in some organizations is the psychology of having full-time people being responsible for leading project teams. Many a Black Belt has confided in me that he or she has encountered difficulty with "baking in" the concepts of Six Sigma. In worse case scenarios, I have been told that Business Process Management responsibilities are delegated to the Black Belt as a Six Sigma "project." In other cases, Black Belts have told me the Six Sigma initiative is in danger of failing in their organization because the employees develop resentment to the Black Belt budget being increased while everyone else's is frozen or cut.

I advocate a Green Belt approach. The Black Belt approach is too close to the perils that traditional quality organizations faced in the mid-twentieth century. In those days, there was too clear a demarcation between production and quality with the former believing they had no responsibility for quality since management had created and financed an entire department for quality. Even if your organization has the fiscal power to finance a Black Belt approach, recognize that once Six Sigma is up and running in your business, you don't want the rank and file to either have animosity to Six Sigma, or have your initiative slowed by thinking there are internal experts that will "do" Six Sigma for you.

■ CONCERN 6—SIX SIGMA EQUALS PROJECTS

The initial steps in setting up a Six Sigma initiative included having the Business Quality Council establish project selection criteria and applying those criteria to select projects to begin work on "fixing" broken processes. Visible, high impact, successful projects are a hallmark of the beginning of a Six Sigma initiative. Projects will continue to be a part of any Six Sigma initiative. Unfortunately, many organizations end up thinking and behaving like Six Sigma equals projects. As we have indicated in Chapter 9, an ongoing responsibility of the Business Quality Council is selection of projects for improvement. This activity does not end over time. However, into the second and third year of the Six Sigma initiative, projects should not be seen as the major evidence of the Six Sigma initiative. High quality Six Sigma initiatives in the second and third years of existence should be highlighted by strong process management systems and the rigor and discipline of the scientific method in everyday activity by all individuals in the organization.

Furthermore, a successful Six Sigma organization has other options to implement at the tactical level. Among the concerns I have with some clients is making all tactical work a three- or four-month DMAIC project. There are other alternatives. For example, there are times when quality tools should be applied to everyday work that could take a matter of minutes rather than creating a full-blown project. Greg Poupard, an executive at Lithonia Lighting often will use the Process Mapping to better understand a process without ending up chartering a team to improve it right away. People like Poupard understand when to use quality tools and when a project needs to be chartered to undergo a substantial improvement in some strategically important process. In the beginning of a Six Sigma initiative, the impression can be formed that projects equals Six Sigma but in short order that must change. Recognize that we have covered in Chapter 2 how projects should be selected as part of the creation and management of the process management system.

At GE, they have as part of their infrastructure a variety of other approaches other than strict DMAIC projects. For example, in the late 1980s and early 1990s, GE implemented "Work-Out," a program whose purpose was to empower employees to improve organizations through two- or three-day problem-solving sessions. I was fortunate to facilitate several Work-Outs beginning in the early 1990s. An area of inefficiency (usually an area top heavy in bureaucracy) was chosen for quick improvements. Management would select a team that would define a problem, analyze its causes, and generate a set of suggestions for improvement that would then be presented to management at the end of two or three days. Management would then rule "thumbs up" or "thumbs down" on a suggestion for improvement in the chosen area. You will notice the methodology uses a similar pattern of a DMAIC project but measurement is not emphasized. Many times while facilitating a Work-Out, we would solicit data, but improvement surrounding the problem was usually not data driven. It didn't have to be. That was the beauty of Work-Out. In a Six Sigma culture, Work-Out should still be an option for the short term, nondata dominant problems (like bureaucratic issues).

Again, one of the problems with Six Sigma is forming a DMAIC team to address all issues surrounding ineffectiveness and inefficiency in the organization. Successful Six Sigma organizations will always have formal projects but they should not be the major sign of Six Sigma a few years into the initiative.

■ CONCERN 7—MANAGEMENT NOT UNDERSTANDING COMMON CAUSE VERSUS SPECIAL CAUSE VARIATION

"The use and understanding of control charts by management is more important than its application by line workers."

—W. Edwards Deming

In our measurement chapter, we discussed how a project team must understand whether they are dealing with a common cause or special cause source of variation. We noted that knowing which of the two types of variation is present would determine the method of problem solving the team would employ.

The good news is that teams have by and large mastered this concept well. The problem is that at a strategic level management hasn't. An example may prove illustrative. During a consulting contract with an executive group the process dashboard in Exhibit 10.3 was presented.

The response from otherwise intelligent management was surprising. They reacted to the downward trend with a call for improvement. A large-scale discussion began while I did some quick calculations. As the management group neared closure on corrective action, I rose to the overhead projector and drew the average sales figure for the data shown and the upper and lower expected levels of variation for the data shown. They are shown in Exhibit 10.4.

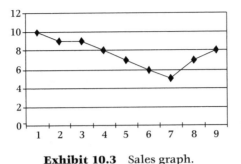

Exhibit 10.3   Sales graph.

With the average and expected levels of variation drawn, the reaction changed. The downward "trend" that prompted the management's reaction was well within the normal range of common cause variation (even taking into account analysis of trends). Corrective action done to a process showing common cause variation has the potential to do more harm than good. Management's lack of understanding of statistical control leads to disastrous results in any organization. All too often management overreacts to common cause variation and makes things worse than better. If Six Sigma does anything to our corporate culture, I hope the concept of common cause versus special cause variation is able to be Six Sigma's legacy. Wall Street and its reactions to a bad quarter by a business is another example of the lack of understanding of common versus special cause variation. Variation exists in all processes. Once the variation extends past the point of common cause variation, it is time to react with corrective action. Wall Street reacts to organizations that don't meet their earnings target

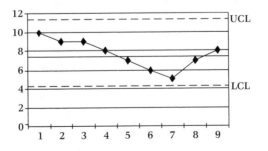

Exhibit 10.4   Sales graph with upper
and lower control limits.

by a penny or don't reach the "whisper number," by having the stock price drop. This would be comical if it didn't have such an impact on our economy. Sadly, I have worked with businesses implementing Six Sigma that have replaced a "Golden Boy" or "Golden Girl" business leader after a bad business quarter despite the bad quarter being due to common cause variation.

In addition, when special cause variation is evident, ignorant management then focuses on people rather than the other M's that are more likely to explain the special cause variation. In a recent seminar with a highly respected Fortune 100 company, as I talked about special cause variation in a call center (these are special 800 phone numbers available to the client that resolve customer issues), an executive who oversees the call center talked about how the people in the process didn't perform to expectations. Instead of focusing on the methods of training or some other element associated with variation in performance, the executive focused totally on the people. Even after talking about deficiencies in the employee acquisition process, the focus was on the poor performance of the people in the call center. This thinking in the early stages of a Six Sigma initiative is expected. This thinking in the later stages of a Six Sigma initiative is fatal.

■ CONCERN 8—FAILURE TO APPLY THE CONCEPT OF CUSTOMER INTERNALLY

Earlier in this chapter, I said that about 30 percent of my clients had achieved a cultural transformation, another 50 percent had achieved tactical improvement, and the rest had basically wasted their money. A key to the first 30 percent is recognition that everyone is a customer to someone else in the organization.

For some organizations, the concept of internal customers is a foreign concept. In seminars when I ask who a customer is, I get as an answer, "the person who pays the invoice." This answer reflects belief in the external customer only. My definition of the customer is anyone who is the recipient of a product or service. In a Six Sigma culture it is critical to have a series of interconnected processes that ultimately lead to the external customer. These interdepartmental, cross-functional processes all have suppliers and customers. The vast majority of these suppliers and customers are internal to an organization. To be exclusively focused on just the external customer without embracing the concept of the internal customer will result in only tactical results in an organization.

The benefits of embracing the concept of the internal customer extend beyond improved effectiveness and efficiency. During a seminar at the IT Distribution division of GE Capital, I asked what the benefits were of being a Six Sigma organization. One of the responses from Sue Recko, an organizational development expert, was right on target, "It's fun working for an organization where you are treated as a customer." For any organization where employee satisfaction is a strategic business objective, this benefit cannot be understated.

■ CONCERN 9— RECOGNIZING MANAGEMENT'S INVOLVEMENT— NOT JUST COMMITMENT

There are seminars in which I ask the following questions:

➤ How many of you are committed to the abolishment of world hunger?

➤ How many of you are committed to the abolishment of child abuse?

➤ How many of you are committed to a cleaner environment?

Virtually everyone in the class raises their hands to these questions. Then I ask the audience how many of them have been *involved* in any activity to improve any of these areas. Far fewer hands are raised. Therein lies the difference between involvement and commitment. Management will find it easy to commit to Six Sigma. Who can be against committing to a course of action that improves the effectiveness and efficiency of an organization? To be committed to a course of action is one thing, but to be successful in implementing Six Sigma there must be management involvement.

We have chronicled how management should be involved in Six Sigma, from the creation and management of the process management system to participation in projects themselves. When an organization only achieves tactical results or fails entirely, the fault lies with management.

In January 1998, we conducted a process management session at the Westin in one of the restaurants in the morning since other conference rooms were unavailable. Late in the morning we took a break and Bill Dougherty had the management group disassemble the room and set it up for the lunch crowd that was soon to be arriving. The picture of vice presidents and directors involved in moving chairs and tables motivated me so much I joined in, albeit for a shorter period of time.

This small but powerfully symbolic visual highlighted for me why the Westin was so successful with their improvement efforts. Management at the Westin saw themselves as participants in the work at the Westin. It's this type of attitude that turns Six Sigma initiatives into the cultural phenomenon that all management desires. When I see management returning late for breaks or missing parts of my seminars to deal with their day-to-day activities, my concern grows exponentially.

■ CONCERN 10—IGNORING THE MANAGEMENT OF CHANGE IN THE ORGANIZATION

In Chapter 8, we covered many of the concepts of change as it relates to implementation of the solutions of a project. We covered management of change at the tactical level. One of the failures in implementing a Six Sigma initiative is not managing change at the strategic level. The tools and techniques are basically the same as the ones we covered but extend further.

In our next book, *Making Six Sigma Last: Managing in a Changing Environment,* we will address managing in a changing environment and how to manage change strategically.

■ SUMMARY

This final chapter has attempted to emphasize some of the pitfalls many organizations fall into in their attempts to achieve the results of a cultural transformation using Six Sigma. We have touched on 10 critical mistakes companies make in their efforts that you should avoid if you expect to be among those minority of organizations that will be looked upon as achieving a true Six Sigma transformation.

KEY LEARNINGS

➤ Be aware that Six Sigma initiatives can fail if the organization believes better quality comes about through more sophisticated statistics.

➤ Six Sigma can fail if the focus of the initiative is cost reduction exclusively.

➤ Six Sigma initiatives fail when process improvement is not considered a part of the job description.

➤ Six Sigma projects can and do fail when the methodology of DMAIC is not followed. The most common technical mistakes are failure to charter teams properly and failure of the teams to conduct root cause validation.

➤ Far more project failures occur when teams ignore soft skills such as good meeting skills, facilitative preventions, and facilitative interventions.

➤ While the concept of the Black Belt can accelerate some Six Sigma initiatives, the far greater danger is seeing the Six Sigma effort being the responsibility of the Black Belt.

➤ When an organization sees Six Sigma as a series of projects, failure is looming around the corner. Projects are the tactical "jump start" for a Six Sigma initiative. Far more important is the focus on process management and instilling rigor and discipline in all processes.

➤ When management fails to understand common versus special cause variation in their management approach, Six Sigma can fail.

➤ The emphasis on being customer focused must extend to the internal customer. When an organization sees the customer solely as the payer of the invoice, Six Sigma cannot flourish.

➤ Management must be actively involved in Six Sigma—not just committed to the allocation of resources. Management's role in creating and managing the process management system is far more important than a rash of successful tactical projects.

➤ Failure to manage change in the Six Sigma organization will result in substandard results, if any.

Appendix

Constants and Conversion Tables

Table of constants: Factors for determining from R the
3-sigma control limits for X bar and R charts.

Number of Observations in Subgroup n	Factor for X bar Chart A_2	Factors for Lower Control Limit D_3	R Chart Upper Control Limit D_4
2	1.88	0	3.27
3	1.02	0	2.57
4	0.73	0	2.28
5	0.58	0	2.11
6	0.48	0	2.00
7	0.42	0.08	1.92
8	0.37	0.14	1.86
9	0.34	0.18	1.82
10	0.31	0.22	1.78
11	0.29	0.26	1.74
12	0.27	0.28	1.72
13	0.25	0.31	1.69
14	0.24	0.33	1.67
15	0.22	0.35	1.65
16	0.21	0.36	1.64
17	0.20	0.38	1.62
18	0.19	0.39	1.61
19	0.19	0.40	1.60
20	0.18	0.41	1.59

Process capability and sigma conversion table.

Capability Index (Cpk)	Process Sigma Short Term	Process Sigma Long Term	Yield	Defects per 1,000,000	Defects per 100,000	Defects per 10,000	Defects per 1,000	Defects per 100
2	6	4.5	99.99966	3	0.34	0.034	0.0034	0.00034
1.97	5.9	4.4	99.99946	5	0.54	0.054	0.0054	0.00054
1.93	5.8	4.3	99.99915	9	0.85	0.085	0.0085	0.00085
1.9	5.7	4.2	99.9987	13	1.34	0.134	0.0134	0.00134
1.87	5.6	4.1	99.9979	21	2.1	0.207	0.021	0.0021
1.83	5.5	4	99.9968	32	3.2	0.32	0.032	0.0032
1.8	5.4	3.9	99.995	48	4.8	0.48	0.048	0.0048
1.77	5.3	3.8	99.993	72	7.2	0.72	0.072	0.0072
1.73	5.2	3.7	99.989	108	10.8	0.08	0.11	0.011
1.7	5.1	3.6	99.984	159	15.9	1.6	0.16	0.016
1.67	5	3.5	99.98	233	23.3	2.3	0.23	0.023
1.63	4.9	3.4	99.97	337	33.7	3.4	0.34	0.034
1.6	4.8	3.3	99.95	483	48.3	4.8	0.48	0.048
1.57	4.7	3.2	99.93	687	68.7	6.9	0.69	0.069
1.53	4.6	3.1	99.90	968	97	10	0.97	0.097
1.5	4.5	3	99.87	1,350	135	13	1.3	0.13
1.47	4.4	2.9	99.81	1,866	187	19	1.9	0.19
1.43	4.3	2.8	99.74	2,555	256	26	2.6	0.26
1.4	4.2	2.7	99.65	3,467	347	35	3.5	0.35
1.37	4.1	2.6	99.5	4,661	466	47	4.7	0.47
1.33	4	2.5	99.4	6,210	621	62	6.2	0.62
1.3	3.9	2.4	99.2	8,198	820	82	8.2	0.82
1.27	3.8	2.3	98.9	10,724	1,072	107	11	1.1
1.23	3.7	2.2	98.6	13,903	1,390	139	14	1.4
1.2	3.6	2.1	98.2	17,864	1,786	179	18	1.8
1.17	3.5	2	97.7	22,750	2,275	228	23	2.3
1.13	3.4	1.9	97.1	28,716	2,872	287	29	2.9
1.1	3.3	1.8	96.4	35,930	3,593	359	36	3.6
1.07	3.2	1.7	95.5	44,565	4,457	446	45	4.5
1.03	3.1	1.6	94.5	54,799	5,480	548	55	5.5
1	3	1.5	93.3	66,807	6,681	668	67	6.7

0.97	2.9	1.4	91.9	80,757	8,076	808	81	8.1
0.93	2.8	1.3	90.3	96,801	9,680	968	97	9.7
0.9	2.7	1.2	88.5	115,070	11,507	1,151	115	12
0.87	2.6	1.1	86.4	135,666	13,567	1,357	136	14
0.83	2.5	1	84.1	158,655	15,866	1,587	159	16
0.8	2.4	0.9	81.6	184,060	18,406	1,841	184	18
0.77	2.3	0.8	78.8	211,855	21,186	2,119	212	21
0.73	2.2	0.7	75.8	241,964	24,196	2,420	242	24
0.7	2.1	0.6	72.6	274,253	27,425	2,743	274	27
0.67	2	0.5	69.1	308,538	30,854	3,085	309	31
0.63	1.9	0.4	65.5	344,578	34,458	3,446	345	34
0.6	1.8	0.3	61.8	382,089	38,209	3,821	382	38
0.57	1.7	0.2	57.9	420,740	42,074	4,207	421	42
0.53	1.6	0.1	54.0	460,172	46,017	4,602	460	46
0.5	1.5	0	50.0	500,000	50,000	5,000	500	50
0.47	1.4	-0.1	46.0	539,828	53,983	5,398	540	54
0.43	1.3	-0.2	42.1	579,260	57,926	5,793	579	58
0.4	1.2	-0.3	38.2	617,911	61,791	6,179	618	62
0.37	1.1	-0.4	34.5	655,422	65,542	6,554	655	66
0.33	1	-0.5	30.9	691,462	69,146	6,915	691	69
0.30	0.9	-0.6	27.4	725,747	72,575	7,257	726	73
0.27	0.8	-0.7	24.2	758,036	75,804	7,580	758	76
0.23	0.7	-0.8	21.2	788,145	78,814	7,881	788	79
0.20	0.6	-0.9	18.4	815,940	81,594	8,159	816	82
0.17	0.5	-1	15.9	841,345	84,134	8,413	841	84
0.13	0.4	-1.1	13.6	864,334	86,433	8,643	864	86
0.10	0.3	-1.2	11.5	884,930	88,493	8,849	885	88
0.07	0.2	-1.3	9.7	903,199	90,320	9,032	903	90
0.03	0.1	-1.4	8.1	919,243	91,924	9,192	919	92
0.00	0	-1.5	6.7	933,193	93,319	9,332	933	93

Index